Happiness, Well-being and Sustainability is the first book aimed at teaching students the new science of happiness and well-being measurement and to think of it in the context of making positive – and sustainable – changes to society. It provides extensive and robust evidence of the theory and metrics underlying the well-being approach, and at the same time links it to those of systemic change. It provides students with lessons on how to be agents of their own destiny, and to use that agency to contribute to the well-being and sustainability of their societies. The authors make their broad objective very eloquently in the introduction by quoting Gandhi: "Be the change you wish to see in the world." It is a refreshing and accessible volume that will provide the next generation with better tools to navigate and improve their collective futures.

Carol Graham, Leo Pasvolsky Senior Fellow,
College Park Professor, University of Maryland

I am speaking today with a group of high-school students exploring ways to create a sustainably happier world. I so wish this book was already here to assist their project. They will learn, I hope, and as the book illustrates, that authentic happiness arises most readily when people work with each other, and not against others, to deliver a better world for generations to come.

John Helliwell, Professor at Vancouver School of Economics,
University of British Columbia; co-editor, *World Happiness Report*

It has long been clear that social change for sustainability requires inner change as well. This is the first book that makes this connection for students, raising many thought-provoking questions about how our personal happiness arises and is connected to larger systems, policies, values, and social change.

Stephen M. Wheeler, Professor, Department of
Human Ecology, University of California, Davis

HAPPINESS, WELL-BEING AND SUSTAINABILITY

Happiness, Well-being and Sustainability: A Course in Systems Change is the first textbook bridging the gap between personal happiness and sustainable social change. The book provides a guide for students to increase their skills, literacy and knowledge about connections between a sense of well-being and systems change. Further, it can help students live a life that brings them happiness and contributes to the well-being of others and the sustainability of our planet.

The book is presented in seven chapters covering the subjects of systems thinking, personal and societal values, measuring happiness, human needs, ecological sustainability and public policy. In addition, each chapter includes engaging exercises to empower students to develop their own ideas, prompts for group discussion, suggestions for additional research and an extensive list of resources and references. The book is written in the context of systems thinking with a style that is approachable and accessible.

Happiness, Well-being and Sustainability provides essential reading for students in courses on happiness, social change and sustainability studies, and provides a comprehensive framework for instructors looking to initiate courses in this field.

Laura Musikanski is the executive director and co-founder of the Happiness Alliance and co-author of *The Happiness Policy Handbook*. She is chair of IEEE P7010 Recommended Practice for Assessing the Impact of Autonomous and Intelligent Systems on Human Well-being. Laura holds a JD and MBA, both from the University of Washington, and is a member of the Washington State Bar Association.

Rhonda Phillips is a community well-being, development and planning specialist and the Dean of Purdue Honors College. She is a three-time Fulbright award recipient and author or editor of 28 books, including co-author of *The Happiness Policy Handbook.* Rhonda holds a PhD in city and regional planning and a MS in economics from the Georgia Institute of Technology. She is a board director of the Happiness Alliance.

James Bradbury is a retired physicist who carried out research at Stanford University, Palo Alto Research Laboratory and the Los Alamos Research Laboratory. Research included the use of accelerator-produced particles for treating cancer and creating fusion energy as a possible renewable energy source. James holds a PhD in physics from Stanford University. He is involved in national climate change policy advocacy and is an emeritus board director of the Happiness Alliance.

John de Graaf is an internationally renowned author, speaker and producer of more than 40 television documentaries. John's books include *Affluenza* and *What's the Economy For, Anyway?* He co-founded the Happiness Alliance, as well as two other nonprofit organizations: And Beauty for All and Take Back Your Time.

Clinton L. Bliss is an administrator and practicing physician who works within the healthcare model of bio-psycho-social systems thinking. Clinton holds an MD from UCLA School of Medicine and a Board Certification in Family Medicine from the University of Washington. He is a board director of the Happiness Alliance.

HAPPINESS, WELL-BEING AND SUSTAINABILITY

A Course in Systems Change

Laura Musikanski, Rhonda Phillips, James Bradbury, John de Graaf and Clinton L. Bliss

Routledge
Taylor & Francis Group
LONDON AND NEW YORK

earthscan
from Routledge

First published 2021
by Routledge
2 Park Square, Milton Park, Abingdon, Oxon OX14 4RN

and by Routledge
52 Vanderbilt Avenue, New York, NY 10017

Routledge is an imprint of the Taylor & Francis Group, an informa business

British Library Cataloguing-in-Publication Data
A catalogue record for this book is available from the British Library

Library of Congress Cataloging-in-Publication Data
Names: Musikanski, Laura, author. | Phillips, Rhonda, author. | Bradbury, James (Sociologist) author.
Title: Happiness, well-being and sustainability : a course in systems change / by Laura Musikanski, Rhonda Phillips, James Bradbury, John de Graaf and Clinton L. Bliss.
Description: 1 Edition. | New York : Routledge, 2020. | Includes bibliographical references and index.
Identifiers: LCCN 2020003525 (print) | LCCN 2020003526 (ebook) | ISBN 9780367488703 (paperback) | ISBN 9780367488727 (hardcover) | ISBN 9781003043232 (ebook)
Subjects: LCSH: Social change. | Happiness—Social aspects. | Sustainable development—Social aspects. | Well-being.
Classification: LCC HM831 .M867 2020 (print) | LCC HM831 (ebook) | DDC 303.4—dc23
LC record available at https://lccn.loc.gov/2020003525
LC ebook record available at https://lccn.loc.gov/2020003526

ISBN: 978-0-367-48872-7 (hbk)
ISBN: 978-0-367-48870-3 (pbk)
ISBN: 978-1-003-04323-2 (ebk)

Typeset in Bembo
by Apex CoVantage, LLC

Visit the website: www.happycounts.org/coursebook.html

To our children, grandchildren and all the young people who will inherit this earth.

CONTENTS

ABOUT THE AUTHORS

Laura Musikanski is the executive director of the Happiness Alliance, a non-profit providing tools and resources for leadership in the happiness movement, including the Happiness Index. She has worked with community organizers, policy makers, educators and students to raise awareness about the happiness movement, measure happiness at a group level and use happiness data to enhance individual and community happiness. She is the co-author of *The Happiness Policy Handbook*, author of two books on sustainability and author of numerous popular and peer-reviewed articles. She has taught at the professional and university level and given numerous talks to audiences around the world. Laura is a recognized member of the happiness movement, an invited participant at the 2012 United Nations' High-Level Meeting Well-being and Happiness: Defining a New Economic Paradigm as well as the 2017 and 2018 Dialogue for Global Happiness held in Dubai, among many other collaborative events supporting the happiness movement. Laura is also a lawyer with an MBA who has owned businesses and worked as a director for sustainability at a national environmental firm. She is also a student of Buddhist Dharma teacher Robert Beatty.

Rhonda Phillips is the dean of the Honors College at Purdue University, and professor, Agricultural Economics Department. Formerly, she served as director and professor of the School of Community Resources and Development and senior sustainability scientist at the Global Institute of Sustainability at Arizona State University; and past president of the International Society of Quality of

Life Society (ISQOLS). Rhonda is a three-time Fulbright recipient, serving as a 2015–2016 and 2012 Fulbright Specialist to Panama and as the 2006 Fulbright UK Ulster Policy Fellow in Northern Ireland at the University of Ulster. Recognitions include induction into the College of Fellows of the American Institute of Certified Planners (FAICP) and recipient of the 2012 International Society for Quality-of-Life Studies' Distinguished Research Fellow. She is the co-author of *The Happiness Policy Handbook* and author or editor of 28 academic books, including the textbook *Introduction to Community Development,* and *Growing Livelihoods: Local Food Systems and Community Development.* Rhonda holds a PhD in city and regional planning and an MS in economics from the Georgia Institute of Technology, as well as an MS in economic development and a BS in geography from the University of Southern Mississippi.

James Bradbury is a retired physics researcher at Palo Alto Research Laboratory and Los Alamos National Laboratory and a global issues instructor at the University of New Mexico and College of Santa Fe. He is a board member emeritus of the Happiness Alliance. James was one of the leaders of an international team that focused on exploring the use of negative neurons in cold fusion for energy, a cutting-edge project at the time. He later led the first physics team in the US to conduct cancer radiotherapy research, testing novel methods for treating cancer with particles. Later in his career, he worked on projects redirecting Russian physicists into peaceful medical and energy research. As an active board member, he has worked in South Sudan to develop sustainable programs for Lone Star Africa Works and helped develop educational programs for the Oppenheimer Institute for Science and International Cooperation. He is currently involved in national climate change policy advocacy as well as working in the happiness movement.

John de Graaf is an author, filmmaker, speaker and activist with a mission to help create a happy, healthy and sustainable quality of life for America. He has been a keynote speaker at numerous conferences and has lectured in more than 100 American universities and in other countries, including Brazil, the UK, the United Arab Emirates, Canada, Hungary, Mexico and Australia. He is the founder of And Beauty for All and Take Back Your Time and co-founder of the Happiness Alliance. He is the co-author of the books *Affluenza* and *What's the Economy For, Anyway?* and has written for the *New York Times*, the *Los Angeles Times*, *The Progressive*, *Solutions Journal*, *YES!*, Grist, Al Jazeera, *Earth Island Journal*, *Experience Life* and many other publications. He is an international public speaker and has taught for Evergreen State College, the University of Washington and Boston University's Center for Digital Imaging Arts.

Clinton L. Bliss is a 13th-generation American. Dr. Bliss is a medical doctor with 25 years of experience in hospital administration, family or primary medicine and emergency medicine. He was trained in the bio-psycho-social model and deeply believes in a holistic and comprehensive approach to allopathic medicine. He earned his medical degree at UCLA School of Medicine, and served his residency at the University of Washington. He is a Certified Diplomate of the American Board of Family Practice. His experience includes acting chief of staff at Walla Walla VA Hospital, director of emergency services at American Lake VA Hospital, director of the Emergency Department Quality Assurance Program at Jefferson General Hospital, and chair of the Swedish Family Practice Quality Assistance Committee at Swedish Home Health (1995–1999), as well as running a private family practice. He is a board member of the Happiness Alliance.

FIGURES AND TABLES

Figures

Tables

TEXT BOXES

ABOUT THE CONTRIBUTORS

Beth Allgood has made it a goal of her career to help policy makers capture a more comprehensive account of the value of vulnerable wildlife populations – and to take action to protect that value around the US and around the world. She has a passion for changing the system and an impressive background in the field of conservation and human well-being. As the US country director of the International Fund for Animal Welfare (IFAW), Beth oversaw the strategy and implementation of IFAW programs across the US and conceptualized and led IFAW's work integrating animal and human well-being to create system change for nearly a decade. Beth has worked in the nonprofit, government and private sectors.

Tom Crompton is the director of Common Cause Foundation. He has worked for NSPCC, Oxfam, Scope and World Wildlife Fund (WWF) on values and social change. He has advised the UK, Scottish and Welsh governments on cultural values and has collaborated with some of the world's foremost academics working in this area. His publications include the reports *Weathercocks and Signposts: The Environment Movement at a Crossroads* (2007) and *Common Cause: The Case for Working with Values and Frames* (2010). Tom holds a degree in Natural Sciences at the University of Cambridge and holds a doctorate in the evolution of altruism from the University of Leicester.

Jean Crowder served as a Member of Parliament for the Canadian Government House of Commons of Canada between 2004 and 2015, having been elected as the New Democratic Party (NDP) Member of Parliament for Nanaimo–Cowichan, British Columbia. She has also served as a councillor in the District Municipality of North Cowichan, BC. Previously, she worked for Human Resources Development Canada and the British Columbia Ministry of Skills Training & Labour and was a human resources consultant and manager at Malaspina University College.

John C. Havens is executive director of The IEEE Global Initiative for Ethical Considerations in Artificial Intelligence and Autonomous Systems and founder of the IEEE P7010 Recommended Practice for Assessing the Impact of Autonomous and Intelligent Systems on Human Well-being. John is also a regular contributor on issues of technology and well-being to Mashable, The Guardian, HuffPo and TechCrunch and is the author of *Heartificial Intelligence* and *Hacking Happiness*. He founded the nonprofit The Happathon Project and is a public speaker. John worked at the executive level in public relations and was a professional actor on Broadway, TV and film for 15 years prior to that.

Marek Havrda is director of AI Policy & Social Impacts at GoodAI, a private R&D company focusing on the development of artificial general intelligence and artificial intelligence applications. He was a contributor to the Impact Assessment of new legislation, sustainable consumption and production policy, and on the use of behavioral economics for policy formulation for the European Commission. Previously, he worked for think tanks and the private sector with multinational innovation leaders in telecom and material industries. He has served as an advisor to the Czech Ministry of Finance and Ministry of Education, and as a member of the Regulatory Impact Assessment Board, he advises the Czech Government on potential impacts of draft legislation. He studied economics, sociology, international relations and public administration at Charles University, Warwick Business School, Johns Hopkins University and Georgetown University.

Lester R. Kurtz is a professor of public sociology at George Mason University Korea, where he teaches peace and conflict studies, comparative sociology of religion and social theory. He has lectured in Europe, Asia, Africa and North America and served as chair of the Peace Studies Association and the Peace, War, and Social Conflict Section of the American Sociological Association, which awarded him its Robin Williams Distinguished Career Award. He is a Distinguished Research Fellow at the Institute of Nanjing Massacre History and International Peace Studies and an ICNC Academic Advisor. He holds a master's degree in religion from Yale and a PhD in sociology from the University of Chicago.

Kate Pickett is a professor of epidemiology in the Department of Health Sciences and the University's Research Champion for Justice and Equality at the University of York. Kate was an UK NIHR Career Scientist from 2007 to 2012, is a Fellow of the RSA and a Fellow of the UK Faculty of Public Health. She served as commissioner for the York Fairness Commission and the Living Wage Commission. She is co-author, with Richard Wilkinson, of *The Spirit Level*, chosen as one of the Top Ten Books of the Decade by the *New Statesman*, winner of Publication of the Year by the Political Studies Association and translated into 23 languages. She is a co-founder and trustee of The Equality Trust.

INTRODUCTION

Happiness, Well-being and Sustainability: A Course in Systems Change is the first course book bridging personal and societal happiness and systems change, bringing together the concepts of positive psychology, sustainability and the happiness and well-being movements with empowering, approachable and actionable lessons. This course book is a comprehensive guide for students and their teachers for improving individual happiness and engaging in societal change for the happiness and sustainability of our systems. The course is designed to inspire and empower students to be change agents for positive social change. The emphasis throughout is to increase literacy, knowledge and skills related to these subjects. The book contains seven chapters with tutorial discussions to explain, in approachable and accessible language, the topic and concepts involved within the context of systems thinking. Each chapter contains thought-provoking questions for students, ideas for group discussion and additional research and an extensive list of references. Within the context of systems thinking, topics covered are values, measurements, individual happiness, societal or community well-being, needs, sustainability and policy.

By the time this course is finished, you will have gained an understanding of what systems thinking is, learned about skills to be happier in your life, and gathered the knowledge, tools and resources to become a change agent for a society in which happiness, well-being and sustainability matter most. This course is designed so that if you are open to learning and willing to put in the effort, you can be happier in your life today and in your future and take action for the well-being of yourself and others and the sustainability of our earth.

Learning how to be happy is the most important lesson in this course. If you do that and you are happier in your life, then these lessons on systems change will have been a success. In the words of Mahatma Gandhi, "Be the change you wish to see in the world." In this book, you will learn about how to be happy and about systems and how to change them. We encourage you to apply the knowledge gathered about systems change to your own life as well as to the systems you want to change.

This book is about systems change for individual and/or societal happiness (some refer to this as well-being or community well-being at the collective level) and planetary sustainability. We use the term *sustainability* to mean the ecological health – or, more simply put, the health of nature – on our planet now and in the future. We use the term *happiness* to encompass these concepts because we believe these concepts and individual happiness are inextricably connected. We discuss research throughout this book to demonstrate the validity of many of these concepts. Some are newer conceptions or not yet researched but are included to provide readers with more context. We believe that many of the connections between individual happiness, that of communities and societies and the sustainability of nature, are not all thoroughly understood but are important to continue to explore.

This book helps span the gap between personal happiness and systems change in societies, economies, governments and other systems. With it, you will learn basic but often overlooked lessons about how to be happy. You will also learn about values, how to measure happiness and the role values and measurements play in personal life and systems change. You will also gain knowledge about human needs, sustainable development, policy and ways to explore connections to happiness and well-being.

Some of these areas of exploration may seem very different, but all contribute to the whole of a system, along with other elements as well. We have selected these to present because they are connected to each other and to individual and societal or community well-being.

Each chapter is written with the intent of inspiring and empowering you to be a change agent in your own life, your career, your community and the world. It is also our hope that readers will consider the validity of the information for their own lives and adapt or change what is learned to empower living life to fullest potential and to encourage positive change in this world.

1

SYSTEMS

Systems learning objectives

The objectives of this chapter are for students to be able to:

- Gain an understanding of what a system is.
- Gain an understanding of what interdependence is.
- Gain an understanding of what leverage points are.
- Understand there are linkages between personal happiness and social systems.

Preliminary questions

- What is the point of life?
- What is the purpose of the government?
- What is the purpose of the economy?
- What is the purpose of school (i.e. education)? Would your answer be different if there were no access to formal education for you?
- What is a system?
- What is systems thinking?
- How is systems thinking different from other types of thinking?
- When would systems thinking be appropriate?
- When might it not be a good idea to use systems thinking?
- How much money do you need to be happy?
- What do you need to be happy?

- Can you make a difference in your own life?
- Can you make a difference in the world?

Introduction to systems

"Happiness is the meaning and the purpose of life, the whole aim and end of human existence" is a statement Aristotle made over 2,000 years ago. The intent of this coursebook is to empower you to explore what happiness is for you personally and for the world you live in through a systems thinking approach and to live a life that is truly happy. The first step of realizing this intent is understanding what systems thinking is.

Intuitively, you probably already know what a system is. Donella Meadows, whose work in systems thinking influenced the sustainable development movement, defined a system as "a set of elements or parts that is coherently organized and interconnected in a pattern or structure that produces a characteristic set of behaviors, often classified as its 'function' or 'purpose'" (Meadows, 2008, p. 188). Everyone's body is a system. A person has a family system. For students, the campus is a system, and for employees, the workplace is a system. Your neighborhood, town and city are systems. The economy, climate and society operate as systems. Systems are dynamic and complex, and when any element of a system changes, the change has an impact on the system. Understanding systems will help build capacity for intentional and impactful system change in your own life and in the world around you.

Systems and elements

To understand systems change, let's first understand what a system is. Donella Meadows defined a system as "a set of things – people, cells, molecules, or whatever – interconnected in such a way that they produce their own pattern of behavior over time" (Meadows, 2008, p. 2). The components of a system are called elements. A system can have many independent elements, such as a child or parent in a family or a river in a landscape. The elements interact. When a child leaves home to go to college, start a job or otherwise live independently, or when a river floods, changes course or is dammed, there is an interaction with some or all of the other elements in the system. Each element has a role to play to keep a system healthy (or unhealthy), to change the system or to end the system.

The interactions of the elements in a system help define what a system is as a whole.

HIGHLIGHT: URBAN OR RURAL PLANNING

Urban or rural planners work with towns, cities, counties or regions to help guide land use and other related development decisions about what will happen in that area in the near and distant future. They use tools such as zoning, incentives and policies to gauge where residential, commercial and industrial buildings will be built; what parts of an area will be kept green; where parks will be established; and where to expand or build airports, public spaces, roads, schools and other public infrastructure. While many aspects of planning are physical in nature, planning also impacts social, cultural, fiscal and other dimensions related to living in communities. There are many other elements of an urban or rural system they must consider, some of which are systems in themselves, such as distribution, energy, information and communication technology, sewage, water supply, waste and recycling systems. The impacts of interactions between the elements of an area and changes in climate, the economy, tourism and other aspects are part of urban or rural planning. Planners may work in government, the private sector (such as housing or development firms) or academia. For most planners, the goal of planning focuses on improving quality of life, which is very similar to goals of happiness and well-being.

Some places are planning for climate change by entirely relocating or buying land to flee to if their land if flooded (Edmond, 2017). Sweden's plans for zero waste includes changes to taxes and energy sources and integrating the concept of a circular economy into policy (Sweden, n.d.). Dubai is integrating artificial intelligence into its banking, education, justice, health care, police and water systems (Smart Dubai, n.d.). Singapore's plans to be a green and sustainable city included zoning laws and educating and engaging youth, resulting in the city transforming from being known for pollution to a model green city with buildings serving as human and plant homes (UN Environment Programme, n.d.).

How would you plan for a city or town that supported your happiness, the well-being of others and ecological sustainability?

Interdependence

The elements in a system interact in ways that are interdependent. Interdependent means that two or more things depend upon each other. The concept of interdependence was conceived by Harold Kelly and John Thiebaut in the 1950s in relation to psychology (*Psychology*, n.d.) and is applied in many fields today. An example of interdependence is a child who needs food and shelter to survive and love to be resilient and happy (Brooks, 2005), which parents or caretakers provide but with varying levels of capacity and competency, or a river that needs trees and other plants on its banks, also called the riparian zone, and land to change its course, which is called the floodplain, to provide healthy water quality, habitats for animals and fish and not destroy roads or homes when it floods (Robbins, 2017). Another example of interdependence is economic interdependence between urban and rural communities and between countries. In 1999, Paul Hawkins and Hunter and Amory Lovins found that in almost all cities, most of the food is imported from farms over 1,000 miles away (pp. 200–201). More recent research shows that the average miles food travels has increased by almost three times in some areas (Hill, 2008). Without the farms to grow the food and the transportation systems to bring the food to the markets in the cities, many people would go hungry. In 2011, a tsunami hit Japan followed by a nuclear reactor meltdown, leaving the nation in devastation. The transportation system is just one of many systems that shut down. The roads were not able to be navigated, and railways were broken. Millions of people in cities and remote areas went days, even weeks, without food (Mimura et al., 2011; NBC, 2011) because the vehicles that brought them food could reach neither the farmers nor the markets. Urban people came face to face with how interdependent they were with farmers, suppliers and the transportation system and how much they need systems to function.

For the past few decades, there has been a growing interdependence between the economies of almost all countries. An example is China and the US, where the US depends on China for much of its manufactured goods, and China has depended on the buyers for goods in the US as well as some agricultural resources, including soybeans, grains, hides, pork and cotton (USDA Foreign Agricultural Service, n.d.). If trade were to suddenly end between China and the US or between any group of nations, life would suddenly be very different in many more ways than you would have considered without knowledge of the system.

HIGHLIGHT: EXPLORING INTERDEPENDENCE

Harold Kelly and John Thibaut were both social psychologists who contributed to the development of their field. Social psychology is the study of our behavior in relation to others and encompasses exploring and understanding the implications and impacts of social norms, attitudes, values and morals on a person or group's behavior. Baron, Byrne and Suls (1989) define it as "the scientific field that seeks to understand the nature and causes of individual behavior in social situations" (p. 6). Kelly and Thibault wanted to better understand why people behaved the way they did in the context of relationships instead of looking at individual actions by individual people.

A famous project named The Harvard Study of Adult Development gathered data for people over the course of their lives to find out what made them happy or miserable. The study found that the most important factor for happiness is relationships (Mineo, 2017). Relationships are characterized, in part, by the interdependence of those in them. For example, how we relate and who we choose to have relationships with in our professional lives can influence our personal relationships (Shragai, 2014). In this exploration, we paraphrase and ask questions for some of the attributes of interdependence that Kelly and Thibaut identified to consider in personal relationships (Kelly et al., 2003; Kelly & Thibaut, 1978; Thibaut & Kelly, 1959):

Control

Control is one basis of relationships. There are two extremes. Dominance is when a person, group or entity has all of the decision-making power and the ability to implement the decision with or without the consent of others. Partnership is the other extreme, when all people, groups or entities cooperate and coordinate to make decisions and contribute to implementing them in a mutually agreeable way.

- How have people or groups that were dominated changed the control basis of societal relationships?
- How would you imagine a person or group that historically dominated changing the control basis from dominance to partnership?

Power

Power contributes to balance in a relationship. If the actions of a person, group or entity have no impact on others, then they have no power over them. On the other hand, if the well-being of a person, group or entity is completely influenced by the action of others, then others have power over them. A balanced power relationship is when both have power over and concern for each other's well-being.

- What is an example of a person, group or entity changing the power another has over them from full power to no power?
- How would you imagine changing the power balance in a relationship between a person, group or entity from full power to balanced power?

Interests

Interests determine the outcome of relationships. When interests conflict and that which contributes to the well-being of a person, group or entity is harmful to others, there is competition and conflict. When all in the relationship have mutual interests, then any action by any person, group or entity can be of benefit to all and there is harmony.

- What is an example of people, groups or entities with conflicting interests, and what were the outcomes?
- How would you imagine people, groups or entities with conflicting interests arriving to a place of harmony?

Clarity of information

Clarity of information is another basis of relationships. When there is no clarity of information, a person, group or entity does not know what others care about, how they feel, what they want or how an action will impact others. When there is clarity in information, all people, groups and entities have enough information to understand each other's interests, feelings, motives and to know about the outcomes of actions. Clarity produces a sense of stability in combination with balanced power, partnership-based control and mutual interests.

- What are some factors that allow for clarity of information between two people, between a person and a group, and between a group and an entity?
- How are the factors different for the different situations, and how are they similar?

Commitment

Commitment determines the evolution of a relationship. When a person, group or entity is not committed to others, they may make decisions about the future that harm the well-being of others. When there is commitment, investments in the relationship itself are made.

- Besides the attributes listed, what is needed for commitment in a relationship?

Recognizing that systems have elements and interactions between elements means that when one element of a system is in play, it has an impact on one or more of the other elements. Instead of focusing on one aspect of a system, a systems thinker considers all the elements they are aware of, the ways that the elements are interdependent and their interactions. This brings us to feedback loops.

Feedback loops

Successive interactions that elicit changes are called feedback loops. There are two kinds of feedback loops. One kind elicits more of something, and the other causes less of something. The kind that causes acceleration, accumulation or amplification is called a positive feedback loop. The kind that causes deceleration, decrease or winding down is called a negative feedback loop. (We define feedback loops in very simple terms for our work together but want you to know there are other ways to define feedback loops, such as through mathematical equations or based on the effect they have on a system.) The two kinds of feedback loops are not called positive or negative because one is good and the other bad. Both can create undesirable outcomes if unchecked. When positive feedback loops are unchecked, they can result in exponential growth and eventual collapse. When negative feedback loops are unchecked, they result in depletion and eventual collapse.

For many systems, positive and negative feedback loops work together to create a steady state, also called equilibrium. You can use the term *dynamic equilibrium* because the way they work together can change as interactions and elements in a system change. Not all systems have feedback loops. Systems that do not have feedback loops are static. An example of a static system is gravity on earth (as long as you consider the system in the time span of our existence). For your entire life, whatever that force is that attracts your body to the center of our planet (which is called gravity), it will not change, and you will not float off or fall into the earth.

A key thing to understand about feedback loops when they operate dynamically to create equilibrium is that they run based on a target. The target is often expressed as a measurement which measures the success of reaching a goal. If feedback loops do not have a target, the system faces the danger of running into a vicious cycle. If feedback loops achieve and maintain a target, they can create a virtuous cycle and maintain or preserve equilibrium (Fig. 1.1).

To better understand how positive and negative feedback loops work to create a dynamic equilibrium, we need to further explain. Let's start with

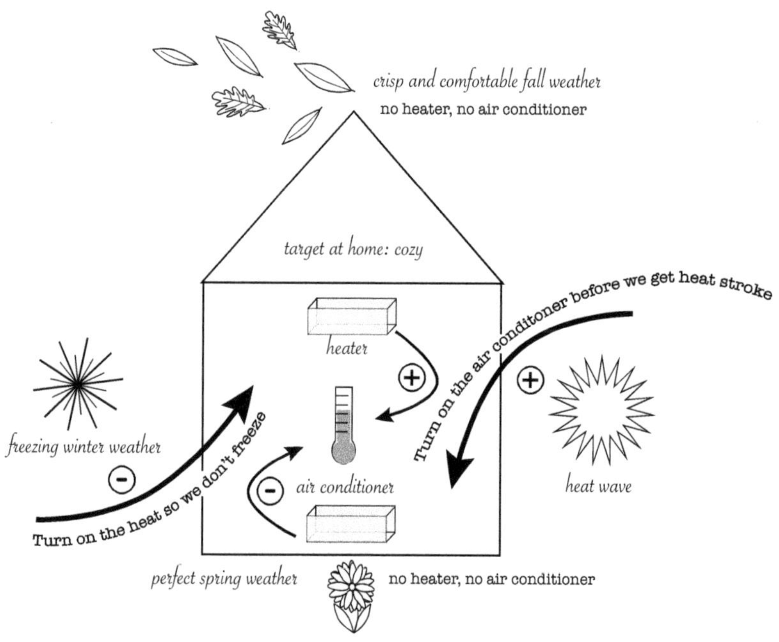

FIGURE 1.1 Feedback and dynamic equilibrium for cozy

positive and negative feedback and explore what happens when there is unchecked acceleration, or exponential growth. Take the example of a room heater. Assume your goal is to be cozy, and for you, that is 72 degrees Fahrenheit/22 degrees Celsius. You set the thermostat for your cozy goal. When you set the target, you are doing two things: (1) telling the heater to start working when the temperature drops below your target and (2) telling the heater to stop working when the temperature reaches your target. In the winter, the temperature in the room drops below your target. The thermostat registers that the temperature is below your target and prompts the heater to pump out heat and continues to do so for a time. This is a positive feedback. If you did not have a target, it would prompt the heater to continue heating the room endlessly, and the temperature in the room would spin out of control until the room was burning hot or the heater broke. Instead, once the temperature reaches your target, a negative feedback is set to motion. The negative feedback tells the heater to stop heating and keeps telling it to stop until the temperature drops again. If the negative feedback were not balanced by the positive feedback, the heater would never turn on again. The heater would no longer operate, and you would never be cozy. Together, the two create equilibrium and a nicely heated room. What if you wanted to change the heating system in your room? The most obvious way would be to change the target for the temperature, or in other words, the thermostat setting.

The example of the heater looked at positive and negative feedback working together to create equilibrium. It did not look at a positive feedback loop operating without a target and spinning out of control. A feedback loop is different from just feedback because with the loop, the feedback triggers more or less of something happening. In our heater example, when the positive feedback is registered for the first time, one heater turns on, and without a target or negative feedback to counter it, the second time positive feedback is registered, assume two heaters turn on, the third time, four heaters turn on, and so on. With exponential growth, by the 10th time 1,024 heaters turn on and by the 100th time this many heaters would turn on:

> 10,715,086,071,862,673,209,484,250,490,600,018,105,614,048,117, 055,336,074,437,503,883,703,510,511,249,361,224,931,983,788,156, 958,581,275,946,729,175,531,468,251,871,452,856,923,1404,35,984, 577,574,698,574,803,934,567,774,824,230,985,421,074,605,062,371, 141,877,954,182,153,046,474,983,581,941,267,398,767,559,165,543, 946,077,062,914,571,196,477,686,542,167,660,429,831,652,624,386, 837,205,668,069,376

The 1,001th time, this number would double, and after not too long, you can imagine what the earth would look like. Clearly, the system would be out of control. The positive feedback loop, left unchecked, would result in exponential growth and eventual collapse. If, in your imagination, you wondered where the resources were coming from to create all these heaters, what happened to broken heaters, and where the energy came from to run those heaters, how the temperature affects people and the planet and what the impacts on the atmosphere might be, then you are tapping into a problem of unlimited economic consequences causing unlimited ecologic consequences (Fig. 1.2).

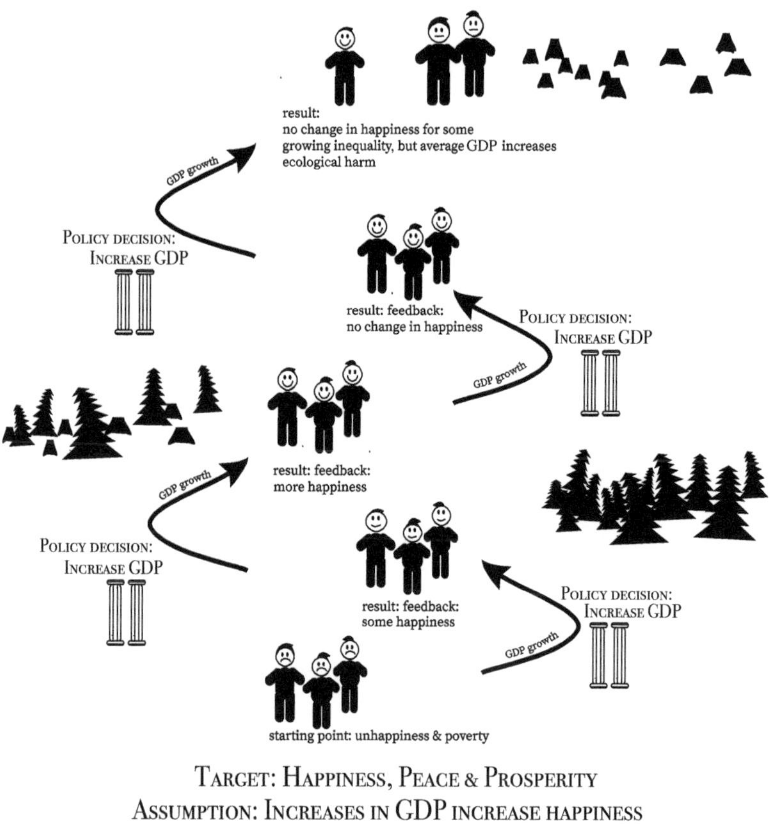

FIGURE 1.2 GDP as happiness loop

Remembering that the key to feedback loops are targets, let's now look at much more complex feedback loops. In this scenario, assume you rule a nation, and your goals are for people to live in peace, realize prosperity and be happy. There are many people in your nation who are living in poverty and not too many who are wealthy. You decide that you will measure the goal by the value of what people in the nation produce in a year. This is called the gross domestic product, which is denoted GDP. It measures the value of the things produced, from a toothpick to a car, and the value of the services rendered, from a street sweeper to a surgeon, in a year. You figure that as GDP goes up, more people will be working, making a better living and able to buy more stuff and services. This will bring people out of poverty, help them realize prosperity and make them happy. You adopt policies that promote and support production of goods and services. For many years, there is a virtuous cycle in the positive feedback loop that you created. You make policies to promote business and production, poverty goes down, prosperity goes up and people are happier. You make more policies, and people get happier; there is even less poverty, and there is more prosperity.

But then something happens. Poverty and prosperity problems appear to have been solved, but people's happiness is not increasing. By this point, you have used the GDP measurement for so long to measure the success of the system that you can't really imagine using a different one. There is a fear too that if a different measure is used, there will be ridicule or attacks by the press and political opponents. You therefore decide to keep going and make more policies to increase GDP. Instead of increasing prosperity for everyone, there is a growing gap between rich and poor, with the poorest getting poorer. Not sure what to do, and noticing the rich are getting very rich, and the average income looks good, you decide to give it one more try and pass policies to increase GDP yet again. After this, you find that the happiness of your people is declining even among the very wealthy, the number of people living in poverty is increasing and the rich–poor gap has widened even more. The positive feedback loop is spinning off into a vicious cycle. One of the problems with the system put in place is that a target was not set for GDP. You assumed that the higher the GDP, the better, but did not check to see if the measurement accurately measured how well the goals were reached.

GUEST COURSEBOOK CONTRIBUTION FROM KATE PICKETT: INCOME INEQUALITY

Kate Pickett is an epidemiologist who focuses on equality. She is a professor, researcher and author and has served in government as a commissioner and for nonprofits in strategic positions. She has been awarded fellowships and awards for her activism for equality. In 2009, she co-founded *The Equity Trust*, a nonprofit, support activist group working towards economic and social equality in the UK with facts, knowledge and the promotion of policies. She wrote this essay to inspire and empower readers of this coursebook.

If someone asked you what gives you the greatest happiness and well-being, you'd probably think first of your family and friends. It's your relationships that give you fulfilment and purpose, not material things, income or wealth. Most people probably don't think that wider issues to do with politics and the economy have a direct bearing on their well-being – but they do.

Income inequality, the gap between rich and poor in a society, causes a wide range of health and social problems – everything from reduced life expectancy and higher infant mortality to worse educational attainment, lower social mobility and increased levels of violence. The differences between more and less equal societies are surprisingly large, and almost everybody seems to be affected by greater inequality, not just those at the bottom of the social ladder (Wilkinson & Pickett, 2009).

Inequality damages the quality of life because it is divisive. It makes social class and status differences more powerful, which in turn makes social comparisons more insidious and increases the social and psychological distances between us (Wilkinson & Pickett, 2018). Inequality strengthens the belief that some people are worth much more than others; simply raising material living standards (even if that could be done for everybody in a sustainable way) cannot produce genuine well-being or quality of life in the face of inequality. Indeed, inequality is a roadblock to creating sustainable well-being economies, as it ratchets up consumerism and consumption and erodes collectivism and social cohesion (Wilkinson & Pickett, 2014). By acting as an enemy between us, inequality prevents us from acting together to create the world we want.

HIGHLIGHT: A SHORT HISTORY OF GDP AS A MEASUREMENT TO GUIDE NATIONS

The reason that governments use GDP is because most believe that economic growth, personal wealth and high consumption rates make people happy and ensure the well-being of all (Layard, 2005). This assumption was the basis for organizations resulting from the Bretton Woods conference convened shortly after the end of World War II. The conference was named Bretton Woods because it was held in Bretton Woods, New Hampshire, in the US.

The Bretton Woods conference brought together 40 countries, including the US, UK, France, Poland, Australia, Canada and New Zealand. Together the leaders of these nations came up with ways to create order out of the chaos that war wrought and to bind nations together so that such a war would never be fought again. The organizations they created were the International Monetary Fund, the World Bank, and, eventually, the World Trade Organization (Bretton Woods Project, 2005). The metric they decided to use to measure the success of their goals was Gross Domestic Product (GDP).

The creator of the GDP metric was Simon Kuznets (1937), an economist and statistician. In the midst of the Great Depression, he was commissioned by the US Congress to come up with a measure to help the government pull the nation out of the Great Depression. At that time, the only way Congress could measure what was being produced was counting box cars as they left the train station. Congress needed to have a better measure to know how much was being produced and what kinds of goods and services were being produced. They needed to pass laws, form incentives and devise programs to aid in the recovery of the economy and help people meet their needs. When Kuznets introduced the measurement to the US Congress in 1934, he cautioned Congress that "the welfare of a nation can scarcely be inferred from a measurement of national income" (Kuznets, 1934). Yet today, almost every nation uses GDP. Like the US, most governments use GDP as their primary measure, thereby putting economic growth before all other goals.

HIGHLIGHT: MONEY, INCOME AND HAPPINESS: THE EASTERLIN PARADOX

There is some truth to the connection between money and happiness, but it does not reflect the full range of truth. Nations with higher per capita incomes have happier people, but this is because they have more resources and more opportunities, not just because they have more money. Research conducted in many different cultures in the world tells us that income, consumption and economic growth are causally related to happiness only up to a certain level of personal income. This observation is commonly called the Easterlin Paradox. It is based on longitudinal data (studies done over the course of many years) collected by Richard Easterlin, an economist.

The Easterlin Paradox tells us that in a stable economy, in which people do not fear losing their jobs, they are happier when they have more money up to a certain amount. After that, happiness increases only marginally, meaning that for large increases in the amount of money one gets, there are smaller and smaller increases in happiness (Easterlin, 2001; Easterlin, 1995; Easterlin, 1974). In the US, that amount is about $75,000 for a family of four; it is £45,000 in the UK. It varies for each nation, but in every nation, there is an optimal income level.

What does this mean in practical terms? If you make less than the optimal amount, an increase in your income is likely to increase your happiness by quite a bit. After you reach that point, to get the same boost in happiness, you will need to make a lot more money, and after a certain point, your happiness may actually decline. This is probably because you are sacrificing other important aspects of life, like spending time with friends and family, learning new things, helping others or developing other aspects of yourself, to make more money. People find it hard to accept that the Easterlin Paradox holds for everyone, even those who are living in areas that are very expensive and so one must make much more money to pay for housing and other living costs. This is because it is hard to change the beliefs and assumptions that underlie values, especially in regards to economic conditions and income. Read more about this in the section on entry points and in Chapter 2 on values.

HIGHLIGHT: WHY CERTAIN NATIONS ARE HAPPIER

Every year since 2012 (except 2014), the *World Happiness Report* gives a ranking of the happiness of nations. Well, actually, it ranks the satisfaction of life of nations, which is different from the feeling of happiness. Satisfaction with life is a measurement based on the question: how satisfied are you with your life? Pretty consistently, the top ten nations are among the wealthiest nations in the world. When researchers study why people in a nation have high or low satisfaction with life, they consistently find that a strong social safety net is the key. If you knew that if you lost your job, could not pay rent or needed health care and did not have enough money to pay for it, you would still have a place to live, food to eat, an opportunity to work and health care, then you have a strong safety net. A strong social safety net also means you have access to education without incurring a lot of debt, you can retire without having to worry about having enough savings, will have time off work if a child or parent gets sick and can find reasonably priced childcare when you need it. Countries that have strong social safety nets are generally wealthier nations with higher incomes, so it makes sense that their happiness, when measured as satisfaction with life, ranks higher.

HIGHLIGHT: WHY SOME POOR NATIONS ARE HAPPIER THAN YOU WOULD EXPECT

Latin American nations are less wealthy, but the happiness levels are high when happiness is defined (and measured) in terms of positive feelings, like feeling joyful or content (Rojas, 2018; McLean, 2014; Diener et al., 2010). Why is this?

Economists and social science researchers have studied this question. Some of the reasons they think that Latin American and other countries have higher levels of happiness than one would expect if based on their GDP are listed here:

- People have similar access to resources and opportunities as people in wealthy nations.

- Families are close, warm, loving and intergenerational. It is not uncommon to live one's entire life with their parents, siblings and other family members, with the household growing as people have partners and children.
- People have warm relationships with their family members, friends, neighbors and co-workers and experience daily doses of positive emotions.
- People generally enjoy taking care of children and want to take care of the elders in their family.
- People spend time with their friends several times a week.
- People have a sense of purpose in life and gather their sense of purpose in life from their relationships and connections to other people.
- People value nurturing personal relationships, and culturally, relationships are of high value.
- Life happens at a slower pace. People accept life as it is and spend their time and energy on enjoying things as they are instead of putting their time and energy into changing their life circumstances.

Let's rethink this scenario by imagining that you add more measurements to measure the success of your system and in reaching the goal of no poverty and increased prosperity and happiness for your people. You add measurements for income equality and happiness. You also decide to set targets for these newly added measurements. You do some research and find that there is an optimal level of income for happiness. You also find that there is an optimal range for the rich–poor gap that gives people a sense of fairness but also allows people to feel encouraged to compete. You find there is an optimal range in levels of happiness and ways to understand and measure happiness that contribute to creating the circumstances where people have the capability to live full lives that addresses groups that are miserable and encourages optimism, hope and productivity for everyone. With these measurements, you can create a system of positive and negative feedback loops and, over time, find an equilibrium where the people do realize prosperity and happiness. The big question that probably arises in your mind for this scenario is how you can do this or even if it is possible? These scenarios and other systems changes are explored throughout this book. But first, let's continue with an orientation to systems thinking.

Leverage points

Leverage points are the places where an effort will cause a change in a system. A leverage point can reveal where you should apply effort so you can make the change you want. A high leverage point is where a small effort causes a big change. A low leverage point is where a small effort causes a small change.

When you combine leverage points with feedback loops, you expand your possibilities for change. This is because feedback loops can amplify a change. An analogy for this amplification would be a ripple effect. When a change is made at a high leverage point, resulting feedback loops can get stronger each time they cycle. In this way, a seemingly small change can have a large impact on a system. This is one reason why it is important to understand the system you are trying to change.

It is possible that an action or change can result in the opposite of what you are hoping or something very different from your goal is (this is referred to as unintended consequences). This is what happened in the GDP scenario when you were the ruler of a nation and decided to pass more policies to increase GDP in the hope it would alleviate poverty as it had in the past. It might also have happened if you used income equality and people's happiness as measurements and target, particularly if you did not have enough information to know if your measurement and target really measured the attainment of goals of no poverty, prosperity and happiness.

Another way to understand the impact of leverage points is to think about your own life when what was anticipated to be a small action caused a large effect. You have probably experienced this when you or someone else said something that elicited a major response. You may also have experienced this when new information or an experience completely changed your perspective on something, breaking open new opportunities and pathways for your life.

A seemingly small effort can also have a large impact over time, and the momentum from feedback loops increases. It may not seem like you are making a big difference at first, but on looking back weeks, months or sometimes years later, you can see how one small action can change a system. This is particularly true for small actions that are repeated over time because they cause an accumulated effect that can be much larger than the sum of the parts (this is referred to as a synergistic effect). Later, individual happiness skills are explored, and you will find that if you make a habit of a happiness practice, it will more than likely have a much larger impact on your life than you initially expected.

HIGHLIGHT: BEEKEEPING AS A LEVERAGE POINT FOR SUSTAINABILITY AND PROSPERITY

South Sudan was founded as a country on July 9, 2011. In this nation ravaged by almost constant civil war, a group of women in a rural community decided to embark upon a sustainable honey production project. They located hives in the wild and constructed some simple wooden hives, ensuring that only wildflowers were utilized by the bees. They marketed the honey, and it became the first export to the US from their region. Sales of honey began in roadside stands, expanded to nearby villages, and in a few years, a shipment of several hundred pounds reached Houston, Texas. The business became profitable with several US firms interested in marketing the product. Unfortunately, civil war killed this endeavor, but let's imagine that it did not, and play out a possible long-term outcome for the women's sustainable honey production project.

Bees play a vital role in ecosystems by pollinating flowering plants and trees. As a result of unsustainable practices and climate change, bee colonies around the world are not thriving, and some species have even disappeared (EPA, n.d.a.). Transporting bees long distances, as well as some pesticides and fertilizers, are bad for bee health. Bee colonies need to peak (meaning the population increases in a colony) at roughly the same time as plant and tree flowering, an occurrence which nature has evolved. Climate change threatens this balance. Sustainable beekeeping is when the human–bee system contributes positively to healthy populations of indigenous bees living in the wild or carefully managed apiaries.

Now imagine that the women's project is very successful. In a desperately poor, traumatized country, the results of this leverage point startup were remarkable: in one town, a few strong women, with help from their children, took the time to develop a sustainable, popular and healthy product. They reinvest their earnings into more hives, gardens and watering systems. This makes the bees happy and neighbors curious. They expand their operation with more women, so that they are producing more honey, growing more food and investing in more stable watering systems. Soon they have extra money to invest in communications technology. Their families are happy to have access to cell phones, and they are happy to be able to control the sales of their honey, keeping tabs on prices and flow of goods. Their gardens are growing, and they are able to sell or trade the extra food. A stable ecosystem is being maintained in which the women have acquired useful skills and knowledge, families a degree of economic security, and, importantly, all are experiencing a sense of bonding with neighbors in pursuit of a sustainable community-based business. A few women run for a position on the local council and win. There are some adjustments in the community, but soon the men and women on the council are enjoying working together and are successful in building up resources for the local schools and health care centers. It's an upward cycle, and soon their town is realizing a sustainable economic, social and ecological boom.

Entry points for systems change

With an understanding of what a system is and that there are feedback loops and leverage points, you might be asking where to start when you want to change a system. Entry points are places for starting. Kambiz Maani and Robert Cavana (2007) both worked as consultants to help governments and businesses organize their processes and people before they came together to identify four leverage points in systems. The four different entry points they identified are paraphrased as:

- Symptoms
- Patterns
- Design
- Values

You can visualize the leverage points as names for four layers in a pyramid. The bottom layer of the pyramid is the biggest, and everything depends on it. This layer can be called *values.* While it is not always the focus when observing the pyramid, it's important to know that when this layer changes, everything else does, too. The top of the pyramid is called *symptoms.* Most of the time when this layer changes, the other layers do not change.

For most people, the most obvious entry point is fixing a problem. This is the entry point of symptoms. Also, most of the time, when faced with a problem, the least obvious (but most powerful) entry point is changing values. Values are high leverage points, and changing them can cause a large change to a system. Changing values is not always easy and often requires shedding light on known and hidden assumptions and shifting beliefs.

(1) Symptoms

Symptoms are the outcomes of a system. They are outcomes because they happen after the fact. An example of a symptom is a fever. Misery and poverty are also often symptoms. Your midterm grades are also a symptom. They happen after you study, learn and take the test. A demonstration or a walk-out happen in protest to a problem in a system and also are symptoms.

You usually fix or react to symptoms. Fixing or reacting to a symptom or event may immediately relieve a symptom or change its immediate course, but it does not necessarily change the system that brought on the problem. You can take medicine for a fever, study to change your grades or use force to disband a march, but the underlying reason giving rise to the symptoms does not necessarily change. Symptoms can be thought of as low leverage points.

(2) Patterns

You know what patterns are but sometimes are not aware that something you do or that happens is part of a pattern. Habits are a kind of pattern that you have in your own life. Habits can be any combination of intentional or unintentional and helpful or harmful. Just like in life, in systems, patterns can be any combination of planned or unplanned and beneficial or damaging.

You change patterns by managing them. Managing a pattern that you want to stop or replace may result in fewer symptoms. Sometimes changing a pattern can result in changing values and so change the reason the pattern emerged in the first place, and sometimes changing a pattern will not get rid of the reason the pattern emerged in the first place and will result in a different but similar pattern.

An example of a pattern that has been managed so it continues is the tax system in the US. When the Internal Revenue Service (IRS) was created, the tax code (code is the word for the laws and rules for governmental agencies, such as the IRS) did not state that people must pay taxes, only that a tax is to be collected. Over time, with the majority of people paying taxes, laws were developed from lawsuits (called case law) that found people are required to pay taxes, and then the IRS created codes so that the pattern of paying taxes every year became a part of the system (IRS, 2018). This way of managing a pattern does not change the values for people who don't pay taxes, although it may influence their decisions and change their patterns.

Sometimes changes in patterns can change people's values. A pattern that is changing in many cities in North America and Europe is disposal of waste. Shortly after GDP was adopted as the primary measure for governments, the pattern of reusing food and other packaging and composting food waste for home gardens was replaced by store-grown food and disposable containers. By the 1970s, garbage was mounting up in cities, and in the US, a law was passed to end open dumping of garbage (EPA, n.d.b.). Calls were made by change agents to start recycling programs with a growing number of cities in the US and nations in Europe creating recycling programs and passing laws that fine people for not recycling (CityLab, n.d.). Some countries are further along in changing disposal patterns. In Germany, there are laws, called the German Packaging Act, that require sellers to take back their packaging and encourage eco-friendly packaging. Sweden's goal for zero waste has led the country to a reduction in its waste by 99% in less than 20 years (TRTWorld, 2019). As the pattern of recycling gets stronger, there is a shift towards the valuing of recycling for economic, environmental and other reasons (Hawkins, 2006).

Patterns can help you understand if a system is healthy or unhealthy and reveal the values held by those in the system. Patterns are not always obvious. If you have ever had the situation when someone told you that you had a habit of doing something, and it was a surprise to you or you thought they were not telling the truth, then you have had the experience of an unknown pattern. In systems, as in life, sometimes you have to do a little digging to discover patterns by gathering data and analyzing it. Patterns can make a large difference because the impact of patterns on a system grows over time when they are regular. When a pattern is well established, it can look like part of the design of a system. This brings us to the next layer of the pyramid: the design of a system.

(3) Design

How a system is designed is like the description of how a system works. Changing a system's design can change patterns and fix the symptoms that you do not want. Once a system is in place, it can be hard to both redesign and implement those designs. It means that people have to change the way they do things – their patterns – and accept different results from their actions. Often there also needs to be significant investment in the design change.

The United Nations Department of Economic and Social Affairs (2019) expects that the population of the world will increase to 9.5 billion by 2050 and 11 billion by 2100. Some cities are already redesigning their transportation, energy, building and land use systems in preparation for increases in population. For the past 50 years, the highly dense city of Singapore has undergone an intense redesign of its systems through laws, incentives, policies and adoption of innovative uses of technology. There are laws for green buildings, incentives for rooftop gardens and policies for affordable housing, public transportation, parks, community and open spaces (Kolczak, 2017).

As with feedback loops, when designing a system, it is crucial to know what your goals are. Some of the goals that cities and nations have set include zero carbon emissions, zero waste, 100% renewable fuel, sustainable transportation and walkability. Once you know your goals, you also need to know what measurements you will use to assess your success in reaching the goals. This allows you to have a better chance of realizing the system change you want. Your goals are directly related to your values, which brings us to the foundation of our pyramid.

(4) Values

Values are the base of the pyramid because they are what drives everything else. For most people, values are based on assumptions and beliefs rather than observations and facts. Assumptions are ideas that are thought to be true without evidence or proof. Beliefs are ideas that people have faith in and hold as true. Both can be difficult to change for a person, a group or in a system. In the chapter about values, values are defined as principles, standards or moral codes that are held in high esteem by an individual or society. Changing assumptions, beliefs or values has a cascading effect on how systems are designed or redesigned, structured or restructured; on our patterns of behavior; and on the symptoms that are a result of the system. The next chapter explores values and how to change values with greater depth.

Change agents

Change agents are people who bring about change. One thing all changes in a system have in common is change agents. Even revolutions that have a great leader, such as Mahatma Gandhi or Ani Pachen, happen because of the leadership of thousands of people who were change agents. A change agent works in many different ways. Some change agents focus on awareness raising, encouraging conversations or educating people. Others focus on gathering data, analysis and publishing information in a multitude of forms from social media to books or ad campaigns. Some change agents are organizers, and some are facilitators. Some change agents are innovators and idea generators, and others are doers who make things happen. Some work within a system, and others work from outside it. There are many ways to be a change agent. Most function in multiple ways, and some expect themselves to be able to do everything. As a change agent, and in life, it's important to do what you love to do and to focus on that instead of trying to do everything.

HIGHLIGHT: DIFFERENT APPROACHES TO CHANGE AGENTRY

Mahatma Gandhi

Gandhi led the independence stuggle of India from Great Britain in a very different way from Thomas Jefferson, George Washington and other American revolutionaries. He based his approach, in part, on the philosophy of Leo Tolstoy, the novelist who wrote *War and Peace*. His approach is called non-violent resistance. He led marches, initiated petitions and went on hunger strikes. Watch the movie *Gandhi*, directed by Richard Attenborough and released in 1982, as a starting point for more information on Gandhi and non-violent resistance.

What are some other ways besides marches, petitions and hunger strikes to non-violently protest? Have you ever participated in a non-violent protest? How?

Ani Pachen

Ani Pachen began and ended her career as a Buddhist nun in Tibet, but at the age of 25, when her father died and her homeland was being invaded by Chinese soldiers, she became a leader of a guerrilla warrior tribe to defend her people and home. She was captured, imprisoned and tortured at the age of 26 and not released until she was 48. After her release, she continued to protest and raise awareness about the independence of Tibet. Read the online graphic novel *The Rejected Princess* by Jason Porath at www.rejectedprincesses.com/princesses/ani-pachen as a starting place to gather more information on Ani Pachan.

What else did Ani Pachen do in her life besides fight and protest? What would you have done if you were Ani Pachen at 25 or 26 years of age? How about at 48? What would you have done differently? Why? What would you have done the same? Why?

Rachel Carson

Rachel Carson wrote the book *Silent Spring*, published in 1962, about the impacts of unrestricted use of pesticides, including DDT. She was a biologist and grounded her book in facts but conveyed her message with stories. She told of a future without birds and with rampant cancer in men, women and children. Her book helped motivate the formation of the Environmental Protection Agency (EPA) in the US in 1970 and environmental protection laws such as the Clean Air Act and the Clean Water Act. The formation of the EPA inspired similar agencies worldwide. Rachel died of cancer in 1964, before she could see the effects of her work. Begin to learn more about Rachel Carson on a website dedicated to her: www.rachelcarson.org.

Why is storytelling often more compelling than facts or data? Are scary stories or stories about bad outcomes more motivating than stories with happy endings or about good outcomes? Why if so, and why if not? How could storytelling have helped climate change scientists and others in the 1990s convey the facts and data? What stories can you tell to facilitate change in your own life or in society for happiness, well-being and sustainability?

GUEST COURSEBOOK CONTRIBUTION FROM LESTER R. KURTZ: PEACEFUL REVOLUTIONS

Lester Kurtz is sociologist who focuses on peace, non-violence and social movements. He is a professor, author and activist in the academic community. He wrote this essay to encourage readers of this coursebook.

A friend of mine met Archbishop Desmond Tutu at a peace conference in the Hague and thanked him for participating. "Mary," he said holding her arm, "when I was a young boy growing up in South Africa, I never dreamed that we would overthrow apartheid in my lifetime. If we can eliminate apartheid, we can abolish war!"

No dream is too big. Our unjust economy and climate crisis were created by human beings; we constructed them, so we can change them. We live in a time of unparalleled transformation as national borders fade and social divides are bridged. The only question is whether or not the global social tapestry will create a planet that is hotter and a more unequal global community.

As a young lawyer, Mahatma Gandhi was too timid to speak in court, but he radically transformed our understanding of conflict by drawing upon age-old wisdom. He inspired non-violent civil resistance that has changed laws, brought down dictators and provided a lifestyle model that promotes fair distribution and ecological sustainability.

The tiny little Himalayan country of Bhutan inspired the global community to make happiness and well-being the goal of an economy rather than ever-increasing GDP in a process that usually concentrates wealth, robs the poor of resources and damages the natural environment. Can we create a world that creates fair distribution and sustainability? Following Gandhi's model, yes, we can listen, analyze and mobilize. We will resist what creates unhappiness by refusing to cooperate with it, through protests, strikes and boycotts as well as by creating and engaging in different ways of doing things. We will construct systems and lifestyles sustainable for all humans, the planet and all of its inhabitants.

It is easy to think that a person cannot make changes in a big system like a national economy or society. But time and time again, it has been proven that even one person can make a difference. While the most powerful people in a system, such as a president, prime minister or other leader of an organization may be able to contribute to change in a system, even they cannot single-handedly make a change. This is because change happens when there are many elements of a system working over a time frame, and each person is an element in that system and has an impact even if they do not see it.

Sometimes change happens quickly and sometimes so slowly it is hard to see the change. The agricultural revolution took a few thousand years, the industrial revolution took almost 100 years and the digital revolution started 50 years ago. These revolutions happened because a few people started doing something new and unheard of, then a few more, and gradually, over time, most everybody was eating food from agricultural sources instead of hunting and gathering, relying upon manufactured goods instead of handcrafted goods, and using information technology. There is no one person one can point to and say *they are the leader of the agricultural, industrial or digital revolution.* There are a lot of different people who were leaders in many different ways, most of them never recorded in history. But that does not mean they did not make a difference.

For the change agent in you, it is important to keep a long timeframe in mind, knowing that systems change slowly over time and that even if you do not see your role as having a noticeable impact, you are part of a tide of changes. We hope to empower you to work towards systems change in ways that bring you happiness. When in doubt, remember the words of Margaret Mead, a noted cultural anthropologist: "Never doubt that a small group of thoughtful, committed citizens can change the world; indeed, it's the only thing that ever has."

Systems change exercises

- Use a piece of paper without lines. In the middle, put down something that represents you – your name, a drawing or symbol. Next, using sticky notes or small pieces of paper, write down at least four or five of the most important things in your life. These may be people, pets, activities, things, places or anything else – a partner, friend, pet, gaming, time alone, reading, sports, your cell phone or perhaps the mountains if you like hiking or the ocean if you love surfing. Put the things that matter most to you closest to you. Next, draw a dotted line around the things that matter to you. Using more sticky notes or pieces of paper, write down the things in your life that you wish were different from how they are, and are not contributing to your happiness – maybe even making you unhappy. These may be an activity you have to do, something someone in your family does, pollution in your neighborhood and on our planet, an aspect of the government in your country or anything else. Place these outside the dotted line. You have just drawn one way to represent elements in your life. Next, change one of the elements or take it away. With a pencil, draw out the impact the change you made has on other elements and describe at least one way that change impacts you.
- In your own life, you can see that when something happens over and over again, over time, it shapes who you are and the world around you. If you don't like what is happening and you have control over the situation, you can change the pattern. Over time with the change in a pattern, you may find that you will change in expected and unexpected ways. Reflect on a pattern in your life that you would like to change. How would you change it? What changes do you expect? What might be some unexpected changes?
- Imagine you are the president of your campus, CEO of a company, executive director of a nonprofit, or the mayor of your city, governor of your region or prime minister or president of your nation. You have experienced living through a global pandemic and just received news that another will occur within the year. What changes will you make to prepare for the impacts on your campus or area's health, economic, social and ecological systems? How does your answer differ depending on the kind of leader you are?
- Imagine that you are an urban planner. Your job is to redesign your city so it is known as a sustainable city where the people are happy. Begin by identifying the goals you want to achieve and the measurements you will use to determine if you reach your goals. Next, identify the elements of the system and form a design. Be bold in your design. You can use the *National Geographic* post *Cities of the Future* (www.nationalgeographic.com/magazine/2019/04/see-sustainable-future-city-designed-for-people-and-nature) as a starting place.

- To change a system in a desired way, it can be helpful to ask three questions:

  - What is the problem?
  - Why is it a problem?
  - When is it not a problem?

  With each answer to a question, you go to the next question, until you have uncovered the assumptions, beliefs and values driving system design, patterns and symptoms. Sometimes it takes several rounds of asking the three questions listed. Understanding of assumptions, beliefs and values will often reveal the high leverage points in a system. Identity a system that you would like to change and use the three questions to discover the underlying values, the changes in design that are needed, how the patterns will change and the cures for the symptoms.
- Graph out the Easterlin Paradox in which income is on the x axis and happiness is on the y axis. Assume that for each increase of $10,000, happiness goes up by 1 point. When you get to $75,000, assume happiness goes up by 0.5 points for the next $10,000, 0.25 for the subsequent $10,000, 0.125 for the next $10,000 and so on, until you reach an effective point at which happiness does not increase. How would you explain this concept to your parents? How would you explain it to a tween? Next, write down your thoughts in a paragraph, bullets, poem or drawings to the following questions: What do you think about the Easterlin Paradox? Will it have an impact on your career choices? How about your choices for how you spend your time? Why do you think most people do not know about the Easterlin Paradox? Do you think it has anything to do with advertising and the media? After you have finished this stage of the exercise, share what you have learned with someone who is not in your class; then share your experiences of explaining the Easterlin Paradox in class.

Systems change discussion questions

- What does it mean when a parent says of their child that they want them to be happy and healthy?
- Is there a connection between an individual's happiness and the happiness of other people? If so, what are the connections? If not, why not?
- Is there a connection between one person's happiness and the sustainability of the planet? If so, why is it? If not, why not?
- The *World Happiness Report* explains happiness levels (meaning satisfaction with life) based on six factors: average GDP, healthy life expectancy (the years a person lives after they lose their health do not count), freedom to make life choices (e.g. getting an education, career choices, having a family, moving, voting), generosity (defined as frequency of donating to

charity), perceptions of corruption in the government and social support (e.g. having someone to turn to when in need). Do you think these six factors are enough to explain the scores? Would you add any factors? Would you take any away? What are some ways the factors that are considered have an impact on the government making policy decisions? What factors explain increases or decreases in your life satisfaction?

- In Latin America, people are happy even though they have a lower average GDP. Do you think the explanations for this in the highlight explain this? If not, what else would explain it? What supports you having positive emotions, such as joy, happiness, contentment or curiosity?
- Draw or write an explanation of your food system starting with one thing you most like to eat or eat most often. Map out the food from its source, such as a cocoa tree and farmers, for chocolate, to your table, and then post consumption, for the packaging, uneaten food and waste.
- What would happen to your food supply if transportation systems to the place where you lived were devastated beyond repair? How would you and the people around you get food in the short term? What would you have to do to have food in the long term? What would need to change?
- Time is another important factor in understanding a system and in systems change. For example, does your understanding about the impact of climate change on human habitats change when your time frame changes from ten years to 100 years? How about from 100 years to 1,000 years? How about from 100 years to 10 billion years? Record your impression of the impact of climate change on human habitats for four different time frames before investigating the forecasted changes; then do some research into what the forecasted changes are. Did your research change your understanding? Does changing the time frame change your understanding of the earth's climate system and your motivation for change?

Systems change resources

Videos

- *What Keeps us Happy and Healthy as We Go Through Life?* by Richard Waldinger, TEDxBeaconStreet. www.ted.com/talks/robert_waldinger_what_makes_a_good_life_lessons_from_the_longest_study_on_happiness?language=en#t-51839
- *The Story of Stuff* by Annie Leonard. www.youtube.com/watch?v=9GorqroigqM
- *Why I Became a Change Agent* by Amanda Nesheiwat, TEDxBergenCommunityCollege. www.youtube.com/watch?v=1aLyRN3hMaM

- *Introduction to Systems Thinking* by Peter Senge. www.youtube.com/watch?v=eXdzKBWDraM
- *Becoming an Agent of Change: A Critique of Sustainability* by Jesse Baker, TEDx UCIrvine. www.youtube.com/watch?v=r8IE7rfKexw
- *The Story of Change* by Annie Leonard. www.youtube.com/watch?v=oIQdYXCKUv0
- *How We Design and Build a Smart City and Nation* by Cheong Koon Hean. https://youtu.be/m45SshJqOP4

Movies

- *Inequality for All* by Jacob Korbbluth (rated PG). http://inequalityforall.com/
- *Where to Invade Next* by Michael Moore (rated R). http://wheretoinvadenext.com/

Reading materials

- *What's the Economy For, Anyway?* by John de Graaf and David Batker
- *21 Lessons for the 21st Century* or *Homo Deus* by Yuval Noah Harari
- *The Book of Joy: Lasting Happiness in a Changing World* by the Dalai Lama and Desmond Tutu
- *How Happiness & Sustainability Connect* by Laura Musikanski. https://medium.com/invironment/how-happiness-sustainability-connect-7c92529d9fca

References

Baron, R., Byrne, D. & Suls, J. (1989). *Exploring Social Psychology*. 3rd Edition. London, UK: Pearson.

Bretton Woods Project. (2005). What are the Bretton Woods Institutions? Retrieved from www.brettonwoodsproject.org/2005/08/art-320747/

Brooks, R. B. (2005). The power of parenting. In S. Goldstein & R. Brooks (Eds.) *Handbook of Resilience in Children*. Boston, MA: Springer. https://doi.org/10.1007/0-306-48572-9_18

Diener, E., Ng, W., Harter, J. & Arora, R. (2010). Wealth and happiness across the world: Material prosperity predicts life evaluation, whereas psychosocial prosperity predicts positive feeling. *Journal of Personality and Social Psychology*, *99* (1), 52–61. doi: 10.1037/a0018066

Easterlin, R. (1974). Does economic growth improve the human lot? In P. David & M. Reder (Eds.) *Nations and Households in Economic Growth: Essays in Honor of Moses Abramovitz* (pp. 89–125). New York: Academic Press, Inc. Retrieved from http://graphics8.nytimes.com/images/2008/04/16/business/Easterlin1974.pdf

Easterlin, R. (1995). Will raising the incomes of all increase the happiness of all? *Journal of Economic Behavior and Organization*, *27* (1), 35–48. doi: 10.1016/0167-2681(95)00003-B

Easterlin, R. (2001). Income and happiness: Towards a unified theory. *The Economic Journal, 11* (473), 465–484. doi: 10.1111/1468-0297.00646

Edmond, D. (2017). 5 places relocating people because of climate change. *World Economic Forum*. Retrieved from www.weforum.org/agenda/2017/06/5-places-relocating-people-because-of-climate-change/

EPA. (n.d.a.). Colony collapse disorder. Retrieved from www.epa.gov/pollinator-protection/colony-collapse-disorder

EPA. (n.d.b.). EPA History: Resource Conservation and Recovery Act. Retrieved from www.epa.gov/history/epa-history-resource-conservation-and-recovery-act

Goodyear, S. (n.d). A brief history of household recycling. *CityLab*. Retrieved from www.citylab.com/city-makers-connections/recycling/

Hawkins, G. (2006). *The Ethics of Waste*. Lanham, Maryland: Rowman & Littlefield Publishers. Retrieved from www.environmentandsociety.org/sites/default/files/key_docs/ethics_of_waste_hawkins.pdf

Hawkins, P., Lovins, A. & Lovins, H. (1999). *Natural Capitalism: Creating the Next Industrial Revolution*. New York, NY: Little, Brown & Company. Retrieved from http://library.uniteddiversity.coop/Money_and_Economics/Natural_Capitalism-The_Next_Industrial_Revolution.pdf

Hill, H. (2008). *Food Miles: Background and Marketing*. Butte, MT: National Sustainable Agriculture Information. Retrieved from https://attra.ncat.org/attra-pub-summaries/?pub=281

IRS. (2018). The truth about frivolous arguments: Section I (a to c). Retrieved from www.irs.gov/privacy-disclosure/the-truth-about-frivolous-tax-arguments-section-i-a-to-c#A

Kelly, H., Holmes, J., Kerr, N., Reis, H., Rusbult, C. & Van Lange, P. (2003). *An Atlas of Interpersonal Situations*. New York, NY: Cambridge University Press.

Kelly, H. & Thibaut, J. (1978). *Interpersonal Relations: A Theory of Interdependence*. New York, NY: Wiley.

Kolczak, A. (2017). This city aims to be the world's greenest. *National Geographic*. Retrieved from www.nationalgeographic.com/environment/urban-expeditions/green-buildings/green-urban-landscape-cities-Singapore/

Kuznets, S. (1934). National income, 1929–1932: Senate Document 124. *US Congress*. Retrieved from https://fraser.stlouisfed.org/files/docs/publications/natincome_1934/19340104_nationalinc.pdf

Kuznets, S. (1937). Introduction to "National Income and Capital Formation, 1919–1935." *National Bureau of Economic Research*. Retrieved from www.nber.org/chapters/c5444.pdf

Layard, R. (2005). *Happiness: Lessons from a New Science*. London, UK: The Penguin Press.

Maani, K. & Cavana, R. (2007). *Systems Thinking, System Dynamics: Managing Change and Complexity*. New Zealand, North Shore: Pearson Education.

McLean, D. (2014). National and international indices of well-being: A critical analysis. *Journal of the Indiana Academy of the Social Sciences, 17* (1), article 5. Retrieved from https://digitalcommons.butler.edu/jiass/vol17/iss1/5

Meadows, D. (2008). *Thinking in Systems: A Primer*. London, UK: Earthscan. Retrieved from https://wtf.tw/ref/meadows.pdf

Mimura, N., Yasuhara, K., Kawagoe, S., Yokoki, H. & Kazama, S. (2011). Damage from the Great East Japan Earthquake and Tsunami – A quick report. *Mitigation and*

Adaption Strategies for Global Change, 16, 803–818. doi: 10.1007/s11027-011-9297-7

Mineo, L. (2017). Good genes are nice, but joy is better. *The Harvard Gazette.* Retrieved from https://news.harvard.edu/gazette/story/2017/04/over-nearly-80-years-harvard-study-has-been-showing-how-to-live-a-healthy-and-happy-life/

National Geographic. (n.d.). From mega-regions to micro-size homes: cities of the future. Retrieved from www.nationalgeographic.com/magazine/2019/04/see-sustainable-future-city-designed-for-people-and-nature/

NBC. (2011, March 13). Millions without food, water, power in Japan. Retrieved from http://www.nbcnews.com/id/42044293/ns/world_news-asia_pacific/t/millions-without-food-water-power-japan/#.Xmq9cJNKi_I

Psychology. (n.d.). Interdependence theory. Retrieved from http://psychology.iresearchnet.com/social-psychology/social-psychology-theories/interdependence-theory/

Robbins, J. (2017). A new way of understanding what makes a river healthy. *Yale Environment, 360.* Retrieved from https://e360.yale.edu/features/new_look_at_rivers_reveals_toll_of_human_activity_yellowstone_river

Rojas, M. (2018). Happiness in Latin America has social foundations. In J. Helliwell, R. Layard & J. Sachs (Eds.) *World Happiness Report 2018.* New York, NY: Sustainable Development Solutions Network.

Shragai, N. (2014). Why we see bosses as parents. *Financial Times.* Retrieved from www.ft.com/content/9cebd9d0-9eda-11e3-8663-00144feab7de

Smart Dubai. (n.d.). AI lab. Retrieved from www.smartdubai.ae/initiatives/ai-lab

Sweden. (n.d.). The Swedish recycling revolution. Retrieved from https://sweden.se/nature/the-swedish-recycling-revolution/

Thibaut, J. & Kelly, H. (1959). *The Social Psychology of Groups.* New York, NY: Wiley.

TRTWorld. (2019). Swedish recycling so successful it is importing rubbish. Retrieved from www.trtworld.com/europe/swedish-recycling-so-successful-it-is-importing-rubbish-24491

UN Environment Programme. (n.d.). 'A city in a garden': Singapore's journey to becoming a biodiversity model. Retrieved from www.unenvironment.org/news-and-stories/story/city-garden-singapores-journey-becoming-biodiversity-model

United Nations Department of Economic and Social Affairs. (2019). Growing at a slower pace, world population is expected to reach 9.7 billion in 2050 and could peak at nearly 11 billion around 2100. Retrieved from www.un.org/development/desa/en/news/population/world-population-prospects-2019.html

USDA Foreign Agriculture Service. (n.d.). China. Retrieved from www.fas.usda.gov/regions/china.

Wilkinson, R. & Pickett, K. (2009). *The Spirit Level: Why More Equal Societies Almost Always Do Better.* London, UK: Penguin.

Wilkinson, R. & Pickett, K. (2014). *A Convenient Truth: A Better Society for Us and the Planet.* London, UK: Fabian Society & Friedrich Ebert Stiftung. Retrieved from www.fabians.org.uk/wp-content/uploads/2014/09/A-Convenient-Truth.pdf

Wilkinson, R. & Pickett, K. (2018). *Inner Level: How More Equal Societies Reduce Stress, Restore Sanity and Improve Everybody's Well-being.* London, UK: Penguin.

2
VALUES

Values learning objectives

The objectives of this chapter are for students to be able to:

- Understand what values are.
- Understand the connections between measurements, values and actions.
- Understand the concept of common values.
- Understand the role of values in systems change.

Preliminary questions

- What are values?
- What are your values?
- What does it mean to be true to yourself?
- What does "an unexamined life is not worth living" mean? Do you agree?
- How would you determine whether you uphold your values on any given day?
- Are there certain values that are common to all people?
- What are some values that are held by some people but not others?
- How do values influence decisions and patterns of behavior?
- Do you think values are drivers of a system? If so, why? If not, why not?
- Do values held by a person or by a society change? If so, what may be some of the reasons for the change?

Introduction to values: setting the stage for a thought experiment

This chapter explores what values are and ways to identify and communicate about values. Let's begin this chapter by setting the stage for a thought experiment. A thought experiment is the term for thinking through the consequences of an idea to understand what the results are, which is different from doing something, such as conducting an experiment, enacting a policy or changing something. Einstein discovered the theory of relativity through a thought experiment (Waldrop, 2017).

For our thought experiment, imagine a world in which your happiness, the well-being of others and the sustainability of nature are the most important things to you, to your professor and to your country. Every year, there is the front-line story on media sites that reports on your nation, state and city or town's levels of happiness, well-being and sustainability compared with others. Every three months, there are updates about changes in these levels.

Imagine that the primary things that policy makers (from the president or prime minister of your country to your city mayor) focus on are happiness for individuals, well-being for communities and sustainability for the environment. Policies, programs and projects are all formed, changed or repealed with the goals of happiness, societal well-being and sustainability.

Imagine that at school, in every grade, happiness, well-being and sustainability are core topics. Since kindergarten, you have developed skills that have supported you in finding and fulfilling your true purpose in life in ways that bring you joy and help others. You have learned how to be a creative problem solver, how to be resilient in the face of trouble and how to form and nurture healthy relationships. You have strong communication skills, a deep capacity for compassion and healthy lifestyle habits. You are able to see things as they truly are with acceptance and discernment.

In this world, the social, economic and governmental systems have shifted. You no longer live in a world where success is determined based on how much money you have, nations are considered developed based on the size and growth of the economy and businesses exist solely to make profit. Instead, all people live in a world where the main goals are happiness for people, well-being for communities and sustainability for the planet. In this world, there has been a fundamental change in the values. Socially, people no longer judge people who are more wealthy, beautiful or famous than others as successful. People see successful people as those who have found their own purpose in life, feel happy about who they are and help others and care for the environment.

What would it take to realize this world? Remember that Einstein, whose discovery changed the world, also said, "Imagination is more important than knowledge. For knowledge is limited, whereas imagination embraces the entire world, stimulating progress, giving birth to evolution" (Vierecj, 1929, p. 117).

The value of values

Tom Crompton is a scientist and change strategist who studies what matters to people, what shapes what matters to people and people's perceptions of what matters to their fellow citizens. He worked with Tim Kasser, a social psychologist and writer, to study the role of values in systems change. What people value is one important factor in determining how they behave. Values are shaped by many aspects of the culture in which we live – including the kinds of measurements that a government uses to determine national progress (Crompton & Kasser, 2009).

This implies that if the government were to change the way that they measure progress, this may contribute to bringing different values to the fore. How would this happen? Let's go back to the scenario in which you are the ruler of a nation. In this scenario, you decide to change the measurements by which the success of the country is measured from GDP to the happiness of your people and ecological sustainability of the natural environment. Resources spent for increasing GDP are now targeted for increasing happiness and ecological sustainability. Soon agencies in the government are thought to be successful when they safeguard or increase both happiness and ecological sustainability and outdated when they predominantly aim for increased GDP. A feedback loop with both positive and negative dynamics is in place. People are rewarded when their agencies successfully meet the goals of happiness and ecological sustainability. Companies that do business with the government, from consultants to contractors, retool their goals to help governmental agencies and people they work with to reach their goals. Your people see that their government highly values happiness and ecological sustainability, and they start to value it as well. Companies that provide goods and services that bring happiness and ecological sustainability are more successful than other companies, and people want to work for these companies because, in part, they will have a more desirable job than by working for companies that don't do this. Soon people's values shift, and their decisions and behaviors change.

As ruler of the nation, you have changed the system of the nation by changing what is measured as well as many other things. How resources are allocated and how agencies and people are assessed is changed, and so their goals and their own measurements for success shift. With this thought experiment, we started with measurements, influenced by the findings of Tom Crompton and Tim Kasser, who study the role of values in systems change.

The last chapter suggested that values are the strongest leverage points in systems. However, there are many other entry points, and sometimes other entry points may be better leverage points, such as when you are not the ruler of a nation and do not have control over what the measurements for success are for a system. Nonetheless, values are important to any system. This brings us to the question: what are values?

GUEST COURSEBOOK CONTRIBUTION FROM TOM CROMPTON: VALUES AND SOCIAL CHANGE

Tom Crompton leads a small non-governmental organization called Common Cause Foundation which works on human values – what matters to people, what shapes what matters to people and people's perceptions of what matters to their fellow citizens. He wrote this essay to empower readers of this coursebook.

There's a danger of seeing action for sustainability as fragmented across different causes (e.g. human rights, biodiversity conservation, renewable energy, animal welfare). These different causes in turn imply different policies and practices, and it's here that work is often focused.

But social psychologists have shown that the values which underpin and energize action on each of the causes are intimately connected. Far from being fragmented, progress on each of these causes relies upon our success in engaging and strengthening interrelated "compassionate" values such as friendship, honesty, social justice, equality and creativity.

In my work with Common Cause Foundation, I've shown how many different kinds of organizations – not just those with an explicit social or environmental purpose – can have a profound impact on the values that we collectively prioritize.

One important element of this work is to help convey a more accurate perception of what other people value. Studies repeatedly find that people tend to underestimate the importance that others place on the "compassionate" values listed earlier while overestimating the importance that they place on "self-interest" values such as social status, image and financial success. This misperception predicts lower concern about social and environmental problems and lowers well-being. Common Cause Foundation shows how any organization can begin to work in ways that strengthen social norms around "compassionate" values – thereby helping to convey the simple truth that most of us care more deeply for one another and the wider world than we currently recognize.

What are values?

The word "value" comes from the Latin verb *valere*, meaning *to be strong, to be worth, to be well.* Value is defined by the Cambridge Dictionary as "importance, worth or benefit" (Cambridge Dictionary, n.d., p. 1). Values have been defined as equivalent to determinants, drives, instincts, interests, motives, preferences, tastes and utility (Hecher, 1993). Values are the basis on which laws, morals, principles, standards and norms are developed, which makes up a value system. Individuals, companies, governments, cities, nations, cultures and society each have their own values. Sometimes a person or entity will know their values and even have a value statement. There are times, though, that people, companies and even cultures are not aware of their values. One way to think of values is as what is important to you.

What may be held as a good value for a person or entity may be considered bad by another. For example, a revolutionary person in a country where the culture values conformity may be considered bad and even imprisoned. People from one culture may condemn another culture for their values, as is sometimes the case in religious-based cultures. This can also happen between political parties or economic and social classes within a culture, country or even family. This subject will be revisited in the section about conflicting values. But now, let's explore your values because knowing your own values empowers you to identify the values of a system.

What are your values?

Knowing your own values helps you to understand how to discover and identify the values that are the foundation of a system and upheld by that system. Your values may mirror those of your family, friends or other group of people or they may be somewhat or entirely different. You have certain values because you learned to care about certain things as a child, through your education or by association with a group, or you may have certain values because of your own experiences or way of being. You know what your values are because they reflect what you care about and what is important to you. So, what are your values? If you are not sure what your values are, there are several ways you can discover them.

HIGHLIGHT: EXPLORING THE ORIGIN OF PERSONAL VALUES

Philosophers and social scientists have sought to understand the origin of personal values for millennia. Philosophers, artists, politicians, religious leaders and others have also sought to shape them. A few theories about the origin of values are very briefly covered here, along with questions for exploring the origin of personal values, and to further understanding of the origin of values within a system.

Genetics

This can be rather controversial, although interesting. A twin study (Renner et al., 2012; Baggini, 2015) indicates that some values may be genetic, in particular, harmony and intellectualism. This means that you are born with certain values. It could also mean that depending on genetic makeup, some values are dominant, and others are recessive. It can influence your nature or disposition. In your family, do you see any similarity in values between generations? Do you see any evidence of recessive or dominant values? Are your values similar to anyone in your extended family whom you have not interacted with much during your childhood?

Family

Your family has a formative impact on your personal values. This is something scientists have found (Parish & Nunn, 1988), but it also makes common sense. You begin to learn who you are and how to be in the world from your parents or guardians. What are the values of your family? How are they similar or different from your values? Do you think that your values come from your family, are in reaction against the values of your family, or come from a different source?

Culture

The culture with which you identify has an impact on your values (Curtis, Conover & Chui, 2012). This means that to some extent, your values will differ from others based on your nation of origin (where you were born and raised), where you live, your schooling and where you work. What are the values of your nation? Of your school? Of your workplace? How are they different? How are they similar?

Soul

Aristotle and Plato postulated that our values are a "psychological good" (Stanford Encyclopedia of Philosophy, 2004 revised 2014, p. 9) that come from our soul. They thought that a person could choose to cultivate them or not but that ultimately their values came from something inside the self, whether immortal or mortal. Do you believe that your values come from something unexplainable inside you, such as a soul? Or something unexplainable outside you, such as a spiritual essence? What are the values that you think would come from a soul or from a great spiritual essence?

These are not all the sources of your values but a start for exploring the source of your values. Others may be your sense of spirituality or religion, friends, a teacher or mentor, your school, your language or of unexplainable origin.

One way to figure out your values is by reflecting on what makes you angry or upset and on what you do not like in the world. If seeing someone treated unjustly makes you angry, then justice and fairness are probably among your values. If it upsets you when someone is mean to another person or an animal, then kindness may be one of your values. If you get angry when someone lies, then truth and honesty are probably your values. If it does not matter to you that someone gets more than their fair share of something as long as they worked for it but you object if someone gets a share when they have not put in an effort, then you may value industry or productivity. On the other hand, you may feel that people should have to work for what they get and should not get more than their fair share, so you value both productivity and fairness equally. If it bothers you that trees are cut down and parks paved for buildings and streets, then nature or environmentalism may be one of your values.

You can also tell your values by what you are willing to stand up or fight for. In the US, the Civil War was fought for the value of freedom, albeit both sides interpreted the value of freedom very differently. One side fought against slavery, as Abraham Lincoln put it in his speech at the site of the Battle of Gettysburg in 1863:

> Four score and seven years ago our fathers brought forth, upon this continent, a new nation, conceived in liberty, and dedicated to the proposition that all men are created equal. . . . Now we are engaged in a great civil war, testing whether that nation, or any nation so conceived and so dedicated, can long endure . . . (and) . . . – that this nation, under God, shall have a new birth of freedom – and that government of the people, by the people, for the people, shall not perish from the earth.
>
> *(Lincoln, 1863)*

On the other side, people went to war for what they thought was their "right to keep slaves and take them wherever they wished" (PBS, n.d.b., p. 5). Of course, there were other values on both sides, some the same and differently interpreted, others in opposition, but on both sides, people fought and died for their values. This is a dramatic example, although it illustrates the point. In your own life, you may have found yourself objecting vehemently to something someone did or said because of the principle of it. If this has ever happened to you or you can imagine it happening, you can reflect on why you object in terms of how it violates one or more of your values and so uncover a value that is important to you.

You can also ascertain your values by your decisions and actions, particularly when you have to choose between two different things. For example, if you choose to spend your spare time alone over going out with friends, you probably value quiet over excitement. You can look at your choices in what classes you take, where you live, how you spend your money and who you choose to have in your life to help uncover your values.

Another way to identify your values is to make a list. This is what Benjamin Franklin did when he was 20. His list of values, which he called *virtues* (some rephrased in modern words), was:

Moderation
Quiet
Order
Determination

Economizing
Productivity
Sincerity
Justice
Moderation
Cleanliness
Peacefulness
Modesty
Humility

(PBS, n.d.a.)

When he first listed his values, he did not include humility; he added this one when a friend pointed out its absence. It was not a value that was in his nature, but that he adopted because it was part of his culture. (Pride probably was a value closer to his nature.) He decided to focus on one value each week of his life, attempting to live it to the fullest. He recorded how well he did by grading his performance for that value. In his autobiography, he wrote about the experience of trying to live the value of humility:

> In reality, there is, perhaps, no one of our natural passions so hard to subdue as pride. Disguise it, struggle with it, beat it down, stifle it, mortify it as much as one pleases, it is still alive, and will every now and then peep out and show itself . . . even if I could conceive that I had completely overcome it, I should probably be proud of my humility.
>
> *(Franklin, 1706–1790)*

If listing your values draws a blank, another way to identify your values is to select from a list. Figure 2.1 shows a compilation of 311 values. See if you can identify the 10 or 20 that are important to you. If you find more than 20, try listing them in order of priority. Then spend time reflecting on each one and contemplate how your decisions and actions reflect that value.

Ten common values

Shalom Schwartz (1994) is a social psychologist who studies cross-cultural psychology. Cross-cultural psychology is the study of how our thinking and acting is influenced by different cultures, with a focus on what is universal

- ABUNDANCE
- ACCEPTANCE
- ACCOMPLISHMENT
- ACCOUNTABILITY
- ACCURACY
- ACHIEVEMENT
- ADAPTABILITY
- ADVENTURE
- ALERTNESS
- ALTRUISM
- AMBITION
- AMUSEMENT
- APPRECIATION
- ASSERTIVENESS
- ATTACHMENT
- ATTENTIVENESS
- AUTHENTICITY
- AUTHORITY
- AUTONOMY
- AWARENESS
- BALANCE
- BEAUTY
- BOLDNESS
- BRAVERY
- BRILLIANCE
- CALMNESS
- CANDOR
- CAPABLE
- CAREFUL
- CARETAKING
- CELEBRATION
- CERTAINTY
- CHALLENGE
- CHANGE
- CHARITY
- CITIZENSHIP
- CLARITY
- CLEANLINESS
- CLEVER
- COLLABORATION
- COMFORT
- COMMITMENT
- COMMON SENSE
- COMMUNICATION
- COMMUNITY
- COMPASSION
- COMPETENCE
- COMPETENCY
- COMPETITION
- CONCENTRATION
- CONCERN
- CONFIDENCE
- CONNECTION
- CONSCIOUSNESS
- CONSERVATION
- CONSISTENCY
- CONTENTMENT
- CONTROL
- CONVICTION
- COOPERATION
- COORDINATION
- COURAGE
- COURTESY
- CREATION
- CREATIVITY
- CREDIBILITY
- CURIOSITY
- DECISIVE
- DECISIVENESS
- DEDICATION
- DEMOCRACY
- DEPENDABILITY
- DETACHMENT
- DETERMINATION
- DEVELOPMENT
- DEVOTION
- DIGNITY
- DISCERNMENT
- DISCIPLINE
- DISCOVERY
- DIVERSITY
- DRIVE
- EDUCATION
- EFFECTIVENESS
- EFFICIENCY
- EMPATHY
- EMPOWERMENT
- ENDURANCE
- ENERGY
- ENJOYMENT
- ENTHUSIASM
- ENVIRONMENT
- ENVIRONMENTALISM
- EQUALITY
- EQUANIMITY
- ETHICAL
- EXCELLENCE
- EXPERIENCE
- EXPLORATION
- EXPRESSIVE
- FAIRNESS
- FAITH
- FAME
- FAMILY
- FAME
- FEARLESS
- FEELINGS
- FEROCIOUS
- FIDELITY
- FITNESS
- FLAIR
- FLEXIBILITY
- FOCUS
- FORESIGHT
- FORGIVENESS
- FORTITUDE
- FREEDOM
- FRIENDSHIP
- FRIENDSHIPS
- FRUGALITY
- FULFILLMENT
- FUN
- GENEROSITY
- GENIUS
- GIVING
- GOODNESS
- GOODWILL
- GRACE
- GRATITUDE
- GREATNESS
- GRIT
- GROWTH
- HAPPINESS
- HARMONY
- HEALTH
- HEDONISM
- HONESTY
- HONOR
- HOPE
- HUMILITY
- HUMOR
- IMAGINATION
- IMPROVEMENT
- INDEPENDENCE
- INDIVIDUALITY
- INFLUENCE
- INITIATIVE
- INNOVATION
- INQUISITIVENESS
- INSIGHT
- INSPIRATION
- INTEGRITY
- INTELLIGENCE
- INTENSITY
- INTIMACY
- INTUITION
- IRREVERENT
- JOY
- JUDGEMENT
- JUSTICE
- KINDNESS
- KNOWLEDGE
- LAWFUL
- LAWFULNESS
- LEADERSHIP
- LEARNING
- LIBERTY
- LOGIC
- LOVE
- LOYALTY
- MASTERY
- MATURITY
- MEANING
- MERIT
- MODERATION
- MODESTY
- MONEY
- MOTIVATION
- NATURE
- NON-VIOLENCE
- NURTURING
- OBEDIENCE
- OPEN-MINDEDNESS
- OPENNESS
- OPTIMISM
- ORDERLINESS
- ORGANIZATION
- ORIGINALITY
- PASSION
- PATIENCE
- PATRIOTISM
- PEACE
- PERFECTION
- PERFORMANCE
- PERSEVERANCE
- PERSISTENCE
- PERSONAL
- PLAYFULNESS
- PLEASURE
- POISE
- POPULARITY
- POSITIVITY
- POTENTIAL
- POWER
- PRACTICALITY
- PRESENT
- PRESERVATION
- PRIDE
- PRIVACY
- PRODUCTIVITY
- PROFESSIONALISM
- PROGRESS
- PROSPERITY
- PUNCTUALITY
- PURPOSE
- QUALITY
- REALISTIC
- REASON
- RECIPROCITY
- RECOGNITION
- RECREATION
- REFLECTIVE
- REGULARITY
- RELAXATION
- RELIABILITY
- REPUTATION
- RESOURCEFULNESS
- RESPECT
- RESPONSIBILITY
- RESPONSIVENESS
- RESTRAINT
- RESULTS
- REVERENCE
- RIGOR
- RISK
- ROMANCE
- SACRIFICE
- SAFETY
- SATISFACTION
- SECURITY
- SELF-AWARENESS
- SELF-CONFIDENCE
- SELF-ESTEEM
- SELF-EXPRESSION
- SELF-IMPROVEMENT
- SELF-LOVE
- SELF-MASTERY
- SELF-RELIANCE
- SELF-RESPECT
- SELF-TRUST
- SELFLESS
- SENSITIVITY
- SENSUALITY
- SERENITY
- SERVICE
- SHARING
- SIGNIFICANCE
- SILENCE
- SIMPLICITY
- SINCERITY
- SKILLFULNESS
- SMARTNESS
- SOLITUDE
- SPEEDINESS
- SPIRIT
- SPIRITUALITY
- SPONTANEOUS-NESS
- STABILITY
- STANDARDIZATION
- STATUS
- STEWARDSHIP
- STRAIGHTFORWARDNESS
- STRENGTH
- STRUCTURE
- SUCCESS
- SUPPORT
- SUPREMACY
- SURPRISE
- SUSTAINABILITY
- SYSTEMIZATION
- TALENT
- TEAMWORK
- TEMPERANCE
- THANKFULNESS
- THOROUGHNESS
- THOUGHTFUL
- TIMELINESS
- TOLERANCE
- TOUGHNESS
- TRADITION
- TRANQUILITY
- TRANSPARENCY
- TRUST
- TRUSTWORTHINESS
- TRUSTWORTHY
- TRUTH
- UNDERSTANDING
- UNIQUENESS
- UNITY
- VALOR
- VARIETY
- VICTORY
- VIGOR
- VISION
- VITALITY
- WEALTH
- WELCOMING
- WINNING
- WISDOM
- WONDER
- WORK

FIGURE 2.1 311 values

Sources: Jeffrey (n.d.); MySelf (n.d.); Threads Culture (n.d.)

among all human cultures. He proposes that there are ten values that are held in common. They are synopsized here as:

- Achievement: success and prosperity
- Benevolence: helping others
- Conformity: restraint and not harming others
- Hedonism: seeking pleasure and avoiding pain
- Power: status and dominance
- Security: safety and harmony
- Self-direction: independence and freedom
- Stimulation: challenge and novelty
- Tradition: respecting one's culture
- Universalism: appreciating and protecting all life and the Earth

(Schwartz, 2012) (Fig. 2.2)

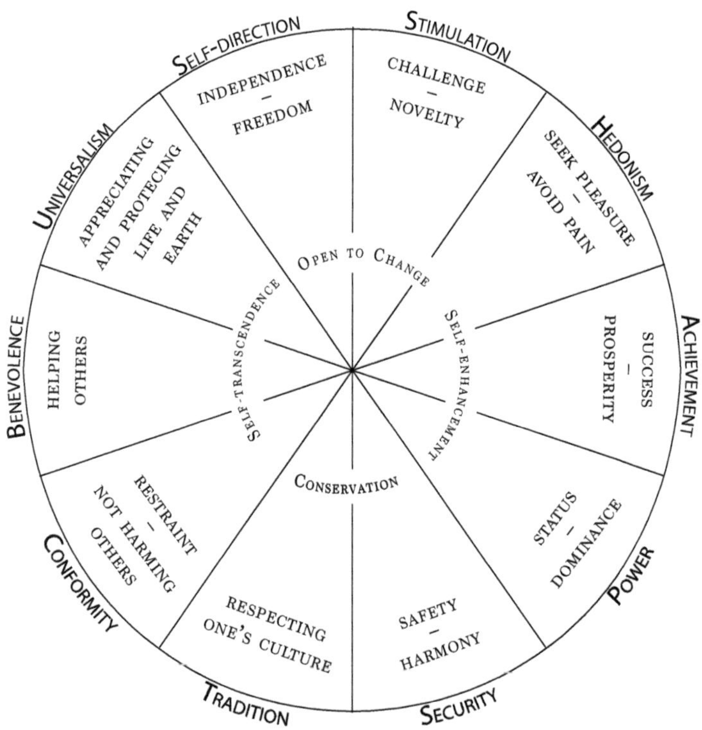

FIGURE 2.2 The ten common values to all human civilization identified by Shalom Schwartz (2012)

Exploring conflicting values

You can see that among these ten values, there can be conflict. The values of self-direction and stimulation may be expressed by an openness to change, which may be in opposition to the values of tradition and security, which may be expressed by a predilection towards conservation. Conflicting values is something everybody experiences in their lives when something they want to do is unconventional or unaccepted by society or by their friends or family. Stimulation can conflict with the value of security. Most people experience this conflict when they want to do something that feels risky, but they are also a little afraid. Someone may choose an unconventional career path or partner in life but otherwise live a very conventional life. Power can come into conflict with benevolence, particularly if someone is seen as powerful when they are able to control or suppress someone else.

Competing values are one aspect of the complexity of humans. This means you do not have to choose some values and ignore others. You have the ability to live with a balance of competing values. Moreover, while values can conflict, they are not de-facto in opposition. A person or society that is open to change may be willing to try new ways to conserve cultural heritage sites, natural environment or other features of society. In a dynamic equilibrium, opposite or different values work in balance.

In your own life, you probably have experienced this in terms of work–life balance, particularly when there is a big project with an impending deadline. Health and leisure time are valued, but you also value productivity, a sense of accomplishment and the reward obtained for completing the project. You work hard to get the project done, foregoing fun, time with friends and family and maybe even exercise and sleep. You feel stressed but know that once the project is done, there will be some time to get caught up on rest, reconnect with the people you love and have fun. Optimally, balance will be restored in your life, working no more than 40 hours a week and spending time resting and enjoying life, maintaining an equilibrium between the values of health and leisure with productivity and accomplishment. However, if as soon as the project is done, another comes along, your level of stress goes up higher than it was before, your sleep deprivation mounts and the effects of time away from family, friends and fun compounds. Eventually, you lose touch with the people you love and forget how good it feels to be rested and have fun. Moreover, life is less ecologically sustainable. You're eating out more often, buying and consuming things as a proxy for fun and producing more waste. It usually takes a major event to bring back balance when this happens, such as a heart attack or a partner leaving.

At that point, values might refocus with limits placed on how many hours worked, on what kind of work will be done and the work environment.

Karoshi is the dangerous cultural phenomena of work–life imbalance that is leading to early death among young people in Japan (Yoshikawaet al., 2018; Otake, n.d.). To change the value system and potentially put an end to the phenomenon of karoshi, the government could put limits on the hours worked each week, require paid vacation time and sick leave and protect job security for people who work part time, job share, or take leaves of absence to care for new babies or ill family members. These policies and laws could promote work–life balance and a balancing of competing values.

HIGHLIGHT: CONFLICTING VALUES AND TRAGEDY

A dramatic example of conflicting values is when a nation places priority on the value of culture, as in the case of Bhutan. In the 1990s, the government of Bhutan expelled or put into camps one sixth of its population in an effort to preserve its culture (Mørch, 2016). Over 100,000 people of Nepali nationality or descendants of Nepalis were put into camps (Shrestha, 2015). In Bhutan, the four goals, called pillars, of the government are good governance, natural environment, national culture and sustainable economic development, which are intended to uphold the goal of gross national happiness for the people of Bhutan (Munro, 2016). The treatment of Nepali people living in Bhutan, some of them born there, in a nation known for putting the happiness of its people above all else continues to be a point of contention for many people. Imagine you were the ruler of Bhutan, and one sixth of your nation's population were from another culture. Your goals are to preserve your culture and safeguard the happiness of all people in your nation. What would you do?

Almost every nation has somewhere in its history a civil war, atrocity or other action that, when looked back on, is hard to explain or understand. These include slavery, massacring of indigenous peoples, ethnic cleansing and other forms of atrocities. This part of a country's history can be hard to understand and hard to reconcile. Reflecting on your own nation or an event that impacted your family, why do you think these things happened? Can the values of the people who committed the atrocities explain it? If so, how? If not, why? If you were ruler of the nation and could steer your country into making different decisions, what would you do?

Two stories

The balancing act of living with a complex value system is experienced by all people on a personal level. Because humans are complex, so are our systems. Choosing just one value at the expense of all others necessitates that one ignores important aspects of society and life. This has been done in countries where GDP is the dominant measure and economic growth is the dominant goal. Today, in many countries, the use of GDP accentuates the values of achievement, power and security over values of benevolence, universalism and self-direction. The use of profit by business and wealth for people does the same. The result is that caring for others and for the environment is not highly valued, esteemed or respected. The rich–poor gap gets wider, and the natural environment suffers. This is an outcome of lack of balance in values. Just as it is possible to have many values, it is possible to have complex measurements that reflect a complex and at times competing set of values. Let's explore this concept with two stories.

Wealth, appearance and status values story

Marley is a successful businessperson who dropped out of school at the age of 17. Marley spent a summer fishing on the Bering Sea, one of the most dangerous jobs in the world but also one of the highest paid. After six months, Marley had earned over $100,000. Marley was able to buy a bulldozer and start a demolition business. At the beginning, Marley did not follow rules on some jobs, which increased profits but put the business at risk for fines and damaged waterways and soil systems on some job sites. Marley got away with it and over time grew the business so that it operates in several states. Today Marley's company employs over 10,000 people. The business expanded to include recycling and clean up on contaminated sites and oil spills. Marley has a reputation for firing high-level employees on a whim, and the company is known for high turnover. Employees usually quit after three years. It is hard to keep people, but the profits are high. Marley earns in the top 10%. Most of Marley's income is reinvested in the stock market, and the rest is spent on lavish homes, vacations, expensive designer clothing and spa treatments. In Marley's mind, there is no such thing as enough money. Marley has been on the cover of *Fortune* and *Forbes*. Every year for about one week, Marley feels like a success because the year's salary and bonus are more than the previous one, and the business has grown compared with the last year. After that week is over, Marley feels driven to make more money. Marley likes being admired by strangers and employees for having lots of money. Marley has a family, but they are like strangers. Marley has to get reacquainted with them each holiday season.

In this story, Marley's primary values are wealth, status and appearance. For Marley, status comes from being wealthy. The society in which Marley lives reinforces Marley's personal values. Marley thinks that the wealthier a person is, the higher their status.

In a society where the primary value is wealth, most people prioritize making money, set their goals to be rich and determine their success by how much money they have, how good they look and what their status is relative to other people. People will feel successful when they increase their wealth or see themselves as richer or more attractive. Often people think that if they get richer, they will be happier. However, most people find that they are never satisfied with how much money they have for long because there is always someone with more.

Care and community values story

River worked hard to get good grades in high school and went to a small but expensive school, accumulating a lot of debt. River graduated from college and took a job at a nonprofit working with children of incarcerated parents. Five years out of college, River still earns less than half the average salary for a graduate with the same degree who works at a private, for profit business. River knows that it will take a lifetime to pay off the college debt and that buying a home is not going to be an option. River loves the work at the nonprofit and has lots of friends. In addition to working, River volunteers at a local shelter for homeless youth and gets a lot of fulfillment. River works and volunteers long hours and often feels exhausted. River feels guilty for taking time off so often works until sick. River has never gone on an expensive vacation or been to a spa. River has to occasionally borrow from family once in a while to cover unexpected expenses. River works off the debt by helping out when there is a big project around the house or baby-sitting. This usually leaves River feeling even more exhausted. River feels important and necessary but undervalued and always a few steps away from a financial crisis.

In this scenario, River's values are care for community and connection to others. River spends a lot of energy and time taking care of other people and trying to make the world a better place, at the expense of making a lot of money. The society in which River lives sends a message to River that River is important but not as valued as people who make a lot of money. River never feels like a real success in societal terms because wealth is how the society in which River lives defines success. River does feel like a success in terms of the community where River works and volunteers.

In communities where people's values are the opposite of the dominant values of society, people often feel that their efforts are important but that they can never do enough. Sometimes this leads to burnout and hopelessness followed by debilitating skepticism.

The dilemma of societal values and happiness

These two stories illustrate a dilemma for most of us. Marley chose to adopt the values of a society where money is the main measure and wealth the primary determinant of success. Marley never feels like a success for long. River rejected the dominant values of society to do work that is helping people and making the world a better place but suffers financially and in other ways.

In the case of Marley, the assumption that more money will make one happier is only partially true. Money does increase happiness up to a certain point, but after that, the increases are only marginal, and for some, after a certain point, more money can lead to decreases in happiness (Easterlin, 1995). In the US, that amount is $75,000 a year for a family of four. In the UK, the amount is about £45,000 a year. In the case of River, not having enough money is a source of unhappiness (Easterlin, 2001).

One of the reasons that being very rich may actually make you less happy is that when there are big differences between how much the highest paid and lowest paid people make in a society, everyone is worse off (Wilkinson & Pickett, 2010). For example, in the US, the top earners make more than $1 million a year. This is 1% of the population. But the bottom earners make about $15,000 a year. This is 50% of the population (Long, 2016). This is the widest gap among the rich countries in the world. In the UK, the top 1% highest earners make about £150,000 a year, and only 15,000 people earn more than £1 million, while the bottom 50% earn about £27,000 a year (The Equity Trust, n.d.).

If River were better rewarded in financial terms for the work of caring for other people, then River might be happier and might enjoy greater work–life balance and a deeper sense of being valued. If Marley lived in a society where balance or family and connections were valued as much or more than income, Marley might stop focusing on accumulating wealth at the expense of other parts of life and find happiness in other pursuits.

When a government focuses on GDP, then the values people prioritize are wealth, appearance and status. The decisions people make and the actions they take will be guided by the goals of increasing wealth, raising status and looking attractive in the eyes of other people. The values of caring for each other, income equity and knowing and living one's inner life's purpose may end up being ignored.

One of the problems with using GDP is that it is an indiscriminate measure. It counts not just the good things that do make us happier and better but also things that make us miserable. When there is an environmental disaster, such as a large oil spill or a terrible flood, GDP goes up because of the costs to clean up, legal battles and fines. When people suffering illness have to sell their homes to pay for health care, GDP goes up. These are just two examples of things that increase GDP but do not make us happier.

GDP also does not count some things that do increase our happiness and well-being. When a person exercises outside instead of buying a gym membership, they are not contributing to the GDP. It also does not include the time and attention of a parent taking care of a child or an adult child taking care of an elderly parent. It does not include time spent relaxing or having fun with friends on the beach or in the park. These are just a few examples that GDP does not count but that are important to happiness.

When well-being and happiness are the primary measures used by a society, then some of the values that people prioritize are self-acceptance, relationships with other people, community and care of the environment. The actions you take will be guided by the goals of taking care of yourself, having fun with family and friends, strengthening your sense of belonging to your community and your connection to nature.

It may seem far-fetched to consider that a government would use happiness and well-being measurements so that they were held as important as GDP or even used as predominant measures. However, if you consider that people value more than just wealth, then the possibility does not seem so remote.

We used two stories in this chapter to illustrate the relationship between societal values, personal values and the kind of life one has. Your values determine your actions and priorities, how success will be defined and measured, and, for the most part, what kind of life you will lead. Over one's life, values will likely change as experience is gained, with aging and as life's circumstances changes. When someone is young, they may want excitement in life. If they have a family, stability may be preferred. Later in life, novelty or exploration may be valued. People can also make a conscious decision to change values. It may be found that a desire for excitement is causing stress and difficulties, so cultivating calmness or reliability is preferred. While you can change your values, can you change the values of a system? And if so, how?

Can values change?

Values in a system, whether a society, culture, nation or entity, do change. Globally, there has been a shift from traditional family to social groups, from monocultures and homogeneity to multiculturalism, diversity and inclusion and from gender inequality to equality (Agents of Change, n.d.). The industrial revolution gradually changed societal values from tradition and obedience (when serfdom and slavery were common in the agricultural era) to individuality and achievement (Littek, 2001). Values also change between generations. The Silent Generation, also called Traditionalists, born between 1900–1945, spans two world wars and an economic depression and is characterized by the values of austerity, hard work and stability. The Baby Boomers were born during a period of economic boom, between 1946 and 1964, and are characterized as valuing gratification, equality and transformation. Members of Generation X were born between 1965 and 1980, and are thought of as balanced, skeptical and independent. Millennials, born between 1981 and 1996, are considered to have the values of civic duty, realism and achievement. Gen Z refers to the youngest people on the planet, those born 1997 and after. These values are very broadly stated and not descriptive of any individual but provided to illustrate how values change. Values in a government, company, campus or nonprofit can change with new leadership, such as a new president, prime minister, executive or director.

While values do change, it is not easy. People define who they are, in part, by their values (Hitlin, 2003). When your values are challenged, you can feel threatened. When you are threatened, you are usually not willing to examine or question your values and are more likely to defend, fight or flee. People have been willing to die for their values, and wars are fought over values (Hutson, 2017; Gómez et al., 2017). If a system is changed in ways that challenge or threaten people's values, it is likely to meet strong resistance. People who are threatened may band together to do what they can to make sure the changes you want to see do not happen. This is one reason it is so important to understand the values of systems and the values of the people who are part of those systems.

To change the values of a system, it is important to know what these are. Knowing your own values empowers an understanding of values for the system you are seeking to change. Once you know, then it is easier to better perceive other people's values. One way to explore values and changing values is through conversations with people who have values you do not agree with or do not understand. If you do have such conversations, a few tips are:

- Seek to understand. Ask questions. State what you understand and then ask if you understood correctly.
- Keep your mind open and reserve judgment. When you disagree, observe instead of object.
- Look for commonalities. Agree wherever you can find a basis for agreement.
- Don't compromise your values but allow yourself to contemplate shifting your own values and what that would look like for you.

The next highlight, Exploring Biases, also gives you some tools for understanding your own and other's values and the reasons for them.

HIGHLIGHT: EXPLORING BIASES

Biases are part of everybody's thinking. Your values can be grounded in biases without your knowing it. The challenge is to become aware of them as there are many kinds. Listed next are three common biases and ways you can explore them.

Confirmation bias

Confirmation bias allows you to interpret reality according to your beliefs and perceived experience. Confirmation bias happens when you see and hear information that supports your beliefs and dismiss anything to the contrary. Thomas Kuhn, a philosopher, wrote about this kind of bias in his book *The Structure of Scientific Revolution*, whereby some scientists could not see evidence for new ways of understanding. To overcome confirmation bias, instead of dismissing others' ideas, try to see things from their point of view. Similarly, if someone is dismissive about your ideas or will not listen to what you say, ask them for their viewpoint and beliefs. Find out if your beliefs are threatening to their beliefs. If a conversation with someone cannot be held, try simulating a conversation with a friend.

Heuristic bias

Heuristic bias allows one to judge about a subject or the future based on the facts as one perceives them. With heuristic bias, you assume that you know all there is to know, instead of opening up to the idea that you do not know what you do not know – the *unknown unknowns*. Daniel Gilbert, a social psychologist, wrote about this and many other ways our thinking can keep us from happiness in his book *Stumbling on Happiness*. To overcome heuristic bias, remind yourself nobody knows everything and take some time to learn. Sometimes this means gathering data and analyzing it for patterns or developing knowledge by studying, thinking about things from a different angle, or talking to people about respective experiences, perspectives and beliefs.

Consensus bias

Consensus bias allows one to assume other people have the same beliefs, see things the same way, generally agree with one's ideas and so feel one is part of a group of like-minded people. Peter Senge, a systems scientist, and his co-authors wrote about how to manage this and other biases in part five of his book *The Necessary Revolution*. To overcome consensus bias, ask friends, family or colleagues who you assume agree with you what they think, keeping in mind that everybody has their own unique perspective, values and beliefs. When asking, use open-ended questions rather than asking if they agree with you to lessen the chance of bias!

Being biased is normal for all humans. Instead of judging yourself or others for having biases, seek to become aware of biases. When you do recognize them, congratulate yourself. The biases listed are just a few of many. Others are anchoring, bandwagon bias, hindsight bias, loss aversion, optimism effect, halo effect, overconfidence, status quo bias and primacy effect. Guess what they are by their names before you research their definitions. When you check your guesswork, see if you fall subject to hindsight bias.

HIGHLIGHT: A FEW INGREDIENTS FOR HAPPINESS AT WORK

It may seem that making a lot of money in any job would make you happy, but it turns out that other factors can turn any job into a bad job and perhaps vice versa. Here are four factors that may be important to your happiness at work.

Equity: Fairness in compensation may be more important than how much one is paid. Fairness has two components. One is being paid fairly for the work done, and the other is in comparison to the compensation others make for the same job (IBM, n.d.).

Given the option of working for two different employers, one where the pay is slightly higher but you make less than others doing the same work and the other where the pay is slightly lower but you make the same as others doing the same work, which job would you choose?

Fit + Purpose + Skills: The combination of liking one's work, feeling the work one does is meaningful and impactful and doing work that demands a high level of skills can bring happiness at work (Stiehl et al., 2019). What jobs would be the right fit for you, give you a sense of purpose and put your skills to work?

Autonomy at work, or being able to decide what you do and when you do it, contributes to happiness at work (Wheatley, 2017). Autonomy has two sides. One is not being micromanaged, and the other is having control over when and how one works. When might being micromanaged help your happiness at work? When would it hurt?

A good relationship with the boss is important to happiness (Ingraham, 2018). It is also important to health. Working for a boss who does not ensure openness and trust can increase your chance of heart disease (Alterman et al., 2019). How does your heart feel when you imagine working for a boss whom you like and likes you, whom you can trust and who listens and lets you know what is happening?

A caveat to these factors is one's value system. If the collective is more important than individualism, then these factors may not be as important. Do you think this is true?

Revising our thought experiment

This chapter began by setting the stage for a thought experiment. Later in this chapter, the idea that the way to change societal values is through changing the measurements used by a government was presented. Let's end the chapter with three sets of questions about a world where happiness, well-being and sustainability are the most important things. There are no right answers to these questions, and you are encouraged to contemplate them in terms of interdependencies and feedback loops:

If the happiness of people increased, what are some ways this could impact the well-being of communities? What are some ways it could impact ecological sustainability? How about the other way around? What are some ways an increase in ecological sustainability could impact the happiness of people? Of communities? How could increases in community well-being impact the happiness of people? Of ecological sustainability?

How would an economy function if the happiness of people, well-being of communities and ecological sustainability were its goals? How would the role of financial institutions, such as banks, credit card companies and the stock exchange, change? What would happen to the goal of economic wealth? What would happen to the way people thought about work?

What would the world look like if there were limitless natural resources, no problems with climate change and zero waste? Would it change how the economy functions? Would it change people's happiness or community well-being? Would you feel differently or make different choices if there were limitless natural resources, no problems with climate change and zero waste?

Values exercises

- Bring to mind two people you know or know about who are very different. Identify one to three values for each person, as you perceive them, and how to measure the success of achieving those values.
- What are your values? If you are not sure, you can use the Carnegie Mellon University Career Path Values Exercise (www.cmu.edu/career/documents/my-career-path-activities/values-exercise.pdf) to identify them. Write down your values. Choose seven and try to live by one each day. Give yourself a grade for how well you did on that day. Do the exercise in successive weeks and see if your grades change.
- Identify at least four of your values. Write down your values in order of priority. Identify your measures for success in terms of living each value. Next, write a short story or list of attributes about a person living your values. What kind of work do they do? What is their family life like? How do they relate to their friends? How do they spend their time?
- Is there a value that your family, friends or culture holds that is not your value but wish it were? If so, what is it, and how would you practice living it?
- Contemplate the ten common values identified by Schwartz listed in this chapter. Define each one for yourself and rate the level to which the value is important to you, with a 10 being you completely agree that the value is important and a 0 being you completely disagree that the value

is important. Then pair up with another person and compare how you are similar and different.

- Go to the OECD Better Life Index at www.oecdbetterlifeindex.org and choose the two topics that are most important to you and slide them to the maximum, leaving everything else at the minimum. Which topics did you choose? What country came out as best places for you to live? What country came out as the worst? Next choose the two topics that are the least important to you.
- Calculate the GDP of your family, assuming your family is the *domestic* in GDP. What are some of the things that go into the GDP that do not contribute to the happiness, well-being and sustainability of your family's life? What are some of the things that do not get included but do make you and your family better?
- The stories about Marley and River were gender neutral. What gender did you assume for Marley and for River? What attributes of the characters lead you to assume these genders?
- If you ask people "In one word, what makes you happy?" it is likely the most popular answer will be *family* or someone in their family. Describe the roles in a family and the values of each role. Are some values more feminine and others more masculine? If so, which are feminine, and which are masculine? How would you describe a man or woman who exemplified both feminine and masculine values?
- Read the article "America in 1915: Long Hours, Crowded Houses, Death by Trolley" by Derick Thompson (www.theatlantic.com/business/archive/2016/02/america-in-1915/462360) and contemplate what life would have been like for you if transported back to 1915. What would you like about life? What would you not like? What does this reveal about your values?
- Conduct a thought experiment by yourself or with one or two other people. Imagine that you lived 40,000 years ago, when humans who looked like us had the same physical and mental capacities as we do today. This is when humans started making cave art. How would your needs differ from today, and how would you meet them? Go through scenarios and see if you can come to a theory about the differences and similarities between people 40,000 years ago and people today. Write down your theory and the rationale for it and share it with one person. Next, imagine that you live 200 years from today, in a world where artificial intelligence has replaced the need for humans to work. Answer the same questions, write down your theory and share it with another person.

- Create a visual representation of the following elements and show how measurements and values can compete:
    - Measurements are determined based on what people value. People measure the things they care about. In this scenario, the two measurements are wealth and health.
    - Values determine the decisions people will make. Imagine someone who values wealth and so chooses to pursue a high-paying job. The same person values friendship and chooses to spend time with friends.
    - Decisions determine actions. When a person decides to do something, then they will most likely act on that decision. For this scenario, the person decides that to become wealthy, they must work long hours and extract the most they can out of their resources. They also want to take care of their health and so eat healthy foods, drink lots of water, get enough sleep, do exercise that is fun, spend time with friends and avoid unhealthy situations.
    - Actions determine outcomes. For this scenario, imagine a person has found a balance between profitable employment and a healthy lifestyle.

Values discussion questions

- Do you agree that there is a relationship between what you measure and what you value?
- Do you agree that there is a relationship between what the government measures and what people value?
- Is it possible to have a society without shared values? Why or why not?
- Do you agree that there are common values?
- What does it mean that there are common values shared by all people in all countries?
- What are the two predominant values of your school? How are they measured?
- What are the two predominant values of your home? How are they measured?
- What is the predominant value for your city or town? How is it measured?
- In Ancient Greece, the value of *arete* (in Ancient Greek spelled ἀρετή) was held in high esteem. It can be interpreted as excellence, and someone was considered highly when they performed excellently and lived their life to their fullest potential. Is this a value of your culture? If so or if not, how do you know?

Values resources

Videos

- *You are Always Changing* by Daniel Gilbert TED talk. www.ted.com/talks/dan_gilbert_you_are_always_changing
- *What Are Your Values? Learn How to Identify Values and Beliefs* by Mind Tools Videos. www.youtube.com/watch?time_continue=32&v=Kz__qGJmTMY
- *Robert F. Kennedy Challenges Gross Domestic Product.* https://www.youtube.com/watch?v=8e0LAoevn8U
- *Riane Eisler: Partnerships in the Post Industrial Economy* by Riane Eisler and Laura Flanders – The Laura Flanders Show. www.youtube.com/watch?v=KyvApqhVDDA
- *Confirmation Bias and Naive Realism* by Sven Van de Wetering & Flora Oswald, TEDxAbbotsford. www.youtube.com/watch?v=6XraX0Hu8zY
- *Our Buggy Moral Code* by Dan Ariely, TED talk. www.ted.com/talks/dan_ariely_on_our_buggy_moral_code?language=en

Reading materials

- *Are Psychological and Ecological Well-being Compatible? The Role of Values, Mindfulness and Lifestyle* by Kirk Brown and Tim Kasser. https://mindfulness.worldsecuresystems.com/publications/pdfs/Peer-reviewed-articles/mindfulness-psychological-ecological-well-being.pdf
- *Affluenza: The All-Consuming Epidemic* by John de Graaf, David Wann, Thomas H. Naylor, David Horsey and Vicki Robin.
- *The Art of Framing Political Debates* by Charlotte Ryan and William Gamson. www.racialequitytools.org/resourcefiles/ryan2.pdf

References

Agents of Change. (n.d.). Changing social norms and values and ethical issues. *European Union.* Retrieved from https://ec.europa.eu/assets/jrc/ilv/edge/aoc/index-16.html

Alterman, T., Tsai, R., Ju, J. & Kelly, K. (2019). Trust in the work environment and cardiovascular disease risk: Findings from the gallup-sharecare well-being index. *International Journal of Environmental Research and Public, 16* (2), 230. doi: 10.3390/ijerph16020230

Baggini, J. (2015). Do your genes determine your entire life? *The Guardian.* Retrieved from www.theguardian.com/science/2015/mar/19/do-your-genes-determine-your-entire-life

Cambridge Dictionary. (n.d.). Value. Retrieved from https://dictionary.cambridge.org/us/dictionary/english/value

Crompton, T. & Kasser, T. (2009). *Meeting Environmental Challenge: The Role of Human Identity*. Devon, UK: Greenbooks (and World Wildlife Fund). Retrieved from http://assets.wwf.org.uk/downloads/meeting_environmental_challenges___the_role_of_human_identity.pdf

Curtis, M., Conover, T. & Chui, L. (2012). A cross-cultural study of the influence of country of origin, justice, power distance, and gender on ethical decision making. *Journal of International Accounting Research, 11* (1), 5–34. doi: 10.2308/jiar-10213

Easterlin, R. (1995). Will raising the incomes of all increase the happiness of all? *Journal of Economic Behavior and Organization, 27* (1), 35–48. doi: 10.1016/0167-2681(95)00003-B

Easterlin, R. (2001). Income and happiness: Towards a unified theory. *The Economic Journal, 11* (473), 465–484. doi: 10.1111/1468-0297.00646

The Equity Trust. (n.d.). The scale of economic inequality in the UK. Retrieved from www.equalitytrust.org.uk/scale-economic-inequality-uk

Franklin, B. (1706–1790). *The Autobiography, and Other Writings: With Selections from Poor Richard's Almanac and Papers Relating to the Junto*. New York, NY: Dodd, Mead (reissued 1963).

Gilbert, D. (2006). *Stumbling on Happiness*. New York, NY: Alfred A. Knopf.

Gómez, A., López-Rodríguez, L., Sheikh, H., Ginges, J., Wilson, L., Waziri, H., Vázquez, A., Davis. R. & Atran, S. (2017). The devoted actor's will to fight and the spiritual dimension of human conflict. *Nature Human Behaviour, 1*, 673–679. doi: 10.1038/s41562-017-0193-3

Hecher, M. (1993). Values research in social and behavioral sciences. In M. Hecher, L. Nadel & R. Michod (Eds.) *The Origin of Values* (pp. 1–30). New York, NY: Aldine de Gruyter.

Hitlin, S. (2003). Values as the core of personal identity: Drawing links between two theories of self. *Social Psychology Quarterly, 66* (2), 118–137. doi: 10.2307/1519843

Hutson, M. (2017). Why do people die fighting for a cause? *Science*. Retrieved from www.sciencemag.org/news/2017/09/why-do-people-die-fighting-cause

IBM. (n.d.). Perception is reality. Retrieved from http://rewardspnw.com/downloads/IBMPerceptionisReality.pdf

Ingraham, C. (2018). Your boss has a huge effect on your happiness, even when you're not in the office. *Washington Post*. Retrieved from www.washingtonpost.com/business/2018/10/09/your-boss-has-huge-effect-your-happiness-even-when-youre-not-office/

Jeffrey, S. (n.d.). Core values list: Over 200 personal values to discover what's most important to you. *CEOsage*. Retrieved from https://scottjeffrey.com/core-values-list/

Lincoln, A. (1863). The Gettysburg address. Retrieved from www.abrahamlincolnonline.org/lincoln/speeches/gettysburg.htm

Littek, W. (2001). Division of labor. In N. Smelser & P. Baltes (Eds.) *International Encyclopedia of Social & Behavioral Sciences* (pp. 8220–8226). Oxford, UK: Pergamon.

Long, H. (2016). U.S. inequality keeps getting uglier. *CNN Money*. Retrieved from http://money.cnn.com/2016/12/22/news/economy/us-inequality-worse/index.html

Mørch, M. (2016, September 21). Bhutan's dark secret: The Lhotshampa expulsion. *The Diplomat*. Retrieved from https://thediplomat.com/2016/09/bhutans-dark-secret-the-lhotshampa-expulsion/

Munro, L. (2016). Where did Bhutan's gross national happiness come from? The origins of an invented tradition. *Asian Affairs*, *47* (1), 71–92. doi: 10.1080/03068374.2015.1128681

MySelf. (n.d.). Values exercise adapted from taproot. Retrieved from www.cmu.edu/career/documents/my-career-path-activities/values-exercise.pdf

Otake, T. (n.d.). 1 in 4 firms in Japan say workers log over 80 overtime hours a month. *Japan Times*. Retrieved from www.japantimes.co.jp/news/2016/10/07/national/social-issues/1-in-4-firms-say-some-workers-log-80-hours-overtime-a-month-white-paper-on-karoshi/#.Xavcr-dKi_t

Parish, T. & Nunn, G. (1988). The importance of the family in forming life values and personal values. *The Journal of Psychology*, *122* (5), 519–521. doi: 10.1080/00223980.1988.10542956

PBS. (n.d.a.). Ben's 13 virtues. Retrieved from www.pbs.org/benfranklin/pop_virtues_list.html

PBS. (n.d.b.). The causes of the civil war. Retrieved from www.pbs.org/opb/historydetectives/feature/causes-of-the-civil-war/

Renner, Q., Kandler, C., Bleidorn, W., Riemann, R., Angleitner, A., Spinath, F. & Menschik-Bendele, J. (2012). Human values: Genetic and environmental effects on five lexically derived domains and their facets. *Personality and Individual Differences*, *52* (1), 9–93. ISSN 0191-8869/

Schwartz, S. (1994). Are there universal aspects to the structure and contents of human values? *Journal of Social Issues*, *50* (4), 19–45. doi: 10.1111/j.1540-4560.1994.tb01196.x

Schwartz, S. (2012). An overview of the Schwartz theory of basic values. *Online Readings in Psychology and Culture*, *2* (1). doi: 10.9707/2307-0919.1116

Shrestha, D. (2015, November 19). Resettlement of Bhutanese refugees surpasses 100,000 mark. UNHRC. Retrieved from https://www.unhcr.org/en-us/news/latest/2015/11/564dded46/resettlement-bhutanese-refugees-surpasses-100000-mark.html

Stanford Encyclopedia of Philosophy. (2004 revised 2014). Ancient ethical theory. Retrieved from https://plato.stanford.edu/entries/ethics-ancient/

Stiehl, E., Jones-Jack, N., Brown, S. & Muramatsu, N. (2019). Worker well-being in the United States: Finding variation across job categories. *Preventive Medicine Reports*, *13*, 5–10. doi: 10.1016/j.pmedr.2018.10.006

Thompson, D. (2016). America in 1915: Long hours, crowded houses, death by trolley. *The Atlantic*. Retrieved from www.theatlantic.com/business/archive/2016/02/america-in-1915/462360/

Threads Culture. (n.d.). Core values examples. Retrieved from www.threadsculture.com/core-values-examples

Vierecj, G. (1929). What life means to Einstein. *The Saturday Evening Post*. Retrieved from https://archive.org/details/WhatLifeMeansToEinstein_201712

Waldrop, M. (2017). Einstein's relativity explained in 4 simple steps. *National Geographic*. Retrieved from www.nationalgeographic.com/news/2017/05/einstein-relativity-thought-experiment-train-lightning-genius/

Wheatley, D. (2017). Autonomy in paid work and employee subjective well-being. *Work and Occupations*, *44* (3), 296–328. doi: 10.1177/0730888417697232

Wilkinson, R. & Pickett, K. (2010). *The Spirit Level: Why Greater Equality Makes Societies Stronger*. New York, NY: Bloomsbury Press.

Yoshikawa, T., Sasaki, T., Matsumoto, S., et al. (2018). 1222 Diagnosis of 1,561 compensated cases for overwork-related cerebrovascular/cardiovascular diseases (CCVDs) known as 'karoshi' in Japan, 2010–2014. *Occupational and Environmental Medicine*, *75*, A122–A123. doi: 10.1136/oemed-2018-ICOHabstracts.347

3

MEASURING HAPPINESS

Measuring happiness learning objectives

The objectives of this chapter are for students to be able to:

- Understand that happiness, well-being and sustainability can be measured.
- Understand why it is important to measure happiness, well-being and sustainability.
- Learn some ways that happiness, well-being and sustainability are measured.

Preliminary questions

- Can happiness be measured? If so, how? If not, why not?
- How would you measure happiness?
- Why would anyone want to measure happiness?
- Can well-being be measured? If so, how? Would measurements for well-being differ from those for happiness?
- How would you measure ecological sustainability?
- What does feeling loved and cared for have to do with happiness? Well-being? Ecological sustainability?
- What does feeling satisfied with life or feeling like your life is worth living have to do with happiness?
- Are there connections between happiness and ecological sustainability? If so, how do you experience them in your life?

- Why would a government care about the happiness of its people? Well-being? Ecological sustainability?
- Is average GDP per capita a good measurement for happiness? If so, why? If not, why not?

Why measure happiness

The chapter about values explored the links between measurements, values and actions. This chapter focuses on measurements. Other words for measurements are indicators, indices, metrics and measurement tools. For simplicity's sake, let's use the term *measurement*.

Can happiness be measured? The answer is yes. In fact, happiness is already being measured.

The idea of measuring happiness gained popularity in 2008, when Bhutan, a small country in the Himalayan mountains north of India and next to Nepal, first measured it. After that, the United Nations General Assembly (2011) passed a resolution called *Happiness: towards a holistic approach to development*. The resolution urges other governments to also measure happiness, with the recommendation "to pursue the elaboration of additional measures that better capture the importance of the pursuit of happiness and well-being" (United Nations General Assembly, 2011, p. 1). In 2012, the first *World Happiness Report* was issued, which shows how countries rate on happiness scales (Helliwell, Layard & Sachs, 2012). Then in 2013, the Organization for Economic Cooperation and Development (OECD), which traditionally issues annual reports comparing nations' GDP, issued the *OECD Guidelines for Measuring Subjective Well-being*, which includes instructions for measuring the feeling of happiness, satisfaction with life and other dimensions of happiness. Thus, one can say that happiness can be measured, but we still have not answered the question of why measure happiness.

HIGHLIGHT: DIFFERENT WAYS NATIONS MEASURE HAPPINESS, WELL-BEING AND SUSTAINABILITY

While many different nations are measuring happiness and well-being, there exists much disparity in approaches. This highlight synopsizes some of those differences identified by Joseph Stiglitz, Jean-Paul Fitoussi and Martine Durand in their book *Measuring What Counts*.

Most nations use a combination of subjective (asking people what they think) and objective (using data already gathered) indicators. For the most part, a national government's department of statistics is responsible for collecting and reporting data, but in a few nations, the finance or other departments take on these duties; others gather and report in partnership with nonprofits or quasi-governmental agencies. While reading this highlight, imagine that you are the president or prime minister of a nation that wants happiness, well-being and sustainability to be its goal. Ask yourself – would you employ either of the two strategies identified here, or would you use a combination or different ones?

Dashboards and reports involve many indicators grouped by themes or domains (e.g. community, culture, education, economy, energy, environment, government, health). Often dashboards are presented in a way where data can be accessed for any single indicator and one can see trends, sometimes interactively online. Some nations have laws that reports or dashboards must be issued. This strategy is being used by Belgium with *Les Indicateurs Complémentaires au PIB* (Complementary Indicators to GDP), Bhutan's རྒྱལ་ཡོངས་དགའ་སྐྱིད་དཔལ་འཛོམས (Gross National Happiness), Germany's *Gut Leben in Deutchland* (Good Life in Germany), Israel's מדדי איכות חיים, קיימות וחוסן לאומי (Well-being, Sustainability and National Resilience Indicators), Luxembourg's *PIBien-être* (GDP-well-being), the Netherlands' *Monitor van Welzijn* (Monitor of Well-being), New Zealand's *Living Standards Framework* and Slovenia's *Kazalniki Blaginje v Sloveniji* (Indicators of Well-being in Slovenia). Online dashboards are issued by Finland in *Findicator* and the UK with *Measuring National Well-being Program.* In the UK, the data are available via an interactive format, with the goal of government departments using the data for policies, programs and projects. Australia also issues an interactive dashboard but with only 30 indicators, called the *Well-being Framework.**

Narrow sets of indicators involve fewer indicators (less than 20), with themes or domains providing snapshots of how a nation is doing. France uses this strategy, with *10 Nouveaux Indicators de Richesse* (10 New Indicators of Wealth) that includes indicators. Others do as well, with Italy's *Benessere Equo e Sostenibile* (Equitable and Sustainable Well-being) including 12 indicators, Sweden's *Nya Mått på Välfärd* (New Dimensions of Welfare) with 15 indicators, and the United Arab Emirates' مؤشر السعادة (Happiness Meter) with one indicator used in Dubai only.

There is less variation in how nations use the data. Almost all use data for understanding and assessing happiness, well-being and sustainability; agenda setting; and in some nations, policy formation. Bhutan, the Netherlands and Scotland use data for evaluation and monitoring of the government or their contractors. Italy, New Zealand and Sweden use the data for governmental budgeting.

*Scotland and Ecuador assess happiness, well-being and sustainability performance, calling it the *National Performance Framework* in Scotland and *Buen Vivar* (Good Life) in Ecuador, but do not appear to use indicators.

There are valid reasons to measure happiness, three are presented next.

The first reason to measure happiness is because what you measure is what you get. Dan Ariely is an economist, author and entrepreneur whose books and talks have given many people insight into how the economy works and why people do what they do. He says, "Human beings adjust behavior based on the metrics they're held against" (Ariely, 2010, p. 5). Intuitively, this probably makes sense in your own life. If your performance at school, access to scholarships and the work you want when you graduate are determined in part by your grades, you will work hard to get good grades, changing what you do for each class based on what it will take to get a good grade. If your performance were determined based on mastery instead of grades, so you had to master one level to proceed to the next, you would stop thinking about grades and focus on levels. In the workplace, the measurement and basis for compensation for the top-level managers who set the goals and performance measurements for everyone else in a company is profit, so this is what they care about, and profit is their goal. Profit is also how they and society judge whether they and their companies are successful. If the measurements of success for companies and for top-level managers were a balance of community well-being and ecological sustainability as well as profit, then they would set goals and compensate their employees based on measurements for these goals. One could also expect that CEOs and other top-level managers would pursue benefiting community well-being and ecological sustainability with the same fervor they pursue profit, seeking to find their own happiness in moving the measurements up and reaching the goals of community well-being, ecological sustainability and profit together.

This still begs the question of why measure, manage or care about happiness? It comes down to something very simple: we believe that happiness is the purpose of life. We began this book with Aristotle's quote stating happiness is the purpose of life. We can't give you research findings that come to a statistically valid conclusion to prove that happiness is the purpose of life, but we can say that it makes the most sense to us, and we can ask you what you think. Granted, everybody will have their own unique way of defining, pursuing and finding happiness, but isn't happiness, however you define it, what you ultimately seek in life? Ask yourself why you are doing what you are doing until you get to the core, most basic and foundational reason. We posit that it will be for happiness, as you interpret happiness for your life. Dan Ariely (2010) tells a story about when he was a professor and gave up his own personal goals of happiness and wealth to get points for teaching as many classes as he could because his performance was measured by how many classes he taught. What was probably in the back of his mind, and driving his choices, was that if he sacrificed his happiness at the moment and got lots of points, he would be happier and wealthier in the end.

The second reason to measure happiness is because happiness is the purpose of government. This idea first came clear when Thomas Jefferson used the phrase *pursuit of happiness* in the US Declaration of Independence. The more commonly used phrase at the time was *pursuit of property* (Kennedy-Townsend, 2011), so replacing the word *property* with *happiness* was a bold move. It was the first time in known history that happiness as the purpose of government was codified. Here are the words from the Declaration of Independence:

> We hold these truths to be self-evident, that all (people) are created equal, that they are endowed by their Creator with certain unalienable Rights, that among these are Life, Liberty and the pursuit of Happiness. – That to secure these rights, Governments are instituted among (people). . . .
>
> *(U.S. Declaration of Independence, 1776, p. 1)*

While the US did not put happiness into its constitution, other governments have. Bhutan, Japan and South Korea, as well as Bolivia and Ecuador – using the term Bien Vivir – have national constitutions that protect people's right to pursue happiness (Pellerin, 2016). Governments that do a good job of governing make their people happy (Ott, 2011, 2010). Governments make policies in the form of laws, regulations and administrative bodies, such as the Centers for Disease Control and Protection and the Environmental

Protection Agency. They also establish subsidies, taxes and permits. In addition, governments create projects such as college grant programs, universal health care, social security and worker training programs. Governments can build infrastructure such as bridges and roads. They can also build and operate energy plants, hospitals, schools and libraries. However, as with the statement that happiness is the purpose of life, there is no scientific proof that happiness is the purpose of government, but ask yourself what you think the purpose of government is and keep asking until you get to the root of why government does what it does. You can also contemplate governments that rule without regard to the happiness of their people, such as governments ruled by tyrants or corrupt leaders, and ask who would want to live under such a government.

If you accept that happiness can be the purpose of government and that you get what you measure, then you can say that governments should use happiness measurements. As explored in the first chapter of this book, after the Great Depression and continuing post World War II, the US and other governments used GDP as a proxy measurement for the goal of happiness, and for a while it was a good proxy (Costanza et al., 2014). However, in 2008, three economists, Joseph Stiglitz, Amartya Sen and Jean-Paul Fitoussi, were asked to study whether or not GDP was still a good measurement for government. They found it was not and issued the *Report by the Commission on the Measurement of Economic Performance and Social Progress* (Stiglitz, Sen & Fitoussi, 2009) unequivocally stating that GDP is not a sufficient measurement for government and that wider measures of well-being and happiness are needed. Within ten years, all the nations in the European Union and all the member nations of the Organization for Economic Cooperation and Development were measuring some dimension of happiness (Durand, 2018). The next step for these governments is to figure out how to use the data and measurements to safeguard and improve happiness, well-being and sustainability. This brings us to the third reason why happiness should be measured.

The third reason that happiness should be measured is that using GDP as a proxy can lead to unhappiness and undesirable outcomes for our communities, climate and planet. As mentioned, GDP includes things that are not supportive of happiness, well-being and sustainability, ranging from the cost of crime to traffic jams, and does not include things that are supportive for happiness, well-being and sustainability, ranging from relaxing, gardening and volunteering to taking care of nature and neighbors. Also as mentioned, income and wealth inequality cause problems and can negatively impact happiness. Continued reliance on GDP comes with increasing production of goods and services and use of natural resources, exponential growth in greenhouse gas emissions, accumulation of plastic and other pollutants in the seas, and decline of species and habitats (Meadows, Randers & Meadows, n.d.; Intergovernmental Panel on Climate Change, 2018). It is fair to say that continued use of GDP instead of measurements for happiness, well-being and ecological sustainability incurs risks to the sustainability of human life and that of many other species (O'Neill et al., 2018). This leads to the subject of connecting happiness, well-being and sustainability through measurements.

HIGHLIGHT: CHANGE AGENCY AND MEASURING HAPPINESS

Laura Musikanski, one of the authors of this book, fell in love with happiness measurements after earning a juris doctor (law degree), master's in business administration and year-long certificates in environmental management and environmental law and regulation. Her focus had been the sustainability movement, and she was building a career in it when she learned about Bhutan's Gross National Happiness index. Perceiving that the economic and social systems today are measurement driven, she was puzzling over why sustainability indicators and data were not having a greater effect towards positive change for ecological health and social equity and equality. She thought that if people have a deeper relationship with indicators and see themselves reflected in the data, perhaps better data would lead to better outcomes.

Since 2010, Laura has worked in communities, with cities as well as national governments to use the Happiness Index, a survey instrument that measures satisfaction with life, feelings, eudaimonia, as well as life's circumstances (community, culture, economy, education, environment, government, health, social support, time balance and work). She does this as part of the Happiness Alliance, a nonprofit that also provides other tools and resources to inspire leadership in the happiness movement.

She has seen how providing people the knowledge, resources and tools to measure and to communicate about happiness has changed lives and changed communities. One of her favorite stories is of a woman who worked for an environmental agency producing reports. She found that her scores in all the areas measured by the Happiness

Index were higher than other people, except her life satisfaction and eudaimonia scores. She was able to see from this data that her life was quite good but that she was not perceiving it as so. She made a promise to herself to change her perception by taking time to care for herself and adopting a gratitude practice. A year later (she is a data person), she took the Happiness Index again and found that her life satisfaction and her scores for eudaimonia had increased. While she knew they had, she said it was nice to see the data.

Another of Laura's favorite stories is about a young woman in New York City who took the Happiness Index. She found that her scores for how her life was going in terms of economics were very high, but in terms of community and social support, she was surprised by how low her scores were. She realized because of the data that she had stopped spending time with her family and friends, and when she reflected on this, she felt sad. Her contemplation about her data caused her to rethink her life and to focus on her personal relationships.

Laura has also seen how the data changes how policy makers make decisions, including budgeting, allocating resources and engaging people in the democratic process. In many cities and regions, it is a slow process, but each step is a step forward. Laura deeply believes that it is individual people and small groups of people working together who make a difference and that the transition in a measurement driven society from measurements of economic growth and financial gain to the development of individual happiness and ecological health will be realized by community activists and change agents.

HIGHLIGHT: TEACHING SUSTAINABILITY

During the years of 2001–2003, James Bradbury, one of the authors of this book, taught a university course entitled Managing Global Issues at the University of New Mexico. James is a physicist who conducted research on cancer treatment at Los Alamos National Laboratory in 1977–1985 and worked on one of the first projects in the US to explore the feasibility of cold fusion energy between 1984 and 1988. In the 1990s, he worked with Russian physicists to explore alternative ways of using nuclear science for peaceful purposes. After retirement, he wanted to teach this course, which today would have the term *sustainability* in its title, to help students think about new approaches for achieving agreement and action on urgent global problems, including population growth, economic inequality, environmental degradation, human rights, nuclear weapons and declines in quality of life. It was an interdisciplinary class at a time when the concept of interdisciplinary studies was new, particularly for undergraduates. Students who attended majored in economics, political science, public administration and pre-med. During this class, students brainstormed after learning about the origins and current status of the problems. They then formed teams, produced plans for action to improve things and presented them to the class. Some of the plans students devised included treaties, unilateral and regional approaches and activism. The class then evaluated their plans for probable effectiveness.

In teaching the course, James wanted to connect with younger generations, to provide them information and to come up with actionable and inspiring solutions. He aspired for a feedback loop that would increase their knowledge and the knowledge base of their generation, leading to greater understanding of the problems and solutions and to increased action that in multiple cycles would produce real change. James did not track the career paths of his students, so one can't say if the students who took this course contributed towards the formation of the field of study that is now known as sustainability in many universities or towards common understanding for business, government and society, but this was James' intent. Many years later, James realized that the course plan had omitted a key component: instilling in the students the concept that thinking and acting for global sustainability contributes mightily to one's satisfaction with life and happiness. That is a major theme of this coursebook.

Connecting happiness, well-being and sustainability through measurements

Now that the question of whether happiness *can be* measured is settled, let's explore *how to* measure it. This begs the question: how is happiness defined? In one sense, it is simple. Happiness is a feeling. In another sense, it is complex. Happiness is about your feelings as well as your health, work, time balance, personal finances, environment, family and friends, culture, community, education and many other aspects of life. When defining happiness in this book, we include individual happiness, societal or community well-being and ecological sustainability. This is because we believe that individual happiness, community well-being and ecological sustainability are inextricably linked. There is research that shows that people are happier when they feel they belong to a community and when their community is vibrant (Lu & Shih, 1997). There is also research that shows how important nature is to happiness and well-being (Kasser, 2010). Experiences indicate that most feel happier when they belong to a community, when that community is doing well and when its natural environment is accessible and healthy. We are not going to try to prove this to you. Instead, we are stating that for our work community well-being, ecological sustainability and individual happiness all influence each other.

That does not stop people from defining these terms differently. Some people distinguish happiness and well-being indicators based on whether they are survey based, also called subjective indicators, or observation-based or objective indicators. Some researchers suggest confining happiness measurements to only those measuring feelings or satisfaction with life and using the terms *well-being*, *quality of life* or *wider measures* for measurements for other dimensions of life. This coursebook does not make these distinctions.

How is sustainability measured?

By now you have probably figured out that sustainability refers to ecological sustainability. Chapter 6 on sustainability delves more into this topic, but sustainability indicators are included in this chapter. Perhaps the most predominant sustainability indicators today are the United Nations Sustainable Development Goal (SDG) indicators. Every nation on earth has adopted the SDGs (National Geographic, 2019). The SDG indicators are used to measure progress towards the 17 SDGs. There are 232 indicators; the majority of them are objective indicators. To provide an idea of what the indicators are, we list two for each of the 17 SDGs (Table 3.1). You can download the entire list of indicators on the United Nations' SDGs website.

The SDG indicators are designed for measuring national level performance towards achieving the SDGs. Another way to measure sustainability is through community-based indicators. The Community Indicators Consortium hosts a webpage with links to over 300 community indicator projects at https://communityindicators.net/indicator-projects. Indicators are often specific to the interests, strengths and challenges of an area, such as salmon runs for

TABLE 3.1 Sustainable development goals and selected indicators

SDG	*Example indicators*
Goal 1: No Poverty	1.2.1 Proportion of population living below the national poverty line, by sex and age 1.4.1 Proportion of population living in households with access to basic services
Goal 2: Zero Hunger	2.1.1 Prevalence of undernourishment 2.4.1 Proportion of agricultural area under productive and sustainable agriculture
Goal 3: Good Health and Well-being	3.4.1 Mortality rate attributed to cardiovascular disease, cancer, diabetes or chronic respiratory disease 3.8.1 Coverage of essential health services
Goal 4: Quality Education	4.3.1 Participation rate of youth and adults in formal and non-formal education and training in the previous 12 months, by sex 4.4.1 Proportion of youth and adults with information and communications technology (ICT) skills, by type of skill
Goal 5: Gender Equality	5.1.1 Whether or not legal frameworks are in place to promote, enforce and monitor equality and non-discrimination on the basis of sex 5.5.1 Proportion of seats held by women in (a) national parliaments and (b) local governments
Goal 6: Clean Water and Sanitation	6.1.1 Proportion of population using safely managed drinking water services 6.4.1 Change in water-use efficiency over time
Goal 7: Affordable and Clean Energy	7.1.1 Proportion of population with access to electricity 7.1.2 Proportion of population with primary reliance on clean fuels and technology
Goal 8: Decent Work and Economic Growth	8.4.1 Material footprint, material footprint per capita and material footprint per GDP 8.5.2 Unemployment rate, by sex, age and persons with disabilities
Goal 9: Industry, Innovation and Infrastructure	9.2.2 Manufacturing employment as a proportion of total employment 9.c.1 Proportion of population covered by a mobile network, by technology
Goal 10: Reduced Inequality	10.1.1 Growth rates of household expenditure or income per capita among the bottom 40% of the population and the total population 10.4.1 Labor share of GDP, comprising wages and social protection transfers

SDG	*Example indicators*
Goal 11: Sustainable Cities and Communities	11.1.1 Proportion of urban population living in slums, informal settlements or inadequate housing 11.7.1 Average share of the built-up area of cities that is open space for public use for all, by sex, age and persons with disabilities
Goal 12: Responsible Consumption and Production	12.1.1 Number of countries with sustainable consumption and production (SCP) national action plans or SCP mainstreamed as a priority or a target into national policies 12.2.1 Material footprint, material footprint per capita and material footprint per GDP
Goal 13: Climate Action	13.1.1 Number of deaths, missing persons and directly affected persons attributed to disasters per 100,000 population 13.1.3 Proportion of local governments that adopt and implement local disaster risk reduction strategies in line with national disaster risk reduction strategies
Goal 14: Life Below Water	14.1.1 Index of coastal eutrophication* and floating plastic debris density 14.5.1 Coverage of protected areas in relation to marine areas *Excessive nutrients in water causing die off of plants and animals in the water.
Goal 15: Life on Land	15.1.1 Forest area as a proportion of total land area 15.5.1 Red List Index* *An index for threatened or endangered species. www.iucnredlist.org
Goal 16: Peace Justice and Strong Institutions	16.1.1 Number of victims of intentional homicide per 100,000 population, by sex and age 16.6.2 Proportion of population satisfied with their last experience of public services
Goal 17: Partnerships to Achieve the Goal	17.8.1 Proportion of individuals using the Internet 17.14.1 Number of countries with mechanisms in place to enhance policy coherence of sustainable development

areas in the Pacific Northwest of the US and diabetes rates for Nova Scotia, Canada. Many campuses also have sustainability indicators, goals, programs and courses. Check to see if your campus has these.

You may have noticed that sustainability indicators often do not include measurements for how people feel or other evaluations of people's happiness. It is our belief that they should and that when sustainability indicators include measurements for people's happiness and community well-being, there will be better data and better decision-making.

Based on analysis of the SDG indicators and happiness measurements, the SDGs are missing measurements for 17 areas commonly measured by happiness indexes (Iriarte & Musikanski, 2019). They are, listed alphabetically:

Feelings
Generosity
Job satisfaction
Life expectancy
Life satisfaction
Mental health
Participation in cultural events
Participation in government
Satisfaction with finances
Satisfaction with housing
Satisfaction with personal relationships
Self-reported health
Sense of belonging to community
Social support
Volunteering
Working hours
Work-life balance

The next section focuses on happiness measurements, with the perspective that happiness, well-being and sustainability are interconnected.

Measuring happiness subjectively

As stated, the OECD (2013) definitively answered the question of whether happiness can be measured, especially in terms of subjective well-being. It is measured through surveys, also called polls or questionnaires. There are three different ways to measure subjective well-being with surveys. They are:

1 Feelings, both positive (happy, joyful, calm, etc.) and negative (anxious, sad, angry, etc.);
2 Satisfaction with life and the conditions of life, also called dimensions of life or domains of happiness. Conditions of life include your economic situation, access to a healthy and safe environment, trust in government, job, time balance, physical and mental health, access to education, sense of cultural heritage, sense of belonging to a community and social support; and
3 Eudaimonia, also called flourishing, which encompasses a sense of worthiness, purpose, achievement, optimism and engagement in everyday life.

The term *subjective* when talking about happiness measurements can lead to misunderstanding. Surveys, polls and questionnaires are not called subjective because the information gathered from the survey is not true or useful but because the information reflects what people think and feel. Gathering these types of data is important to foster understanding of what people think and feel, whether people are happy or not and what makes them so. For example, if it turned out that people in your class are unhappy and angry, this would be important information. Anger, like other negative emotions, can point the way for needed change.

For example, suppose your teacher asks each student if they are satisfied with the lessons and then tells them that their replies do not count because they were based on their opinions. If, on the other hand, the teacher used this information to learn more about how to construct lessons that gave greater satisfaction, then students may believe they are valued. Subjective data can be gathered for a group, such as for your entire class, or for a geographic region, such as a city or state, and used in many ways to guide decision makers. Some of these ways are explored in this section.

Conditions of happiness can also be measured with objective indicators. These are measurements of such things as income levels; healthy years of life expectancy; employment; education levels; voting participation; rates of the diagnosis of depression or other mental illness; toxicity levels in water, air and soil; and many other aspects of life that impact our happiness and well-being.

These kinds of subjective happiness data provide varying information that can be used for different purposes. Objective indicators give us information you can use alongside the subjective data to get a balanced picture. The next sections uses stories to show the differences.

Using satisfaction with life data

Satisfaction with life and the conditions of life is a way to define and measure happiness and well-being. It is measured by asking people to answer questions about how satisfied they are with their lives and aspects of their life. One question often used to measure satisfaction with life is:

> On a scale of 0 to 10, with 0 being the most dissatisfied and 10 being the most satisfied you could possibly be, answer these three questions:
>
> 1 Overall, how satisfied are you with your life?
> 2 How satisfied are you with your school?
> 3 How satisfied are you with extracurricular activities?

When these questions are answered, it causes one to pause, even if for just a moment, and think about the answers (Kahneman & Riis, 2005). This is because satisfaction questions are reflective. This is an important characteristic of this type of questioning because it implies people draw on their memories to answer.

Levels of satisfaction with life or with a condition of life will have an impact on what decisions are made. Take, for example, after-school activities at your school. If you choose a low-ranking score for satisfaction with extracurricular activities, this probably means you will not continue doing them. This kind of information can be very important for policy and decision makers. For example, if your whole school rated their satisfaction with extracurricular activities with a very low score, it would mean the school should think about changes.

HIGHLIGHT: CHOICES AND SATISFACTION WITH LIFE

Are you are satisfied with your life? This is a reflective question, which means it requires you to look back on your experiences to decide. A few things to think about when reflecting on such questions are the following two areas.

Your choice of focus

In her book *The Myths of Happiness*, Sonja Lyubomirsky writes: "What you choose to focus on becomes a part of your life, and the rest falls out" (p. 187). This is also true for when you reflect on your life. When looking back on the past week, month, year or all of your life, you can change how you feel about your life by focusing on the good things. You may find that your mind has a tendency to focus on the bad things, particularly if you have unresolved loss, anger or hurt feelings. When this happens, which it does in life, it is important to process the trauma by talking about it and working it out. However, when life is going well, someone can increase enjoyment of life by training their mind to reflect on good things that have happened when thinking about the past.

Your life investment choices

The book *Origins of Happiness* (Clark et al., 2018) by three economists and two other scholars studied what made for high life satisfaction. They found that being physically and psychologically healthy and having healthy relationships were the most important things. Other important factors are employment and education: when education obtained enables someone to do the things in life they love to do and to have a job they enjoy or like. In terms of employment, their analysis indicates that unemployment has a large and sometimes lasting negative impact on satisfaction with life, which leads them to suggest that even a bad job is better than no job. However, other research says that a person's relationship with their boss at work has a large impact on satisfaction with life, in part because so much time is spent at work (Ingraham, 2018). Putting the pieces together, to be happy in terms of satisfaction with life, it's important to take good care of yourself, foster healthy relationships, have stable employment and work for a boss you like and who likes you.

Everybody is different. How do these factors – your choice of focus and life investment choices – coincide or differ from what you think is important in your life? If they are different from what is important to you, how so, and is it contributing to satisfaction with life?

HIGHLIGHT: HAPPY JOBS

How will you choose which kind of job to do? You may be battling between how much money you can make at a job and what kind of job is best suited to your personality. For the latter, Career Zone's online tool, the Interest Profiler, may be of help: www.cacareerzone.org/ip.

Have you considered which job brings the most happiness? What if your school gave you information every year on which jobs bring people the most happiness and life satisfaction, as many schools do for which jobs have the highest wages? This is something a few job placement companies provide data on but there is not a great deal of data. Two placement companies in the US, CareerBliss and PayScale, have published reports over the years.* Here is a compilation of some of their findings:

Happiest jobs

Teacher | Teaching Assistant
Software Developer | IT Specialist
Researcher | Analyst | Technical Writer
Manager | HR Manager | Project Manager | Property Manager
Nurse | Physical Therapist | Dietitian

Unhappiest jobs

Accountant | Administrative Associate | Legal Assistant
Security Guard | Dispatcher | Truck Driver
Cashier | Server | Food Service Staff
Buyer | Merchandiser | Salesperson | Clerk
Customer Service Specialist | Technical Support | Nursing Home Assistant

Which people in your life have a job that gives them happiness and satisfaction with life? Why do you think this is? What job would give you happiness and satisfaction with life? Why?

*The data collected for jobs and happiness (and satisfaction with life) are being collected by placement companies, so there may be problems with the reliability of the data. The companies may be collecting data from people and for jobs that will support them in furthering their business interests. Moreover, there are many factors that influence happiness and satisfaction with life besides what kind of job one has. (Note that you may be miserable in a job on the happiest list and find great happiness on a job in the unhappiest list.)

How would you like to see data collected for happiness in jobs? What information about jobs and happiness would be helpful to you in making your career choices?

Data for satisfaction with life and the conditions of life can be useful for policy and other decision makers (O'Donnell et al., 2014; Diener et al., 2009). As discussed in Chapter 1, let's imagine that you are the prime minister or president of your country. You want to do something to increase people's happiness. You have been told that one of the most important things for a person's happiness is jobs and that the more satisfied a person is with their job, the happier they are. You have a report on your desk that says that unemployment levels are forecasted to go up significantly in the next three years. This is objective data. Digging deeper into the report, it is discovered that the reason for increasing unemployment is artificial intelligence replacing many jobs, from food and retail services to accounting, business analysis and some legal and medical services.

Next, a report of subjective data provides data on how satisfied people are with their jobs. You find that the kinds of jobs in which people are most satisfied share a common theme: people are caring for each other. These jobs include special education and college teachers, physical therapists, psychologists and community organizers. A second theme is creativity. These jobs include information technology (IT) designers, artists and web developers. You also can tell from the subjective data that the jobs that yield the lowest satisfaction include many of the service jobs that are disappearing. Because you want to run for reelection, you want to form policies that will encourage the creation of jobs people love. This may mean investing in mental and physical health care centers and increasing access to creative IT education for people of all ages. This is just one example of how objective and subjective data can tell a story and point the way for decisions that increase people's happiness and well-being.

Using data about how you feel

In the last section, when asked how satisfied you are with your life, likely you paused to reflect, even if only for a moment. This is not the case if you were asked about a feeling. One way to get data about how people feel is by asking them. To gather data about a feeling, set up a scale as is done for satisfaction with life. Let's say that 0 means you do not have even a trace of the feeling, and 10 means you completely feel the feeling. Right now, how happy are you, on a scale of 0 to 10? How anxious are you? How about sad? How about angry? You probably did not have to think about it when you answered. If you did, it was not to reflect but to check in with yourself to find out how you are feeling, which is different from what you think about your feeling. When asking enough people in a group about their feelings, data that represents the entire group's feelings can be gathered.

Another way to get data about how people feel is by mining online data, which is also called big data, generated from billions of little pieces of data. A piece of data is generated each time you like something on Facebook, from each word you use in a post, or when you reply to something or do not reply. More data is generated from the time, location, and from your profile. All of these data together from many people collected over a time span becomes big data. This means people's viewpoints collected together, when used for policy purposes, can influence change. On the flip side, social media platforms can manipulate people's feelings, beliefs and decisions, so it is important to keep this in mind when using big data.

GUEST COURSEBOOK CONTRIBUTION FROM JOHN C. HAVENS: PERSONAL DATA OWNERSHIP

John C. Havens is an author, speaker and executive director of The Global Initiative on Ethics of Autonomous and Intelligent Systems, a program of the Institute of Electrical and Electronics Engineers (IEEE). His career has gone through many evolutions, from being an actor on Broadway and in films, manager at a public relations firm, and journalist, to bring him to see the importance of ethics and well-being in the field of technology. He wrote this to inspire readers of this coursebook.

Like many people, I was teased at a young age. It was a daily occurrence for playground bullies to give me the invisible treatment, standing directly in front of me and pretending I didn't exist. This left me feeling I did not count, but it also instilled a deep passion in me to help all people be genuinely recognized for their true worth. In the age of the algorithm, our personal data is gathered, used and sold in ways we often don't fully understand. This, combined with agreements to use technology that forces our uninformed consent, represents a form of modern bullying that lets other people determine our personal algorithmic identity.

My work for over ten years has been to put people at the center of their personal data and ensure we control our own algorithmic identity. While the subject of privacy is complex, it is not a mystery how an entire economic ecosystem has been built to profit from your data while you are losing the ability to be genuinely informed what your digital identity is and how algorithms influence your thoughts, behavior and choices. Some of this is helpful to you, such as book recommendations that match your tastes. Nonetheless, collecting, tracking, selling and using your personal data in ways you don't understand or control can erode your agency and increases a general malaise that diminishes your well-being. As these trends continue with advances in artificial intelligence (AI), we must claim the right to access and control our personal data to take back control of our digital identity. I am one of many working to make this happen.

GUEST COURSEBOOK CONTRIBUTION FROM MAREK HAVRDA: FUTURE OF AI

Marek Havrda is a sociologist and economist with a master's in public administration. He works as a policy advisor to governments and, more recently, in research and development of AI, with the company GoodAI. He specializes in governance and social impacts of AI, AI ethics and the future of jobs. He wrote this essay to inspire and guide readers of this coursebook.

Today, AI is being used to optimize energy consumption or detect illegal logging, and it is being considered to be deployed for better design and maintenance of our homes, cities and mobility systems to minimize negative environmental impact. Indeed, AI can help us significantly improve environmental efficiency of everything we do, starting with how we consume and produce. This is particularly important because thus far, some of our efforts to improve our well-being have brought about damage to our planet, to our own ecosystem, and in some cases, even to our own long-term well-being.

AI can help us overcome some of the conditions we humans are born with, such as myopia, biases and unhealthy preferences. It can also help us understand the complexities of dynamic, complex and uncertain systems – from particle level to species interactions – and thereby arrive at better ex-ante assessments of our impact on the environment and increase the probability of bringing about desired system level changes – capacities that are simply beyond our human ability.

Together with Michiel De Smet of the Ellen MacArthur Foundation, a mathematician who works as a policy advisor and expert in the circular economy theory, we formulated three priority areas for near future research and innovation in AI. They are:

1. *Fix the chaos at the end of the material flow: AI is directly used along the whole life cycle to eliminate all waste. One start towards this is ZenRobotics, a use of AI to automatically sort waste into piles of valuable materials.*
2. *Design new materials and products: AI helps to develop new molecule, polymer or material for ecologically caring production, delivery, use and end of life of products and packaging.*
3. *Design novel solutions to societal or personal needs: AI is deployed to assist humans to identify novel ways of meeting needs – often*

> *possibly redesigning related supply chains – in a way that is ecologically beneficial and enhances human well-being. An example would be significant reduction of transport of goods and food waste, solving water scarcity, contributing to species protection and maintenance of biodiversity and so on.*
>
> *You may not be aware that AI is already part of your life – through your use of information and communication technology and in everyday life with the Internet of Things (IoT), ranging from wearable devices to traffic management and investment trading. I encourage you to seek ways to include AI in your life and work and discover how you want to use it for your own good and the good of the planet. This can be the first step towards realizing happiness, well-being and sustainability with AI.*

Data about feelings is important to people who want to know how a situation or place affects a person (MacKerron & Mourato, 2013). This time imagine you are the mayor of your city. There is a large city block that is undergoing redevelopment. Redevelopment means building new structures in an area, usually an area that is dilapidated or no longer used. The area of focus had a very large warehouse and parking lot, but now the structure is dilapidated, and shrubs and trees are growing in the parking lot. The city's planning department has provided a report with objective data about the area. You know that there is an issue with homelessness in the area and that the neighborhood is busy during the day, with offices nearby and lots of small restaurants open for lunch, but essentially deserted at night, except for people who are homeless. Crime rates in the area are low.

A report with subjective data tells another side of the story. It says that people are least happy during their commute and generally angry or anxious during the commute time. It also tells you that the places where people rate their happiness levels highest are in natural settings, such as parks where there are trees and open green spaces, or at home. You also learn that people perceive crime rates in the area to be high during the night. A light bulb goes off in your head.

You call your planning and permitting department together with your city council members to see what you can do to encourage the development of mixed-use space with changes to permitting and zoning. An example of mixed-use space is buildings that have retail space for offices, stores, restaurants, a day-care center and a theater for movies or plays on the ground level; offices and a space that can easily be developed into a school on the middle levels; and residential units on the top levels. You want the development to include inclusionary housing, which means low-income housing or homeless shelters, and an outreach center so the people living and working in the space have easy opportunities to volunteer. You ask them to find ways to encourage shared green space, so that buildings are built around a park where people can rest, children can play and birds and other animals can live. This way people can live very close to where they work, which cuts out the commute and the misery of it. Homeless people have more opportunities for housing. You could work with the permitting department to find ways to encourage renewable energy and closed-loop water and energy systems, green roofs and low emissions in construction and long-term functioning of the redevelopment to enhance sustainability aspects.

This is one story of how happiness data about how people feel can inform public policy and our lives.

Using eudaimonia, flourishing and other data for a good life

Happiness can be measured by gathering data for satisfaction with life and the conditions of life. These kinds of data help us understand what people may do in the future. Happiness can also be measured by gathering data about how people feel. This data can also be helpful in designing experiences and places that make people feel good. In both cases, objective data is useful to get a balanced picture of people's happiness. There is a third way to define and measure happiness. This is called eudaimonia or flourishing.

The word eudaimonia comes from *eu* for good and *daimon* for spirit. The word eudaimonia means happiness that comes from living a virtuous life. This type of happiness is sometimes called flourishing. This is the happiness that is meant in the statement in the US Declaration of Independence that all people have inalienable "right to life, liberty and the pursuit of happiness" (U.S. Declaration of Independence, 1776, p. 1).

Another way to define happiness in terms of eudaimonia or flourishing is to measure it. Some questions to measure eudaimonic happiness are:

Do you feel that your life is worthwhile?
Do you feel a sense of purpose and meaning in your life?
Do you feel interested in the daily activities of your life?
Do you feel positive about yourself?
Are you optimistic about your life?

Eudaimonic data allow policy makers and others to understand what motivates people. It also reveals whether a population is flourishing or not (Huppert & So, 2013). It can be used alongside objective data to understand how different demographics of populations are doing, and thus, understand what policies, programs or projects may work well for some people and not for others. Some examples of objective data are income levels, literacy levels and voter participation.

HIGHLIGHT: FOUR KINDS OF HAPPINESS–HEDONISM, EUDAIMONIA, FLOW AND CHAIRONIC HAPPINESS

There are many ways to be happy. The pitfalls and paths back to happiness for four ways are briefly explained here. Seek for a balance among all four throughout your life.

Hedonism

Happiness from hedonism is found in pleasure or avoidance of pain. This kind of happiness includes pleasure and avoidance of pain from activities necessary for life such as eating, drinking, moving and sleeping. It also includes other pleasures, such as getting intoxicated or high, acquiring new things, partying, dancing, singing, learning something new, helping others and so on.

Pitfalls: hedonic treadmill and unhealthy pleasures

A pitfall to happiness found in pleasure is the hedonic treadmill. The hedonic treadmill is the situation where you have to keep getting better things, more intense experiences or more stuff to get the same amount of happiness. You have probably experienced this with technology, when you were thrilled to get your first cell phone but wanted an upgrade once you found out about something better. Then once you got that, after a while you wanted the next upgrade. Another pitfall to hedonic happiness is in addictive or self-destructive activities.

Getting back to happiness with hedonism

Ask yourself if you are setting unrealistic goals for yourself. Are you trying to look or be perfect or have the best thing? Are you trying to be better than everyone else? Ask yourself if you are overindulging yourself. Are you trying to always feel intense pleasure and doing everything you can to never experience calmness, quiet, dullness or pain? If so, check in with yourself to see if your pleasure seeking is doing harm to your health and your relationship with others and is something that if everyone did it, would do harm to the planet.

Eudaimonia

Eudaimonia happiness is found from living a life with a sense of purpose and meaning and when in doing so you also help others. It can be found if you feel like you are contributing to something positive for the world and you are making a difference. Aristotle used the word eudaimonia when he said that the purpose of life is happiness, and this is also the meaning of happiness that Thomas Jefferson was thought to have meant when he wrote the Declaration of Independence (Frost, 2004).

Pitfalls: burnout and negativity

Finding happiness through eudaimonia can put you at risk for doing too much for other people or the planet, sacrificing your well-being and burning out. You can also end up spending too much time exposing yourself to and contemplating things that cause misery, such as social ills, ecological disasters or injustices, and become bitter and negative.

Getting back to happiness with eudaimonia

While you can get insight from contemplating what is wrong with the world, if you spend too much time on it, you can stop seeing what is possible and end up stuck in what is wrong. If you recognize that you are getting bitter about the problems you want to help solve, limit your exposure to bad news, and limit the time you spend dwelling on it or talking about it. Pursue happiness through hedonism, flow or numinous experiences to get some distance and perspective.

Flow

Flow is the kind of happiness felt when you are immersed in what you are doing so that you are attuned with that activity and nothing else matters. You may lose track of time and forget to eat or even go to the bathroom. It helps to have just the right amount to challenge and the resources you need to meet that challenge to experience flow. Mihaly Csikszentmihalyi, a psychologist, identified the term flow to describe this kind of happiness by studying athletes and other performers.

Pitfalls: excess and imbalance

A pitfall to flow is excess. You may find yourself excessively watching television, gaming, working or any other activity. You have fallen into imbalance when you have made a pattern of ignoring hygiene, not taking care of your health by eating poorly and not exercising, sacrificing sleep or ignoring other activities in life to keep pursuing happiness through flow. When you are really in the pit, you don't see any point in doing anything other than pursuing your happiness through your one activity.

Getting back to happiness with flow

Check to see if the way you are experiencing happiness through flow is aligned with your values and gives you a sense of purpose and worthiness in life. Check also to see if it is supporting your happiness in terms of relationships with the people in your life whom you love, your access to nature and your sense of being a part of something bigger than yourself and making a positive contribution to the world. If not, see if you can find other ways to find happiness that are aligned with your values and give more balance in your life.

Chaironic happiness

Chaironic happiness is found when you feel a sense of awe and wonder or a sense of the divine. It can be described as feeling at one with nature, spirit, a higher power or God. Chaironic happiness can be experienced when in a place that is spiritual to you, with a profound experience or in community when you feel a sense of oneness. Carl G. Jung, a contemporary of Freud, used the word *numinous* to describe something intangible and divine.

Pitfalls: doubt or dogmatism

Pitfalls to happiness found through spiritual or divine experiences can be doubt or, on the flip side, rigid and dogmatic thinking. Doubt can leave you feeling sick, angry, hopeless or empty when something you believed in suddenly seems different. You may feel doubt in your concept of the divine, doubt in yourself or both. On the other hand, you can become rigid in your thinking and unkind in your treatment of others who do not believe the same if you cannot consider that you may not be right or what you believe is not a truth all people should also believe.

Getting back to chaironic happiness

If you experience doubt, then talk to people who also have experienced chaironic happiness to get a new perspective. If recognized that you have become rigid and dogmatic, talk to someone with whom you are safe being honest and vulnerable about what you are afraid of, why you feel a need to control, why you feel angry or other difficult feelings.

* * * * * *

Which kind of happiness is most relevant to your life today? Are you using a balance of these four ways of happiness? If not, how can you bring balance? What are some other kinds of happiness that you experience that do not fit into these four categories?

In this story illustrating how to use happiness and well-being data, imagine that you are the director of a nonprofit organization that serves homeless youth. Your organization works with homeless youth who have left their families by giving the youth a steady and safe place to live, career counseling and mental health counseling. You are going to meet with your board of directors for your annual strategic meeting, where the goals and programs for the year will be set. It is up to you to prepare the board and to suggest the direction for the next year.

The objective data gives high school dropout rates, youth health care costs, and mental illness and mental health care use rates. You traditionally use this data to measure the success of your programs. Recently, you have started to gather subjective data measuring youths' sense of purpose, autonomy, optimism and self-respect as well as belonging to community and satisfaction with life. You plan to use this data to hone the services and to add the subjective metrics to the objective ones to measure the success of the organization.

Your data shows that youth who have experienced being homeless for over six months have lower scores in all of the subjective measurements than others. It shows that young people who leave home have a similar sense of optimism, autonomy and self-esteem as youth who live at home, but within two months, their scores for these three measurements plummet. Homeless youth who have been homeless for over six months have a harder time recovering in terms of optimism and satisfaction with life than those who have a steady and safe place to live but also have increased scores for the measurement of sense of belonging to community.

You decide to ask for more resources to reach out to youth when they first experience homelessness. The nonprofit's governing board is behind a new project to build on the sense of community that homeless youth gain after they experience extended homelessness. You want to start a boarding school that will help young people with their transition to self-sufficiency by providing opportunities for housing and food, work training and jobs to pay for housing and food, and a sense of community that serves the needs of belonging, esteem and respect. This redesign could encompass offering students choices among formal education, skill development, job training or work. You are planning for a campus that includes buildings and space for housing and light industry, farming and other operational and business functions where students could learn how to work different jobs while also earning money to pay for room and board while getting their education. It would also entail processes to foster strong and healthy relationships with others and oneself so that each student had the opportunity to feel a sense of belonging and learn how to meet their esteem and respect needs in safe and healthy ways. You know that this kind of school system has been successful when designed for specific populations such as members of a religion, at-risk youth or for military training. You plan to develop it so that it will be a place for homeless youth, as well as youth who are at risk of homelessness, so your organization can serve youth before they experience homelessness.

This story shows another example of how happiness and well-being data can guide decision makers. There are many other ways that happiness data can help us to better understand what you can do in your life, community and government for the happiness of all.

Roles for measurements in system

We have presented quite a few concepts and examples in this chapter. This includes considering that government's use of happiness, well-being and sustainability measurements instead of GDP could influence people's values. When values change, people's behavior and actions also change. With the adoption of happiness and well-being metrics by government, the goals of government become the happiness and well-being of people, and so governments form policies that encourage and support the development of individual happiness skills. Governmental policies promoting individual happiness and well-being increase people's opportunities and capacity to meet their basic and higher needs. When people's capacity to meet their basic and higher needs increases, policy makers also have higher capacity to meet their own basic and higher needs. People and policy makers have a greater capacity for helping others and a deeper understanding of the connection between their own happiness and the well-being of others and the sustainability of the planet. They also have greater capacity to take action to help others and to protect and preserve nature now and in the future (Fig. 3.1).

What do you think? Can you come up with a different way to describe the dynamics of the system?

FIGURE 3.1 Chain of reactions

Measuring happiness exercises

- What is a resolution? Have you ever made a resolution, such as a New Year's resolution? Read the United Nations Resolution 65/309 *Happiness: towards a holistic approach to development* (https://documents-dds-ny.un.org/doc/UNDOC/GEN/N11/420/70/PDF/N1142070.pdf?OpenElement). Now imagine that you are the president or prime minister of your country and rewrite the resolution in simpler and clearer words. Include a recommendation for how governments can use happiness, well-being and sustainability data in your declaration.
- Take the Happiness Survey (www.happycounts.org/take-the-happiness-survey.html). Choose the option of creating a profile and save your results. Look at the two or three domains where you score highest. What are you doing in your life that is helping to make those scores high? Now look at the two or three domains where you score lowest. What are some things you could do differently to increase those areas' scores? Write these down. Try making one or two changes for one week and take the survey again. Save your results and analyze the two different scores from the two times you took the survey. Was there any change? If so, what do you attribute this to? If no, why do you think there was not?
- Use the Happiness Index for your entire class by requesting a unique URL at info@happycounts.org. Gather the data for your group, analyze it and then present it to the group. Where did your class score higher than the average? Where did it score lower? What are some ideas people have for why your class scored higher or lower in areas? What are some ideas your class has for increasing scores?
- Review the SDG indicators (https://unstats.un.org/sdgs/indicators/indicators-list) and select at least one for each SDG that you think is related to happiness and well-being. For each SDG, develop a plan, policy or activity that would contribute to realizing that goal in ways that would be beneficial to individual happiness, community well-being and ecological sustainability.

Measuring happiness discussion questions

- What objective indicators or data do you use in your life? How about grades? Your weight or height? The amount of money you have saved or spent? How do the objective indicators and data impact your life?
- What do you do to be happy? How would you measure the happiness this activity gives?

- What activities do you think give you the deepest sense of satisfaction with life? Remember that satisfaction with life is a remembered experience. Why do these activities do this?
- What activities give you a sense of purpose and meaning in life? If responding that you do not have any in your life right now, what activities would give you a sense of purpose? What activities do you see other people doing that appear to give them a sense of purpose and meaning?
- Consider the lines from the US Declaration of Independence: "We hold these truths to be self-evident, that all (people) are created equal, that they are endowed by their Creator with certain inalienable Rights, that among these are Life, Liberty and the pursuit of Happiness. – That to secure these rights, Governments are instituted among (people). . . ." What do they mean to you?

Measuring happiness resources

Videos and movies

- *Happy – The Movie, The Movement* by Roko Belic
- *This Country Isn't Just Carbon Neutral – It's Carbon Negative* by Bhutan's Prime Minister Tobagy, Tshering, TED2016. www.ted.com/talks/tshering_tobgay_this_country_isn_t_just_carbon_neutral_it_s_carbon_negative/discussion?langu
- *Influencing Well-being Policy on a Global Scale* by Lord Gus O'Donnell and Legatum. Institute. www.youtube.com/watch?v=k5BIqewfeSw
- *What is Gross National Happiness?* by Morten Sondergaard. www.youtube.com/watch?v=7Zqdqa4YNvI

Reading materials

- *World Happiness Report*. 2012–2017. http://worldhappiness.report/
- Resolution 65/309. *Happiness: Towards a Holistic Approach to Development*. 2011. United Nations. www.un.org/Docs/journal/asp/ws.asp?m=A/RES/65/309
- *Gaian Economics*. 2014. Jonathan Dawson, Helean Norberg-Hodge and Ross Jackson, editors. www.skalaecovillage.com/wp-content/uploads/2015/10/Gaian_Economics.pdf

Websites

- Authentic Happiness Questionnaire center with multiple surveys for well-being at www.authentichappiness.sas.upenn.edu/testcenter
- The Happy Planet Index at http://happyplanetindex.org/

References

Ariely, D. (2010). Column: You are what you measure. *Harvard Business Review*. Retrieved from https://hbr.org/2010/06/column-you-are-what-you-measure

Clark, A., Flèche, S., Layard, R., Powdthavee, N. & Ward, G. (2018). *Origins of Happiness*. Princeton, NJ: Princeton University Press.

Costanza, R., Hart, M., Kubiszewski, I. & Talberth, J. (2014). A short history of GDP: Moving towards better measures of human well-being. *Solutions Journal, 5* (1), 91–97. Retrieved from www.thesolutionsjournal.com/article/a-short-history-of-gdp-moving-towards-better-measures-of-human-well-being/

Diener, E., Lucas, R., Schimmack, U. & Helliwell, J. (2009). *Well-Being for Public Policy*. Oxford: Oxford University Press.

Durand, M. (2018). Countries' experiences with well-being and happiness metrics. In J. Sachs, A. Adler, A. Bin Bisher, J. de Neve, M. Durand, E. Diener, J. Helliwell, R. Layard & M. Seligman (Eds.) *Global Happiness Policy Report*. New York, NY: Sustainable Development Solutions Network.

Frost, M. (2004). Frost's meditations: Eudaemonia, the good life: A talk with Martin Seligman. Retrieved from www.martinfrost.ws/htmlfiles/mar2009/eudaemonia-good-life.html

Helliwell, J., Layard, R. & Sachs, J. (2012). *World Happiness Report*. Retrieved from http://worldhappiness.report/

Huppert, F. & So, T. (2013). Flourishing across Europe: Application of a new conceptual framework for defining well-being. *Social Indicators Research, 110* (3), 837–861. doi: 10.1007/s11205-011-9966-7

Ingraham, C. (2018). Your boss has a huge effect on your happiness, even when you're not in the office. *Washington Post*. Retrieved from www.washingtonpost.com/business/2018/10/09/your-boss-has-huge-effect-your-happiness-even-when-youre-not-office/

Intergovernmental Panel on Climate Change (IPCC). (2018). Summary for policy makers of IPCC special report on global warming of 1.5 C approved by governments. Retrieved from www.ipcc.ch/2018/10/08/summary-for-policymakers-of-ipcc-special-report-on-global-warming-of-1-5c-approved-by-governments/

Iriarte, L. & Musikanski, L. (2019). Bridging the gap between the sustainable development goals and happiness metrics. *International Journal of Community Well-Being, 1*, 115–135. doi: 10.1007/s42413-018-0012-2

Kahneman, D. & Riis, D. (2005). Living and thinking about it: Two perspectives on life. In N. Baylis, F. Huppert & B. Keverne (Eds.) *The Science of Well-Being* (pp. 285–301). Oxford, UK: Oxford University Press.

Kasser, T. (2010). Psychological need satisfaction, personal well-being, and ecological sustainability. *Ecopsychology, 1*, 4. doi: 10.1089/eco.2009.0025

Kennedy-Townsend, K. (2011, June 20). The pursuit of happiness: What the founders meant-and didn't. *The Atlantic.* Retrieved from www.theatlantic.com/business/archive/2011/06/the-pursuit-of-happiness-what-thefounders-meant-and-didnt/240708

Lu, L. & Shih, J. (1997). Sources of happiness: A qualitative approach. *The Journal of Social Psychology, 137* (2), 181–187. doi: 10.1080/00224549709595429

Lyubomirsky, S. (2013). *The Myths of Happiness.* New York, NY: Penguin Press.

MacKerron, G. & Mourato, S. (2013). Happiness is greater in natural environments. *Global Environmental Change, 23* (5), 992–1000. doi: 10.1016/j.gloenvcha.2013.03.010

Meadows, D., Randers, J. & Meadows, D. (n.d.). A synopsis: Limits to Growth: The 30 year update. *The Donella Meadows Project.* Retrieved from http://donellameadows.org/archives/a-synopsis-limits-to-growth-the-30-year-update/

National Geographic. (2019). Sustainable development goals. Retrieved from www.nationalgeographic.org/article/sustainable-development-goals/

O'Donnell, G., Deaton, A., Durand, M., Halpern, D. & Layard, R. (2014). Wellbeing and policy, Legatum Institute report 2014. *Legatum Institute.* Retrieved from http://li.com/docs/default-source/commission-on-wellbeing-and-policy/commission-on-wellbeing-and-policy-report-march-2014.pdf

OECD. (2013). OECD guidelines on measuring subjective well-being. In *OECD.* Paris, France: OECD Publishing. doi: 10.1787/9789264191655-en

O'Neill, D., Fanning, A., Lamb, W. & Steinberger, J. (2018). A good life for all within planetary boundaries. *Nature Sustainability, 1,* 88–95. doi: 10.1038/s41893-018-0021-4. Retrieved from https://tinyurl.com/y3jg44wn

Ott, J. (2010). Happiness, economics and public policy: A critique. *Journal of Happiness Studies, 11* (2), 125–130. doi: 10.1007/s10902-008-9125-2

Ott, J. (2011). Government and happiness in 130 nations: Good governance fosters higher level and more equality of happiness. *Social Indicators Research, 102* (1), 3–22. doi: 10.1007/s11205-010-9719-z

Pellerin, C. (2016). Constitutional considerations of happiness. *Columbia Undergraduate Law Review.* Retrieved from https://blogs.cuit.columbia.edu/culr/2016/02/16/constitutional-considerations-of-happiness/

Stiglitz, J., Sen, A. & Fitoussi, J. P. (2009, September). Report by the commission on the measurement of economic performance and social progress. Retrieved www.stiglitzsen-fitoussi.fr/documents/rapport_anglais.pdf

United Nations General Assembly. (2011, August 25). Happiness: Towards a holistic approach to development (Resolution 65/309): 64th session: 109th plenary meeting. Retrieved from www.un.org/ga/search/view_doc.asp?symbol=A/RES/65/309

United Nations Sustainable Development Goals. (n.d.). SDG indicators. Retrieved from https://unstats.un.org/sdgs/indicators/indicators-list/

US Declaration of Independence, Paragraph 1. (1776).

4

INDIVIDUAL HAPPINESS

Individual happiness learning objectives

The objectives of this chapter are for students to be able to:

- Understand that people have a certain amount of decision-making power about their own happiness.
- Learn different ways to be happier.
- Learn some of the pitfalls of seeking happiness.
- Understand how to develop communication skills.

Preliminary questions

- Is happiness something you can choose or not?
- Does happiness matter? If so, why? If not, why not?
- What makes you happy?
- Are some people born happy?
- If a person is born with an unhappy disposition, can they ever be happy?
- What do your needs being met or not being met have to do with effectively communicating?
- What do feelings have to do with effectively communicating?

Individual happiness introduction

This coursebook started by stating that happiness is the purpose of life. This chapter contains information and resources for happiness skills development in three sections on mindfulness, gratitude and generosity. Each section also contains an overview of researchers' findings and caveats. The chapter ends with a section on communication skills. But first, let's look at the question of whether it is worth the effort to develop happiness skills.

For most people, it is common sense to want to be happy and not to be miserable. Research findings indicate there are good reasons to be happy. Happy people are more resilient, creative, better at problem solving and healthier (Cohn et al., 2009; Carnegie Mellon University, 2006; Kyriopoulos, Athanasakis & Kyriopoulos, 2018). Happiness science tells us there are three different sources of happiness, also called determinants, and that some of them can be changed to a certain extent (Lyubomirsky, 2007). The three determinants are (1) genetic set point, which is determined by DNA (deoxyribonucleic acid is the hereditary material in people and other living organisms); (2) the circumstances of life, such as opportunities for education, work, health care, participation in governance, access to nature and so on; and (3) decisions about what to feel, think and act. Some researchers say that up to 50% of happiness is due to genetic set point (Lyubomirsky, 2007), but others, using twin studies, suggest about 33% of happiness comes from genes (Bartels, 2015). Research indicates that as little as 10% of happiness may be influenced by life circumstances, and more than 40% of happiness may be determined by personal decisions (Lyubomirsky, Kennon & Schkade, 2005; National Geographic Live, n.d.). It is possible that the lines between genetics, life circumstances and personal decisions are quite blurry, but suffice to say that some part of happiness is determined by genetics, and some part is under an individual's control. This means a person can change how happy they are. More good news is that given all the studies in happiness, you can learn how to develop happiness skills.

HIGHLIGHT: WHY NOT BE HAPPY?

Why wouldn't a person want to be happy? There are times when it is not appropriate to be happy or to focus on the good things in life. The quality of relationships has a large impact on a person's happiness (Treleaven, 2018). If a person is in a relationship with someone who physically or psychologically abuses them or a person is abusive to someone, then it would not be appropriate to be happy. Domestic violence affects about one quarter to one third of people in relationships (National Coalition against Domestic Violence, n.d.). This means that in any group, it is likely at least one out of four people have or will experience being victims or victimizing their partner, family member, friend or roommate. If you are not sure what domestic violence is, the Duluth Power and Control Wheels can help clarify at www.theduluthmodel.org/wheels, as can the National Coalition Against Domestic Violence factsheets at www.ncadv.org/statistics. If you are in an abusive relationship, reaching out to find the people and resources you need to safely move into safety, and waiting until you are safe, or, if you are abusive, reaching out to find support and help so you stop hurting people is likely more important than learning happiness skills. (Note that if you are a victim, you may put yourself at the highest risk by leaving, challenging the abuser or asking your abuser to stop, so be sure to have resources to be safe.) In some areas, police are still not responsive to domestic violence calls, but many areas have shelters and resources to help. Wikipedia has links to many domestic violence hotlines at https://en.wikipedia.org/wiki/List_of_domestic_violence_hotlines.)

Another time when it is not necessarily helpful or appropriate to develop happiness skills is when someone is struggling with depression or anxiety. It is the authors' opinion that happiness skills should not be used as a way to get over depression or other mental illness. For example, meditation should not be used as an alternative to medication. Depression is an illness which can and should be treated. Symptoms of depression vary a lot. They can include feeling detached or as if one is living apart from themself; not feeling interested in anything; having a really hard time getting going; being unable to concentrate; feeling overwhelmed and lacking confidence most of the time; feeling tired, run down or sick all the time; having problems sleeping (e.g. waking up too early) or sleeping too much; losing or gaining a lot of weight; or not having real enjoyment in anything. Life can be really hard, and very few people have the skills to bounce back when things get really tough. Almost everyone suffers from depression, anxiety or some sort of mental illness at some point in their lives. Medical treatment and talk therapy can be life changing and even life saving. If you suffer from depression, anxiety or other problems, seek medical help.

There are many other reasons not to be happy: war, the extinction of species, ecological disasters, social injustice, the news and hard things happening in life are just a few. It is important to be able to feel and express the unhappiness, sorrow, anger, hurt and loneliness that come with living life. However, this does not mean a person cannot also learn happiness skills, cultivate happiness in life and develop greater resilience to hard times. Victor Frankl (1984), a psychiatrist and neurologist who was put into Nazi camps at the age of 37 for three years and survived, said it best: "Everything can be taken from a (person) but one thing: the last of the human freedoms – to choose one's attitude in any given set of circumstances, to choose one's own way" (p. 75).

HIGHLIGHT: THE DOCTOR BLISS DOCTRINE

Clinton L. Bliss, MD, one of the authors of this book, is an emergency and primary care physician. He provides care using the bio-psycho-social model, meaning he takes into account his patients' physical health, mental state and life circumstances. He has found from treating thousands of patients each year for over 25 years that people's health problems are often deeply connected to unprocessed grief.

Grief has many causes: not having experiences you wanted to have, having experiences you did not want to have, not being with someone you want to be with or being with someone you do not want to be with. Sometimes there is grief because of a health problem, and sometimes health problems arise from unprocessed grief. Grief can come from major events in life, such as the loss of a family member, or from something that seems trivial, such as losing a piece of jewelry. And grief can be hidden in an event that we expected to happen that did not, such as not having a baby, a broken promise or not getting a job.

An important lesson about happiness is that to feel truly happy, you have to also allow yourself to feel sadness and all the other difficult feelings (Brown, 2012). Emotions can be likened to a river of life that flows within you. When your emotions flow freely, they act as a kind of personal compass that leads you to meaning and purpose in life. Without this compass, you feel lost and confused.

Everyone, even the most fortunate of us, experiences devastating losses in this life. When you lose something or someone important, you experience many overwhelming and often conflicting feelings such as anger, guilt and sadness. In response to this emotional tidal wave, you typically go into a state of denial, which acts like an emotional dam that protects you.

Unfortunately, this dam also keeps you from experiencing your positive feelings such as love, forgiveness, happiness and hope. While in this state, you tend to feel dead inside, leading a zombie-like existence, going through the motions of your life as if it were someone else's. If you do express feelings while in this state, they often come out sideways, or like an uncontrolled gush over the top of the dam, and you may react in ways that you later come to regret. The only way to get through this process is to experience your emotions fully.

The process of grief is one that takes time, patience and attention. To get through it, you must go over and over it. There is no shortcut or escape. If necessary, grief will wait a lifetime for you.

Dr. Bliss created a grief process that he uses with his patients to help them find happiness when they are stuck in sadness, numbness or other difficult feelings such as anger. We call it the Doctor Bliss Doctrine. It has four steps, listed next. Please note that each person is unique, and this is just one way to process your grief.

1 **Feel your feelings.** All feelings are valid. Allow anger, fear, disbelief, confusion and every other feeling to be felt. Do not judge feelings. Actions may be judged but not feelings. Suppressing feelings sends a message to yourself that your feelings do not matter, so you do not matter. When you do not matter, you go through life feeling dead inside. Moreover, ignored and suppressed feelings do not go away. They just come out sideways, like in depression, unexplained anger and annoyance or overly risky behavior and sometimes in aches in the body, sickness or disease.
2 **Express your feelings.** When you express your feelings, you feel valued. Talk about your feelings with someone who is trustworthy, cares about you and will not judge you. If it is too uncomfortable to talk about, start by talking about the feelings of discomfort, but whatever the case, find a way to talk about your feelings.

3 **Consider the impacts** of your options for action, including impossible options, things you would never do, things you feel ashamed to admit you think about doing, as well as doing nothing. Play out the ultimate conclusion of each of the options and consider the outcomes. Answer the question of what would happen if you actually did each option and how you would feel once it was fulfilled. Often ethical dilemmas arise in the process. Consider whether it would be worth acting on each option.

4 **Act.** After you have fully felt and expressed your feelings and considered the impacts of your options, you are now able to act in ways that bring fulfillment to you and others and can often avoid harmful outcomes and unseen consequences. Processing your feelings of grief brings you back into balance and you can again feel and act in true integrity within yourself and with compassion towards others.

The science behind mindfulness

Happiness science indicates that practicing mindfulness leads to happiness (Huppert,2017; Fredrickson, 2008). Research into the brain has found that mindfulness changes the brain so the patterns of activity in the brain are similar to those of calm and happy brain patterns (Lutz et al., 2004; Richard, 2003). But what is mindfulness?

Jon Kabat-Zinn, a medical professor, is credited with popularizing mindfulness as a stress-reduction technique. He defines mindfulness as "paying attention in a particular way: on purpose, in the present moment, and non-judgmentally" (Kabat-Zinn, 1994, p. 4). Another word for mindfulness is meditation. Meditation is often associated with Buddhism, but there are many ways that mindfulness is taught and practiced that are not Buddhist. Jon Kabat-Zinn advocates for a science- or evidence-based rather than spiritual-based approach to mindfulness. One of the core teachings in Buddhism is called the Kalamas lesson. In this lesson, Buddha is said to have recommended (paraphrased here): don't believe something just because it has been told to you. Try practicing mindfulness and see if you find there is less suffering and more happiness in your life. If it works, keep going. If it does not, find something else to ease suffering and find happiness.

Some of the benefits that can come from mindfulness are stress reduction, stronger concentration skills, better problem solving, improved memory, better sleep, psychological resilience, better mental health, better dietary habits, increased capacity for compassion and better functioning in relationships (Goldman & Davidson, 2017; Smith et al., 2017; Stierwalt, 2018). One of the reasons companies and sports teams provide mindfulness trainings to employees or, in some cases, use mindfulness to begin meetings or the day is that mindfulness is thought to increase productivity and concentration and to decrease sick days (Kersemaekers et al., 2018; Kachan et al., 2017; Wei, 2018; Levin, n.d.; Christensen, 2017; Daily, 2019).

A few caveats about mindfulness. Mindfulness is not for everyone. There are times in life and people for whom mindfulness can be unhelpful and damaging (Foster, 2016). When there is unresolved trauma in a person's life or someone is living in a situation in which they must ignore their feelings and thoughts in order to survive, practicing mindfulness can be unhelpful. Also, if a person has a psychological disorder, such as bipolar disorder, schizophrenia or a personality disorder, then while mindfulness may be helpful for managing anxiety and other symptoms (Brown et al., 2010; Johnson et al., 2009; Perich et al., 2012), it may also be destabilizing, depending on how it is practiced. As stated earlier, the authors advise that mindfulness should not be used as an alternative to prescribed medication.

Mindfulness as a theory of positive change

Having covered some of the benefits and a few caveats for mindfulness, we present our theory of how mindfulness works in terms of systems change. First, we will define mindfulness in our own way. We define mindfulness as seeing things as they truly are and being present in the moment with friendliness towards yourself and others. Our understanding is that mindfulness is experienced through awareness of one's thoughts, emotions and life's circumstances with an understanding that one is not solely defined by their thoughts, feelings or the roles they play in life, such as daughter or son, student or employee, athlete or artist. Some people mistakenly, in our view, think that mindfulness is a way of escaping from everyday life by escaping from thoughts and feelings and achieving a state of bliss or mindlessness. It's actually just the opposite. Mindfulness is not about separating oneself from daily life or one's thoughts and feelings. We propose that mindfulness is about being more present in daily life. By practicing mindfulness, you can train your mind to be able to see things as they truly are in everyday life, and with this ability, you may find that you are able to manage yourself more wisely, which in turn leads to feeling happier.

Our theory for how mindfulness works and can lead to happiness and empowerment as a change agent begins with training oneself to be mindful.

This is the first change. Practicing mindfulness trains the mind to be mindful just like practicing to take a test trains one to be a good test taker and lifting weights results in muscle strength. By practicing mindfulness a few minutes each day, one slowly teaches oneself to become aware that feelings arise from a set of circumstances and to develop the ability to allow feelings and thoughts to occur without immediately acting on them or reacting to them, such as when feeling fear and immediately getting anxious or feeling angry and bursting out. The feelings do not dissipate, but an awareness that there are feelings increases. With more practice, one's capacity to be in the present with feelings and thoughts increases, even with big feelings, without being overtaken by them. As mindfulness is practiced a few minutes a day for weeks on end, you start to see patterns in how your own mind works. Insights are gained into oneself, other people and the circumstances of life. This is because a key part of practicing mindfulness is noticing patterns of feelings, thoughts and impulses. The benefits of practicing mindfulness are seen because one is better able to handle situations and able to get over difficulties with less stress and strain. This is positive feedback. This inspires practicing for a bit longer each day, and with more practice, we are able to see things more clearly more often and to better understand what to do and what *not* to do in everyday life. We can become more powerful in our intentions and actions. With this, we start to see how our presence, actions and words affect other people in positive ways when they are mindful, and in negative ways when they are not, which fuels greater appreciation and practice of mindfulness. Eventually, we want to practice for a longer time each day or as many days a week that we can. With practicing for a longer time, we may notice bigger changes in life and over time and that there is more peace, ease and balance in life.

This is just a theory, but we have found in our own lives and observed in the lives of others how this theory sometimes proves to be correct. It doesn't mean that practicing mindfulness leads to perfection, never making mistakes, or having a perfect life without hardship. However, we have seen how regular mindfulness practice can create a positive feedback loop and a gradual change towards less suffering, more ease and happiness and greater empowerment as a change agent. Find a mindfulness practice that works for you and come up with your own theory.

The next sections explain four ways to practice mindfulness. They are all just starting places provided with the intent that they are a way to explore and find ways to practice mindfulness that work for you. But first, another caveat. Even though mindfulness can lead to happiness, it is not easy for most people. In fact, for most people, it is incredibly hard. This is because when a person starts to practice mindfulness, a lot of feelings, thoughts and impulses come up. For most people, it is a very slow process. Moreover, practicing mindfulness can be particularly hard when a person is feeling bad or when life is hard. However, when one practices mindfulness even for one minute in the hard times, there can be benefits.

Four ways to practice mindfulness

Four ways to practice mindfulness are breath, loving kindness, body sweeps and walking meditations. Each of the four ways to practice mindfulness is different. Try each to find which suits your personality and life circumstances best. Breath meditations are often better for when you are needing some quiet time. Loving kindness is often good for when you are having negative thoughts about yourself or others. Body sweeps are often good when you are feeling anxious or restless or cannot sleep. Walking meditations are often good when feelings are strong, such as when you are angry or upset.

Breath meditation

With breath meditation, focus on the breath. Take three deep breaths and focus on how the air feels going into the body as you breathe in and then out. Try counting each in-breath and out-breath or silently saying *breathing in* and *breathing out* up to ten breaths; then start again. You will be a rare person if you can get to ten easily! It is more likely your mind will stray somewhere between the first and third breath. Don't worry. This is normal. Each time your mind strays, begin again at the first breath. It is inevitable that the mind will stray. It is also inevitable that you will have thoughts and feelings about the mind straying, such as *I am bad at meditating*, *I'm doing this wrong* or *this is stupid*. When your mind strays and the thought comes, notice that thought and the feeling that comes with it and return to the first breath again. Over time, you will begin to notice a predominance of certain feelings, thoughts or impulses. You may notice that at certain times in your life, you have lots of feelings of anger or wanting for things to be different. At other times, you may notice lots of thoughts about things you need or want to do or lots of worry. Sometimes you may get sleepy or space out every time you meditate or the idea that meditating is a waste of time might come up a lot. Notice the patterns of these or any other feeling, thought or impulse and bring your focus back to the breath. This is how you train yourself to be mindful. Each time you bring your mind back to the breath, it is like lifting the weight another time to become stronger.

A reason breath meditation is so popular is that there is no need to go anywhere or get anything. Breath is always there. Breath meditation can be done anywhere at any time: standing in a line, waiting for the bus, at the dinner table, the moments before you go to sleep. However, many people practice in a quiet place and alone because it is easier to focus without lots of distractions.

Loving kindness

Loving kindness practice involves a mantra. The mantra begins with yourself, then a person or animal who you love, then someone you do not know well, then someone you do not like, and then for the whole world, over and over again. The mantra is: May I be happy, may I be healthy, may I be at peace; may (name of the person or animal you love) be happy, may (name) be healthy, may (name) be at peace; may (name of someone you do not like) be happy, may (name) be healthy, may (name) be at peace; may all beings be happy, may all beings be healthy, may all beings be at peace. There are many versions of this mantra. This is just one. While you are saying the mantra, your mind will wander. Each time your mind wanders, bring yourself back to the mantra, starting with yourself again but without chastising yourself for a wandering mind. As your practice develops, take some time between each phrase to notice the thoughts and feelings that come up; then return to the phrase. At first, this practice may seem artificial or insincere, but over time, it creates neural pathways that bring real feelings of love and friendliness for yourself and others and will help you see the people you do not like more clearly and so be able to react to them in ways that are better for you (Lutz et al., 2008; Garrison et al., 2014).

Body sweep

A body sweep is a mindfulness practice that involves being aware of parts of the body. It usually starts by bringing the attention to the toes on the left foot, then the right foot and so on for both sides and all body parts. This meditation can be done very slowly, starting with each toe and working up to the top of the head, or more quickly going from feet to legs, torso, arms, neck and shoulders and head. If you get bored doing this meditation or are having a hard time getting to sleep (and want to sleep), focus on each part of your body, sense without words how it feels and then thank each body part. You can also give thanks for each of your organs and each muscle and sinew. Each time your mind wanders off, begin at the part of the body you last remember focusing on.

Walking meditation

Walking meditations involve focusing attention on the way the feet are moving when walking. They can be practiced when angry or upset by walking with big stomping steps; paying attention to how each foot feels each time one stomps the foot down; noticing the contact with the ground; and noticing the foot lifting off the ground, in the air and then on the ground again. Each time feelings or thoughts take the focus away from walking, the walking meditator brings their focus back to the next step. Walking meditation can also be practiced when someone is calm. Then with each step, one focuses on each step with great curiosity, noticing each discrete part of a step. Like with breath, you can try to focus for ten steps but will likely lose focus after the first, second or third step. Then just bring your focus back to the next step.

A few last words on mindfulness

If you practice mindfulness for three to five minutes every day, you may notice a change in your ability to deal with the stresses of life. Three to five minutes a day may not sound like a lot of time, but it will be a lot at the beginning. Actually, for most people, even that is too hard and a good way to start is to use guided meditations. There are myriad different recorded guided meditations online, apps and other resources you can download, buy or borrow online, at libraries, bookstores and maybe even in your friend or family's bookshelves or media files. (Note: Never listen to guided meditations while driving, bicycling or doing any activity that requires your attention and focus.) It is important to find a meditation guide whom you like and feels right for you, so try a few until you find the right one for you.

The science behind gratitude

Scientific research tells us that practicing gratitude gives many of the same benefits as mindfulness. Practicing gratitude can lead to more happiness and satisfaction with life, less anxiety, better relationships, better sleep and healthier immune systems (Watkins, McLaughlin & Parker, 2019: Wood, Joseph & Maltby, 2009; McCullough, Emmons & Tsang, 2002; Harvard Health Publishing, n.d.; Miller, 2014; Lambert, Fincham & Stillman, 2012; Sarafia, 2014).

However, like with mindfulness and any happiness skill, there are some times when gratitude practice is not appropriate. Feeling pressured to be grateful, even when self-imposed, can lead to feeling stressed or inadequate instead of happy (Miller, 2014). Similarly, overdoing it, such as expressing gratitude for the sake of it instead of out of the genuine feeling, does not yield happiness (Lyubomirsky, Sheldon & Schkade, 2005). In addition, when gratitude is used as a way to mask feelings or cover up an unhealthy relationship, it can lead to unhappiness. An example is using gratitude to try to manage an unhealthy or harmful relationship or situation, when it would be better to change the situation or find a different one.

Our theory for how gratitude can lead to happiness goes like this. By practicing gratitude, relationships can be strengthened with other people and nature. Within a few days or weeks, one sees the good things about their life and their world in ways they had not before they practiced gratitude. With this, one begins to have deeper appreciation for themselves, others and nature. This appreciation strengthens relationships and is empowering as a change agent. One now focuses on what they do want in their life and on the planet instead of all the things that are wrong. With a habit of gratitude established, it becomes second nature to thank people and to appreciate oneself, others and nature and to simply feel thankful. With this, one's actions as a change agent for good become more powerful, and one is happier with the outcomes of their actions. It is just a theory of how gratitude practice can empower a person's life and actions, and we do not have scientific research findings to prove it. Try practicing gratitude for a while and then come up with your own theory.

This brings us to gratitude practices. The next sections explore two categories of gratitude practices: reflective and expressive. As with the mindfulness practices, these are just starting places. You can use them as a way to learn and explore in your own life and find gratitude practices that work for you.

Reflective gratitude practices

Reflective gratitude practices are done alone. Three reflective gratitude practices are gratitude journals, gratitude posts and counting your blessings. Try these out, and if they do not work, come up with your own ways.

Gratitude journals

One of the more popular reflective gratitude practices is keeping a gratitude journal. A gratitude journal is just like any other journal, except it contains journal entries about the people, things or events for which one is grateful. Martin Seligman, one of the founders of positive psychology, which is a refocusing of psychology on what makes people mentally healthy instead of mentally ill, identified a structure for gratitude journals in which one writes down three things that went well in the day and then, for each thing, a reason why it went well (Seligman, 2011). If you do not like to write in journals, you can do this as a reflection before you go to sleep or when you wake. Psychologists Sonja Lyubomirsky and Martin Seligman both found that for some people, writing in a gratitude journal or reflecting each morning or night gives them happiness, and for others, limiting journal entries to a few times a week gives optimal benefits to happiness (Lyubomirsky, 2013; Seligman, 2011). Try both for a few weeks and record how you are feeling at the end of the week to find which is better for you.

Gratitude posts

For those who enjoy using social media, another way to practice gratitude is by posting on favorite feeds. A way this is done is with a challenge to make a gratitude post or tweet once a day or three times a week. Because publishing online and posts or tweets will be seen by friends, followers and maybe the public, depending on profile settings, this practice has an added dimension. For some, it leads to feeling one must censor or polish their posts or to a sense of obligation, fatigue or even dread. If you decide to try this way of practicing gratitude and you start to censor or feel obligation or dread, switch to a different happiness skill. On the other hand, if you love it, you will find lots of *how to* and informative articles and resources online to keep you inspired.

Count your blessings

The saying *count your blessings* is thought to have been made popular from a song written in 1897 (The St. Augustine Record, 2014). With this practice, one lists the things that are going well in their life when they are disappointed or unhappy about things. Two ideas behind the concept of listing the good things in life when feeling downtrodden, unlucky or ungrateful concern reorienting the mind and comparisons. Thinking about the things that are going well in life can reorient the mind and feelings. (Note that counting blessings should not be a substitute for processing feelings and grief but can be useful for little things or to get a new perspective on bigger things.) Thinking that things could be worse gives a perspective on one's situation and can help one feel better about their predicament. Studies show that there are benefits to contemplating how one's life could be worse, such as by comparing oneself with others who are worse off (Watkins, Grimm & Kolts, 2004; Bauer & Wrosch, 2008; Bauer, Wrosch & Jobin, 2008).

However, there are downsides to comparing oneself with others, and it is often best to avoid this. Comparing with people who may be better off in any way will, in general, lead to unhappiness (Alderson & Katz-Gerro, 2017). For example, if you compare the amount of money you have with someone richer than you, you will probably feel like you do not have enough. Once you have as much as the person you were comparing yourself to, you will most likely start comparing yourself with someone who has even more, and the dissatisfaction will begin all over again. This is the same for the kind of clothes you have, your looks or weight, and any other aspect of your life. If you tend to compare yourself with other people, try comparing your predicament with an imagined and much more difficult predicament or replacing this habit with a different happiness skill and see if this brings more happiness.

Expressive gratitude practices

Expressive gratitude practices are done in the company of other people and as part of a relationship with them. In addition to bringing happiness, this kind of gratitude practice often helps strengthen relationships, which are important to happiness (Treleaven, 2018).

Say thank you

Perhaps the most obvious and simple way to practice expressive gratitude is to say *thank you*. The practice of saying *thank you* can help us to see more clearly all of the good things people do to help make each day go smoothly. A way to practice this form of gratitude is to set a goal of saying *thank you* to everyone who does something for you, the bus driver, a professor, a clerk at the store, the janitor on campus, a colleague at work and so on. For people who habitually do things for you, such as a friend who spends time with you, a partner or roommate who does the dishes or a child who give you a hug, a simple statement such as "Thank you, and I appreciate you" or "I am grateful for you" might help convey gratitude more clearly, especially if you do not have a habit of saying thank you. See how you feel at the end of the day.

Gratitude letters

Gratitude letters are letters written to express gratitude to the recipient. Research indicates that writing three letters over the course of three weeks will bring lasting happiness (Toepfer, Cichy & Peters, 2012). Gratitude letters are usually about 100 words. They include a description of what the recipient did for you, how they affected you and what you think about them. For at least one of the letters, choose someone who is still alive, and after you have written the letter, ask to meet with them so you can read something to them. Don't tell them what it is, and then read the letter out loud to that person. If you can't meet in person, then read the letter over the phone. Happiness research says that just doing this will increase happiness (Seligman, 2011). Another way to express gratitude to others is with short notes. This can be done via text or email or with cards or sticky notes. Including a sentence about why one is grateful can increase the happiness effect for both the person who is thanked and the person expressing gratitude.

Say nice things about the people you love

Saying nice things about somebody is another way to express gratitude. It also can strengthen relationships (Benson, 2017). This practice was devised by John and Julie Gottman, a couple who studied and wrote about what it takes to have a happy or unhappy relationship. Together they founded the Gottman Institute and have written a number of books. Their research findings include that there is a magic ratio of positive to negative interactions in a relationship. The magic number is five to one (Benson, 2017). This means for every negative interaction, there should be a minimum of five positive ones.

To practice gratitude in this way, first notice when you talk about your partner, friend or family member in daily conversation. Notice whether it is easier for you to list the good things or bad things about them. When you talk about them, record the number of good things you say about them and the number of bad things, including the things that are funny but a little demeaning or said with the intention of helping them be a better person. If you are saying less than five good things for every bad thing, then set a goal of changing your ratio. Each time you notice the impulse to say something negative, see if you can resist or say something positive. Notice if your feelings about that person, your relationship with them and your sense of happiness change when you change how you speak about them. A technique you can use to replace the negative things you say with positive ones is expressing appreciation. This may seem awkward at first, but if you speak honestly, it will come naturally over time. You can start a sentence with "What I appreciate about you is . . ." or just say, "I appreciate you."

There are three important caveats about this gratitude practice. If you are in a relationship with someone who is abusive to you or whom you are abusing, then the way you are speaking about this person is more than likely a symptom of a deeper problem; do not to use this practice as a way to stay in an abusive relationship or keep someone in an abusive relationship with you. The other caveat is that you should not use this practice as a way to avoid problems in relationships. All relationships have problems and conflict. Addressing problems instead of avoiding them can strengthen relationships. This chapter includes some information and tools for communicating that can be helpful for addressing problems and managing conflict.

Avoid certain negative interactions

In their research about relationships, John and Julie Gottman also found that there are different impacts on relationships from varying kinds of negative interactions. In all relationships, some negative interactions are inevitable, such as sadness, frustration, irritation or guilt. However, John and Julie Gottman found that not all negative interactions have the same impact on relationships (Lisitsa, 2013). There are four kinds of negative interactions that are particularly harmful to relationships. These four should be avoided. The four negative interactions are (1) criticism, (2) contempt, (3) defensiveness and (4) stonewalling (refusing to talk or do something or being evasive).

In relationships in which these interactions are common, it is usually both sides that are engaging in some form of criticism, contempt, defensiveness or stonewalling. If you want to break these patterns, you can only control and change your own behavior. Next, each interaction is briefly explained. You will probably easily recognize these behaviors in other people. Try to see if you can identify them in yourself. Recognizing your behavior is the first step towards changing it.

Criticism is disapproving, demeaning or judging. For people who are used to criticizing, it may feel like telling the truth or a necessary function in relationships. Some people take pride in their ability to criticize. That is one reason this negative interaction can be hard to identify and hard to stop. Critical interactions can also be difficult to identify when they are couched in advice or humor. If you find you are using advice or humor as a way to criticize, even if the person you are making fun of also finds it funny, first recognize that you are being critical. You may think that your intent is to help someone, but unless your advice is requested and welcome, it is more than likely taken as a form a criticism by the person you are advising.

Contempt is an expression that conveys that someone feels another person is beneath them or worthless. It can show disrespect, scorn, disgust or a sense of superiority. Contempt can come in the form of words, but more often, in our experience, it comes across in body language, usually in the face. The face shows contempt when one side of the top lip is curled up or only one side of the mouth smiles and the eyes do not wrinkle a little, like they do when one genuinely smiles. You can experiment by making this expression on your face or looking online for facial expressions of contempt. One way to understand if someone is expressing contempt to you is by mirroring their facial expression, and this often reveals how they are feeling.

Defensiveness is a way of protecting or defending and is expressed when one feels attacked. Body language and verbal responses are ways to tell if someone is being defensive. Defensiveness comes across in body language when the arms are crossed in front of the body or on the hips or the body is turned away and closed off. Defensiveness comes across as a verbal response with objections, agreements, protestations or attacks. Being defensive can be very hard to identify because you usually feel attacked or afraid even if you are not under attack. It is hard not to be defensive if someone is criticizing you or being critical, which may be the case if negative interactions are common in a relationship. A way to identify when you are defensive is to imagine you are back in an interaction where you objected or argued, and even if you were right, see how it affects your body and how you are feeling. This will help you to notice when you are being defensive in the future.

Stonewalling is refusing to do or say anything. It can be obvious, such as with silence, avoidance, threats or changing the subject. It can also be less obvious, such as spending a great deal of time talking about something when you know you will not change your mind or saying you will do something when you know you will not do it (and not doing it). One thing all forms of stonewalling have in common is that there is no intention of doing what the other person is asking.

It can be really hard to stop being critical, contemptuous, defensive or stonewalling in relationships, especially if these are ways of expressing yourself. The first step is to recognize when you are being critical, contemptuous, defensive or stonewalling and to keep recognizing it each time. The next is to understand the underlying reasons for being critical, contemptuous, defensive or stonewalling. If you do this, you may find that the reason has nothing to do with the other person. This is usually not easy to do, and for many people, it helps to talk to someone trusted and who will not judge. Once you see the underlying reason, you may find that solutions to the problems that gave rise to your criticism, contempt, defensiveness or stonewalling are much different and much more rewarding.

A few last words about laughter in terms of interactions. Laughter can be a powerfully positive interaction (Butler, 2005) and makes you happy but just make sure that what you are laughing about does not belittle anyone. All of these negative interactions can be couched in laughter, so it is important that when you are making someone laugh or laughing, your humor is respectful as well as funny so that laughter strengthens relationships and brings happiness.

A few last words on gratitude

As gratitude practices become a part of daily life, you may occasionally experience yourself humming with gratefulness and deeply appreciating goodness in the world. That said, often when someone feels the benefits of practicing gratitude, they stop. Then stressful things happen in life, and you may not feel like there is much to be grateful for. This happens to almost everybody. When this happens to you, try to find one thing to be grateful for and then build on that. If you cannot, then it might be better to use a different happiness skill. It is also important to process your grief when hard things happen in life. Sometimes we stop practicing gratitude and things are still pretty good in life. If this happens, notice that you stopped and then pick up your gratitude practice again, knowing it is normal to stop and start.

The science behind generosity

Research about generosity tells us that being generous leads to greater happiness (Akin, Dunn & Norton, 2012; Park et al., 2017; Dunn, Aknin & Norton, 2008).

Generosity is defined in this book as an act of giving without expectation of getting anything back. The expectation to get something back can be overt, such as expecting an exchange or someone to pay back what is owed. This expectation isn't hard to recognize. Some people give with an expectation that good things will happen or other people will recognize them as a good person. There is nothing wrong with exchanging good acts or doing something to be recognized as a good person, but the definition of generosity in this book excludes giving with expectation of an exchange or getting something in return. Being generous in this way can yield benefits to happiness that are bigger and longer lasting. This section covers four ways to be generous, but first, a theory for generosity and a few caveats.

Our theory of generosity is that giving is something that humans are born wanting to do, as much as humans are born wanting more. However, in a society where wealth, income and materialism are the measures by which success is determined, it is normal to focus on having and getting stuff at the expense of giving. However, there is a balance between giving and getting. When you are in balance, the quality of what you give and receive goes up, and so does the quality of life for everyone in your life. This theory says that when one gives freely (without expectation of return) and in a balanced way, generosity extends to oneself, and one takes good care of oneself. Life flows more easily, and there is less struggle and misery. When hard times do come, one is more resilient and a better problem solver because one has taken care of oneself and is living in balance. As with mindfulness and gratitude, we encourage you to find ways of practicing generosity that work for you and to come up with your own theory for generosity, happiness and systems change.

Two caveats for generosity both concern over-giving. The first is about over-giving of yourself. Being generous should fill you and never deplete you. You should feel more energetic and better about yourself because of your generosity. It is common for people who want to help others to give to the point that they are exhausted or burnt out. This is called compassion fatigue, and the Compassion Fatigue Awareness Project has resources about it at www.compassionfatigue.org. Taking care of yourself is a generous act. Taking care of yourself is not selfish. When you are healthy and happy, you are in a better place to give to others, and what you give is of higher quality. Getting enough sleep, taking the time to do fun things and saying nice things about yourself are just three ways to be generous to one's self.

The second caveat concerns over-giving to one person or entity. In every adult relationship, there is a happy balance of reciprocity. When one person gives too much, it can cause entitlement and resentment, which may seem contradictory, but are often both present in a recipient who feels they cannot give back to even the scales. The giver also can feel unappreciated, over-extended, exhausted or like they can never satisfy the other person or entity. If this is happening, then focus on taking care of yourself, consider using some of the other happiness skills in this book and reflect on the underlying reason for imbalance in your relationship and what you (not the other person or entity) can do to find balance.

Generosity practices

Generosity comes in many forms. It includes giving to others and giving to yourself. This section provides information about giving in terms of things that can be bought as well as ways to give that do not cost money.

Spend your money on experiences over stuff

Happiness researchers found that spending money on experiences gives a longer lasting sense of happiness than buying stuff (Dunn, Aknin & Norton, 2008; Howell & Guevarra, 2013). This finding can be useful when there is extra money to spend or when buying someone a gift. There are a number of reasons that one gets a longer sense of happiness from experiences than from stuff. The hedonic treadmill is one reason, in which the joy one gets from the latest technology acquisition or much desired pair of sunglasses wears off quickly, and soon one wants the next best thing. Another reason happiness from experiences lasts longer than from things is that it creates a memory, which can last longer than any object. A good memory also brings happiness.

Spend your money on donations over experiences

Researchers who contrast spending money on stuff or experiences with donating money find that the happiness from giving money away lasts longer than happiness from buying things or experiences (Harbaugh, Mayr & Burghart, 2007). This is true even if someone donates to a charity on behalf of another person for their birthday gift or as a celebratory present. The happiness benefit from giving away money can last for years. Research findings suggest that for most people, even though they may not like it that their present was a charitable donation to a cause, over the years, when they look back on it, they get a positive feeling from having been part of a contribution to something that was helping others.

A way scientists conduct their research is to give people a small amount of money and ask them to either spend it on themselves or on someone else. The people who spend the money on someone else end up happier. In other studies, people plan to spend their own money on someone else or themselves. The people who planned to spend money on someone else ended up happier and often did spend money on someone else. You can experiment with this by planning to spend a small amount of your own money on someone else in the next week. It doesn't matter how much money; it just matters that you make the plan. In the next week, do what you planned or something similar and test to see if you feel happier. If you do feel happier, then do the same thing the next week. Ask yourself at the end of the second week whether you feel happier. If this giving practice works for you, then make it a regular thing to plan to spend a little of your money on someone each week or so and then do it.

Give your time

Researchers have found that volunteering can bring happiness (Thoits, 2012; Thoits & Hewitt, 2001). Volunteering can take many forms, from volunteering for a nonprofit once a week to occasional random acts of kindness. This section covers a range of ways to volunteer. Do the one that excites and inspires you and that does not seem like a chore or make you feel anxious. If none inspire you, come up with an idea on your own. After some time, check in with yourself and see if feelings about yourself improve and you feel happier. It is important to give your time to someone you really enjoy spending time with and who leaves you feeling good about yourself. Do not volunteer with people who leave you feeling drained, depressed or bad about who you are. Scientific research tells us that you end up being a lot like the people with whom you spend time (Riess & Neporent, 2018). This is called the empathy effect, and it holds true not just for volunteering but for all aspects of our lives.

One way to give time is to volunteer for a nonprofit. This kind of volunteering can involve training and a commitment to volunteer for a period of time. When volunteering, it is important to choose a nonprofit that is doing work you believe is important and aligned with your values. For example, if you love animals, volunteer at a local shelter. If you love being in nature, volunteer for environmental nonprofits or at your local park department.

Another way to give time is to volunteer informally. Offering to help an elderly person, such as a grandparent, or someone who has small children, such as a friend or sibling, with household chores or errands, spending time with them discussing a subject they are interested in or playing a game they enjoy are a few ways to give time. Doing an errand or dropping off dinner or a snack to a friend who is going through a hard time or a particularly hectic time are also ways to give time informally.

Focusing on the people you love is another way to give time. Giving someone 30 minutes or an hour to completely focus on them and to listen to what they have to say without offering advice or feedback unless they ask for it can be an expression of generosity. Other ways to give time are to make a date with a friend or family member whom you enjoy being with and instead of going out, sit and talk about what is happening in their life.

Random acts of kindness

Random acts of kindness are small and easy things a person does as part of their daily life, without going far out of their way. Small acts of random kindness also have a ripple effect, inspiring others to also be kind (Tsvetkova & Macy, 2014). Studies about random acts of kindness find that they bring at least as much happiness to the person doing the act of kindness as to the receiver (Lyubomirsky & Layous, 2013). Examples of random acts of kindness are paying for someone's coffee at the coffee shop, buying lunch for a homeless person, putting change in a vending machine, holding a door open for someone, giving a heartfelt compliment, picking up litter, giving something away or smiling at someone. There are countless ways to practice random acts of kindness as part of everyday life.

For some people, one kind of random act of kindness is easy for them; for another, the same act would be a challenge. It is important to find the right random act of kindness that is both easy and fun for you. When choosing a random act of kindness, find the one that feels right for you and practice it when it is safe and easy. The next day, try setting a goal of five random acts of kindness in a day and see how you feel at the end of the day. As you experiment with practicing random acts of kindness, you will find the ways that feel right for you. Then, when you find you have fallen out of the habit, you can pick it back up and experiment again to find a new way of practicing random acts of kindness. Consider giving yourself the challenge of making random acts of kindness a normal way to live.

A few final words on generosity

These are just a few ways to be generous. There are myriad ways to practice generosity. Some of them you already do as a regular part of your life. We encourage you to reflect on the good things you have done over the course of your life on a regular basis. This is not a common thing to do in most cultures, and this suggestion may seem objectionable to you. By reflecting on the good things accomplished, a positive feedback loop is created.

Communication

This section focuses on communication. Communication is something that all sentient beings do, but not all do it well. All children talk and listen but do not necessarily learn how to communicate well. Most adults find that sometimes one's words cause misery to oneself and others. Researchers have found that good communication skills can add to your happiness (Segrin & Taylor, 2007), but you probably already know this. As a change agent, it is important to communicate well. This section provides some resources and tools to develop good communication skills. You may find it useful to use this section as a starting place and develop your own methods to skillfully communicate.

There are two sections, one for listening and the other for talking. There are many other aspects of communication that are crucial to good communication. Body language, tone of voice, proximity to another person, touch, appearance and smell are often more powerful communicators than words. The intent of this section is to inspire you to learn and explore good communication skills in all these aspects.

Active listening

Perhaps the most effective and important communication skill is listening. However, it does not come naturally for most people to listen. For many people, when someone is talking, they are not listening but waiting for the other person to stop talking so they can talk. Few people listen to understand. One reason people may not listen is that they rarely feel understood. Our theory is that by learning to listen, one can be better understood.

Active listening is listening to understand what the other person is saying and what they mean. It includes listening to their words as well as observing other aspects of communication: their body language, their tone and pitch of voice, the emotions with which they speak, their facial expressions, whether and how they make eye contact, the proximity of their body and their appearance. It is important to keep in mind that active listening does not entail preparing a response or a list of ways someone can improve their appearance, posture, facial expressions and so on. This would be a form of not listening but judging and multitasking. Active listening also entails bringing the focus back to the person being listened to each time one feels an impulse to come up with a response.

Active listening cannot be done when multitasking because active listening requires full attention. When one gives their full attention, they are using both the left and right sides of the brain. They are both analyzing and synthesizing, understanding sequentially and intuitively, perceiving the parts and the whole of what someone is saying at the same time. When one listens fully, one does not multitask by thinking about other things, such as how to fix the speaker's problem, or how to respond to a list of things to do. We should also not check email or social media, play a game or do a household chore.

With active listening, when a person is finished talking, the listener first reflects back to them what they heard the speaker saying. Then they ask if they understood correctly. The listener might try saying something like "So, if I understood you, you said [and then repeat what you heard]. Did I understand correctly?" The listener should try to say what they heard the speaker say without adding or interpreting. The speaker and listener can go back and forth until the speaker feels that the listener correctly understood. After this, the listener can ask if the speaker wants to hear what they have to say. If the speaker feels understood, they may be more likely to listen.

A caveat about active listening concerns people who are difficult to be around or who persistently leave you feeling bad about yourself. The people listened to influence how you feel about yourself (Hatfield, Rapson & Le, 2009). If you are being honest, non-judgmental and caring with someone and they do not respond in kind, try a new course of action. You can quietly pay attention while they speak and then leave their company. If it is too hard to listen to them, you can appear to listen until you can excuse yourself or, if you cannot leave, divert the conversation to another topic. This does not mean you should not listen to people when there are hard things to talk about or avoid conflict in a healthy relationship. Difficult interactions are part of every long-term relationship and can be springboards for personal growth. Resolving conflict through good communication skills can strengthen relationships and lead to greater happiness.

Speaking

The second communication lesson is about speaking. There is a story about a woman who is comforting a wounded child, when a great warrior comes along and tells her that what she is saying is useless. She turns to him and says, "You are a stupid and worthless man." This enrages him, and he lifts his sword to kill her. She yells, "Stop!" and then says to him, "With those seven words, I was able make you ready to murder a stranger. Now do you see how a few words can change everything?" This story illustrates how words can do great good or deadly evil. Learning to speak in a way that does no harm is an art. We humans are born with the ability to talk but must learn how to speak to do no harm.

This lesson breaks communication into four steps following a communication technology developed by Marshall Rosenburg (Rosenberg, 2003). Rosenberg was an innovative psychologist and teacher who sometimes used puppets to teach his technique to adults. The four steps are not easy to learn for most people because they are a completely different way of communicating and take time. When learning this way of speaking, it is likely that there will not be anyone to practice with on a regular basis because it is so different. Try taking the time to go through the steps on your own when there is something difficult to communicate and you want to be understood. If done regularly, you may find that you can use these steps with some facility in everyday life, and gradually communications skills will improve.

Step one: observing without judgment

The first step is to state an observation of what has happened. This entails making a statement with neutral words and in a neutral tone and without judgment. It can be hard to know when one is judging or not. One way to keep from judging is to state simple descriptions of what is observed and keep away from assumptions, adjectives and adverbs used to describe what is observed. In particular, the words *always* and *never* can denote judgment. Another way to tell if one is judging is to ask if one is allowing feelings and desire for things to be different to influence how one describes what they observe. An example of an observation would be "I noticed the door was shut loudly when you came in today" or "I noticed that there was a loud sound when the door shut today." An example of judging rather than just observing would be to say, "You must have been angry because you keep slamming the door" or "You slammed the door again. Why do you always slam the door?"

Step two: state your needs

The second step is to state one's needs using the very simple sentence "I need . . ." (state your need in one word). A needs inventory is provided in Figure 4.1, which is adapted from Rosenberg. It is important to be clear

SELF-ACTUALIZATION NEEDS

ADVENTURE	CONSCIOUSNESS	HUMOR	PROGRESS
AWARENESS	CONTRIBUTION	INTEGRATION	PURPOSE
BEAUTY	CREATIVITY	LEARNING	RELAXATION
CELEBRATION	DISCOVERY	MOURNING	SPIRITUALITY
CHALLENGE	FUN	PARTICIPATION	STIMULATION
CLARITY	GROWTH	PRESENCE	

ESTEEM NEEDS

AUTONOMY	DIGNITY	FREEDOM	RESPECT
CHOICE	EFFICACY	INDEPENDENCE	SELF-RESPECT
COMPETENCE	EFFECTIVENESS	PURPOSE	SELF-EXPRESSION

LOVE & BELONGING NEEDS

ACCEPTANCE	COMMUNICATION	EMPATHY	PARTNERSHIP
AFFECTION	COMMUNION	FAMILY	SUPPORT
APPRECIATION	COMMUNITY	FRIENDSHIP	TRUST
BELONGING	COMPASSION	INCLUSION	UNDERSTANDING
CARE	CONNECTION	INTIMACY	WARMTH
CLOSENESS	CONSIDERATION	NURTURING	

PHYSIOLOGICAL NEEDS

AIR	SEX
CARE	SHELTER
FOOD	SLEEP
MOVEMENT	TOUCH
REST	WATER

SAFETY NEEDS

BALANCE	HOPE
EASE	ORDER
EQUANIMITY	PEACE
FAITH	SECURITY
HARMONY	STABILITY

*A HOLISTIC INTEGRATION OF MASLOW'S NEED HIERARCHY AND ROSENBERG'S NEEDS INVENTORY

FIGURE 4.1 A holistic needs inventory – an integration of Maslow's Hierarchy of Needs and Rosenberg (2003)

Source: Formulated by the authors

about the difference between one's own needs and blaming or complaining about what one wants someone else to do or how one wants someone else to be. A way to do this is keeping a need statement to these words: "I need . . ." (state need in one word).

Simply stating needs can be hard to do, especially when not sure about one's needs. It is easy to get confused, especially when not sure or ashamed about one's needs. When this is the case, try to state your needs as simply as possible and not explain them. Try checking off the needs that are important to you using the needs inventory; then start with the most important one and make your need statement.

Step three: state your feelings

The third step is to identify and state your feelings using the very simple sentence "I feel . . ." (state the feeling in one word). This may seem like a really simple step, but it is very hard for most people.

Feelings can be confusing. A person can have contradictory feelings at the same time. For example, you can feel happy and sad or stressed and excited. Having contradictory feelings does not mean that feeling does not count because you are also experiencing the opposite feeling. All of the feelings we have are our own.

Shame can also make it hard to state feelings. If shamed for feelings in the past, we may have learned to suppress or ignore them. You may not even know how you are feeling because it's been learned that it is not safe or acceptable to express your feelings.

Strong negative or unpleasant feelings can also make it hard to state feelings. Strong feelings of anger, hatred, fear or other unpleasant feelings can cause the body to put energy into the part of the brain that prepares for fight or flight (the amygdala) and less energy in the part of the brain that thinks creatively and logically (the prefrontal cortex). This is one reason most people's tendency when feeling strong negative emotions is to say something like "You make me feel . . ." This is a blaming statement and usually ends up causing the person listening to have strong feelings, too. The result is that when the speaker speaks, they are not heard because they are not listening. In this situation, it is good to take a break to calm down. It can take between 20 minutes and an hour and a half to calm down, depending on one's personality type.

For most people, it takes a lot of practice and the right circumstances to be able to make a simple statement such as "I feel afraid" or "I feel joyful." Practice alone or with someone you trust to get comfortable stating your feelings. You can use Figures 4.2 and 4.3. Sometimes it is helpful to use a list and circle the words for your feelings; then make your feelings statement.

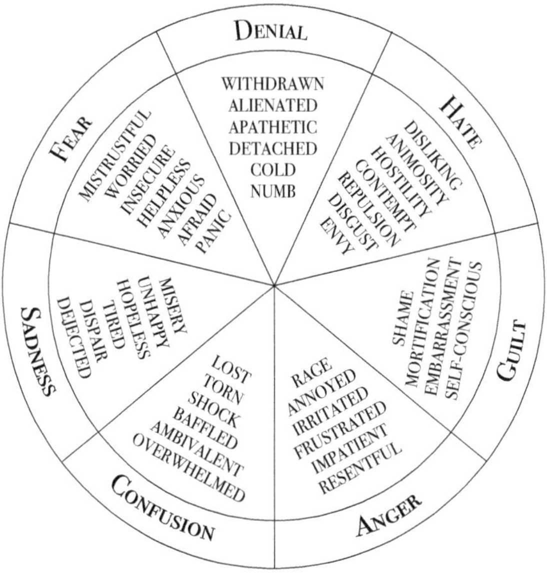

FIGURE 4.2 Unpleasant or negative feelings

Source: Formulated the authors

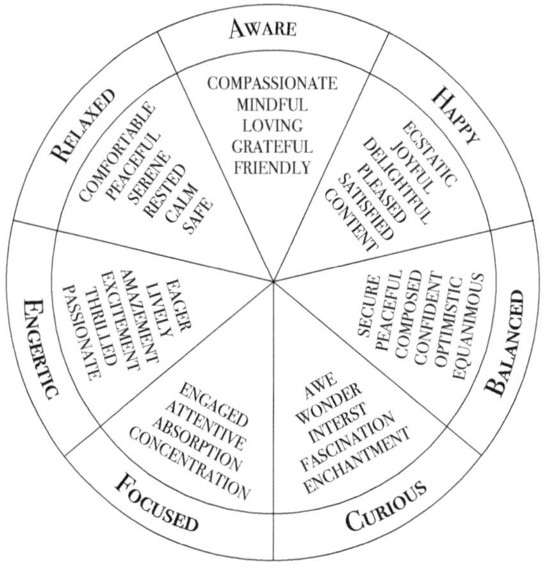

FIGURE 4.3 Pleasant or positive feelings

Source: Formulated by the authors

Step four: state your request

The fourth step is to state what you would like to do or what you would like someone else to do. It is important to remember that this is a request, not a command. For requests, say something like "Would you be willing to . . ." or "Would it work for you to . . ." For an action you would like to do, say something like "Would you like it if I . . ." or "Would it be good for you if I . . ."

Requests should be made in positive terms, that is, in terms of what to do, not in terms of what not to do. Requests should not be made in negative terms, such as telling someone to stop doing something. For the example of the slammed door, a request might be "Would you be willing to agree to shut the door quietly tomorrow?" and not "Would you be willing to quit slamming the damn door all the time?"

When making a request, it is good to keep it in the short term and avoid asking for something forever. A request might go something like this: "Would you like it if I changed my schedule so I come home tomorrow after you do?" instead of "How about if I came home an hour after you from now on?"

Breaking down speaking into four steps can be clumsy and slow, and it requires that all in the conversation agree to listen to each other's observations, feeling, needs, and respond to requests. In some situations, it will be better to go through the process by yourself. Try writing down your observations, feelings, needs and requests and then ask the person or people if they are willing to listen to you. With difficult people or difficult situations, you might try rehearsing. If you had a difficult interaction that you wish had gone differently, go through this process retrospectively, and the next time you may be better prepared to address the problem.

Benefits of individual happiness skills checklist

We explored happiness skills. When developing these skills, how do you know if they are working? For one thing, you will feel happier. Satisfaction with the conditions of your life will also increase, in part because you are in a better position to see and take advantage of opportunities to pursue happiness.

But life's events will happen, and at times you will not feel happier. These skills will help with navigating the inevitable difficulties of life.

There are other benefits and other ways to determine if developing happiness skills is working for you:

- You are resilient in the face of disappointments, failures, losses and other difficult things that inevitably arise in life. Resilience means that you are able to process feelings and bounce back emotionally, as well as gain insights and develop compassion from the difficulty that arose in life.
- You get along with the people you love. You are discerning and place your efforts where they are valued.
- You are more empathetic and compassionate towards others and yourself. *Empathy* can be defined as being able to identify with how others are feeling. *Compassion* can be defined as taking action to help someone who is hurting, including yourself. You help people who are in need.
- You are generous without an expectation of return. You also do not allow people to take advantage of you. When your generosity is reciprocated, it is appreciated. You do not give when doing so would hurt you emotionally, physically or financially.
- You are curious and open to learning. You are not threatened by being wrong or frightened to be wrong but see being wrong as an opportunity to learn and grow.
- You are courageous and willing to be vulnerable, even when it is frightening to do so.
- Your self-esteem improves, and you think and say fewer unkind things to yourself. You also have a sense of humor about yourself and take the situations in life more lightly.
- You take care of yourself, treating yourself as you would someone you deeply love. You eat enough healthy foods, get enough sleep, do exercise that is fun and are gentle with yourself when you make mistakes.

Individual happiness exercises

- In 30 seconds for each category, write down ten things, ten activities and ten people for which you are grateful. Fill up each category; if not, reflect on which ones were easier to fill.
- For one week, practice mindfulness, gratitude or giving every day. For one week, record how you are feeling each day, writing down your feelings. At the end of the week, share your experience with someone.
- For one week, practice the communication skills in this lesson with one person or by yourself once a day. Keep a record for one week, noting

each day a one-sentence reflection about your ability to communicate. At the end of the week, share your experience with someone.

- Research online about a sports team or business that is using mindfulness. Write a half-page report about your findings and share it with a small group. Did you learn anything from the group that was unexpected or helpful?
- Pair up with another person and stand silently facing each other for 30 seconds. What do the body language and posture, facial expression, type of eye contact or appearance communicate to you about the other person? Silently reflect about the other person. Notice the thoughts and feelings that arise in you. Repeat this with at least three other people.
- Bring to mind a difficult interaction in which you wish you had behaved differently and write out how you would have liked to communicate using the four steps listed in this chapter.
- There are many other happiness skills that can be developed. Here is a list, organized by domains of happiness. Do they make sense for you? For each domain, come up with skills that fit for your life.

    - Community – Do a random act of kindness for someone in your neighborhood without any expectation of a thank-you or reciprocity.
    - Economy – Living standard: Save 10% of your earnings or allowance in a savings account.
    - Education – For one week, take an online entertainment fast and read a book that you have been meaning to read.
    - Environment – Eat vegetarian once a week and contemplate for one minute the fact that producing one gram of meat protein from meat takes 20 to 30 times more natural resources than one gram of plant-based protein.
    - Governance – Get on the newsletter list for your neighborhood's elected leader. Write at least one email or make one call to them about an issue that is important to you.
    - Health – Make a new friend by reaching out to someone you like but with whom you are not yet friends and do something outside or that involves movement, such as taking a walk, exploring a new part of town or going to a festival.
    - Social support – Refrain from social comparisons.
    - Time balance – Make up on sleep at least once a week by carving out at least one day to sleep for the amount of time you have missed sleeping in that week. For example, if you need 8 hours a sleep a night but got only 6 for three nights in a row, take a day to sleep 14 hours (8 hours plus 6 hours of missed sleep) to get caught up.
    - Work – At school or work, take a gossip fast for one day this week, two days next week and so on until gossiping is no longer a habit.

Individual happiness discussion questions

- Scientific research tells us that some of the benefits of happiness are resilience, creativity, problem-solving skills and health. In your experience, what are other benefits of being happy?
- What are some of the ways you practice gratitude or giving in your life?
- Do you think there is a connection between fully grieving the difficult things in life and happiness? If so, what is the connection between grief and happiness? If not, why not?
- What do you think about the idea of active listening? When does active listening come easily to you? When is it hard for you to actively listen?
- What do you think about the four steps for communicating? When would going through the steps be helpful?
- What do you think about the definition of mindfulness in this chapter? How do you define mindfulness?
- Look at the Benefits of Individual Happiness Skills Checklist. Do you agree? Is there anything missing or anything you think should not be in the list?

Happiness resources

Videos

- *How Mindfulness Meditation Redefines Pain, Happiness & Satisfaction* by Kasim Al-Mashat, TEDx Talks. www.youtube.com/watch?v=JVwLjC5etEQ
- *The Power of Vulnerability* by Brene Brown, TEDx Talks. www.ted.com/talks/brene_brown_on_vulnerability
- *Vulnerable Honesty* by Yoram Mosenzon, TEDxAmsterdamED. www.youtube.com/watch?v=LSGfqyhleUA&vl=en
- *How to Buy Happiness* by Michael Norton, TEDxCambridge. www.ted.com/talks/michael_norton_how_to_buy_happiness
- *The Habits of Happiness* by Matthieu Ricard, TEDxTalks. www.ted.com/talks/matthieu_ricard_on_the_habits_of_happiness
- *Want to be Happy? Be Grateful* by David Steindl-Rast, TEDGlobal 2013. www.ted.com/talks/david_steindl_rast_want_to_be_happy_be_grateful
- *Flow, the Secret to Happiness* by Mihaly Csikszentmihaly, TED 2004. www.ted.com/talks/mihaly_csikszentmihalyi_on_flow
- *Positive Emotions Transform Us* by Barbara Fredrickson Greater Good Science Center, 2011. www.youtube.com/watch?v=hKggZhYwoys
- *Positive Emotions Open Our Mind* by Barbara Fredrickson Greater Good Science Center, 2011. www.youtube.com/watch?v=Z7dFDHzV36g

- Dacher Keltner, TEDxBerkeley, 2010. www.youtube.com/watch?v=KsFxWSuu_4I
- *The How of Happiness* with Sonja Lyobomirsky, PhD, at Happiness and its Causes, 2016. www.youtube.com/watch?v=F7JDbP_x8So

Reading materials

- *The How of Happiness: A Scientific Approach to Getting the Life You Want* by Sonja Lyubomirsky
- *The Subtle Art of Not Giving a F*ck: A Counterintuitive Approach to Living a Good Life* by Mark Manson
- *Authentic Happiness: Using the New Positive Psychology to Realize Your Potential for Lasting Fulfillment* by Martin Seligman
- *The Little Book of Hygge: The Danish Way to Live Well* by Meik Wiking
- *Positivity* by Barbara Fredrickson and the website for the book with online quiz at www.positivityratio.com

Websites

- Greater Good Science Center's The Science of Happiness Course at https://ggsc.berkeley.edu/what_we_do/online_courses_tools/the_science_of_happiness
- The Pursuit of Happiness website with teaching resources and information about happiness at www.pursuit-of-happiness.org
- The Positive Emotions and Psychophysiology Laboratory website contains research and information about Barbara Fredrickson's work at http://peplab.web.unc.edu and the Social Psychology Network has more information about Barbara Fredrickson's research at https://fredrickson.socialpsychology.org
- Positive Psychology Center about Martin Seligman's work at https://ppc.sas.upenn.edu
- Sonjua Lyubormirsky's website at http://sonjalyubomirsky.com

References

Akin, L., Dunn, E. & Norton, M. (2012). Happiness runs in a circular motion: Evidence for a positive feedback loop between prosocial spending and happiness. *Journal of Happiness Studies, 13* (2), 347–355. https://doi.org/10.1007/s10902-011-9267-5

Alderson, A. & Katz-Gerro, T. (2017). Compared to whom? Inequality, social comparison, and happiness in the United States. *Social Forces, 95* (1), 25–54. doi: 10.1093/sf/sow042

Bartels, M. (2015). Genetics of wellbeing and its components satisfaction with life, happiness, and quality of life: A review and meta-analysis of heritability studies. *Behavior Genetics, 45* (2), 137–156. doi: 10.1007/s10519-015-9713-y

Bauer, I. & Wrosch, C. (2008). Making up for lost opportunities: The protective role of downward social comparisons for coping with regrets across adulthood. *Personality and Social Psychology Bulletin, 37* (2), 215–228. doi: 10.1177/014616721039256

Bauer, I., Wrosch, C. & Jobin, J. (2008). I'm better off than most other people: The role of social comparisons for coping with regret in young adulthood and old age. *Psychology and Aging, 23* (4), 800–811. doi: 10.1037/a0014180

Benson, K. (2017, October 4). The magic relationship ratio according to science. *The Gottman Relationship Blog.* Retrieved from www.gottman.com/blog/the-magic-relationship-ratio-according-science/

Brown, B. (2012). *Daring Greatly: How the Courage to be Vulnerable Transforms the Way We Live, Love, Parent, and Lead.* New York, NY: Gotham Books.

Brown, L., Davis, L., LaRocco, V. & Strasburger, A. (2010). Participant perspectives on mindfulness meditation training for anxiety in schizophrenia. *American Journal of Psychiatric Rehabilitation, 13* (3), 224–242. doi: 10.1080/15487768.2010.501302

Butler, B. (2005). Laughter, the best medicine? Retrieved from https://scholarsbank.uoregon.edu/xmlui/bitstream/handle/1794/7422/laughter.pdf

Carnegie Mellon University. (2006, November 8). Happy people are healthier, psychologist says. *ScienceDaily*. Retrieved October 21, 2019 from www.sciencedaily.com/releases/2006/11/061108103655.htm

Christensen, J. (2017). For greatness on the gridiron, NFL teams turning to mindfulness. *CNN.* Retrieved from www.cnn.com/2017/11/23/health/nfl-football-mindfulness/index.html

Cohn, M., Fredrickson, B., Brown, S., Mikels, J. & Conway, A. (2009). Happiness unpacked: Positive emotions increase life satisfaction by building resilience. *Emotion, 9* (3), 361–368. doi: 10.1037/a0015952

Daily, T. (2019). Meditation coaches, the next frontier in major league sports. *Tricycle.* Retrieved from https://tricycle.org/trikedaily/meditation-for-athletes/

Dunn, E., Aknin, L. & Norton, M. (2008). Spending money on others promotes happiness. *Science, 319*, 1687–1688. doi: 10.1126/science.1150952

Foster, D. (2016). Is mindfulness making us ill? *The Guardian.* Retrieved from www.theguardian.com/lifeandstyle/2016/jan/23/is-mindfulness-making-us-ill

Frankl, V. (1984). *Man's Search for Meaning.* 3rd Edition. New York, NY: Touchstone.

Fredrickson, B. (2008). Promoting positive affect. In M. Eid & R. Larsen (Eds.) *The Science of Subjective Well-Being* (pp. 449–469). New York, NY: Guilford Press.

Garrison, K., Scheinost, D., Constable, R. & Brewer, J. (2014). BOLD signal and functional connectivity associated with loving kindness meditation. *Brain Behavior, 4*, 337–347. doi: 10.1002/brb3.219

Goldman, D. & Davidson, R. (2017). *Altered Traits.* New York, NY: Avery.

Harbaugh, W., Mayr, U. & Burghart, D. (2007). Neural responses to taxation and voluntary giving reveal motives for charitable donations. *Science, 316* (5831), 1622–1625. doi: 10.1126/science.1140738

Harvard Health Publishing. (n.d.). Giving thanks can make you happier. Retrieved from www.health.harvard.edu/healthbeat/giving-thanks-can-make-you-happier

Hatfield, E., Rapson, R. & Le, Y. (2009). Primitive emotional contagion: Recent research. In J. Decety & W. Ickes (Eds.) *The Social Neuroscience of Empathy*. Boston, MA: MIT Press. Retrieved from www.neurohumanitiestudies.eu/archivio/Emotional_Contagion.pdf

Howell, R. & Guevarra, D. (2013). Buying happiness: Differential consumption experiences for material and experiential purchases. In A. Columbus (Ed.) *Advances in Psychological Research* (Volume 98, pp. 57–70). New York, NY: Nova Science Publishers Retrieved from https://tinyurl.com/y3n64fgz

Huppert, F. (2017). Mindfulness and compassion as foundations for well-being. In M. White, G. Slemp & A. Murray (Eds.) *Future Directions in Well-Being*. Cham, Switzerland: Springer International Publishing.

Johnson, D., Penn, D., Fredrickson, B., Meyer, P., Kring, A. & Brantley, M. (2009). Loving-kindness meditation to enhance recovery from negative symptoms of schizophrenia. *Journal of Clinical Psychology, 65* (5), 499–509. doi: 10.1002/jclp.20591

Kabat-Zinn, J. (1994). *Wherever You Go, There You Are: Mindfulness Meditation in Everyday Life*. New York, NY: Hyperion.

Kachan, D., Olano, H., Tannenbaum, S., Annane, D., Mehta, A., Arheart, K., . . . Lee, D. J. (2017). Prevalence of mindfulness practices in the US workforce: National health interview survey. *Preventing Chronic Disease, 14*, E01. doi: 10.5888/pcd14.160034

Kersemaekers, W., Rupprecht, S., Wittmann, M., Tamdjidi, C., Falke, P., Donders, R., Speckens, A. & Kohls, N. (2018). A workplace mindfulness intervention may be associated with improved psychological well-being and productivity: A preliminary field study in a company setting. *Frontiers in Psychology, 9*, 195. doi: 10.3389/fpsyg.2018.00195

Kyriopoulos, I., Athanasakis, K. & Kyriopoulos, J. (2018). Are happy people healthier? An instrumental variable approach using data from Greece. *Epidemiol Community Health, 72*, 1153–1161.

Lambert, N., Fincham, F. & Stillman, T. (2012). Gratitude and depressive symptoms: The role of positive reframing and positive emotion. *Cognition and Emotion, 4* (26), 615–633. doi: 10.1080/02699931.2011.595393

Levin, M. (n.d.). Why Google, Nike, and Apple love mindfulness training and how you can easily love it too. *Inc.* Retrieved from www.inc.com/marissa-levin/why-google-nike-and-apple-love-mindfulness-training-and-how-you-can-easily-love-.html

Lisitsa, E. (2013). The four horsemen: Criticism, contempt, defensiveness, and stonewalling. *The Gottman Institute*. Retrieved from www.gottman.com/blog/the-four-horsemen-recognizing-criticism-contempt-defensiveness-and-stone walling/

Lutz, A., Brefczynski-Lewis, J., Johnstone, T. & Davidson, R. (2008). Regulation of the neural circuitry of emotion by compassion meditation: Effects of meditative expertise. *PLoS One, 3* (3), e1897. doi: 10.1371/journal.pone.0001897

Lutz, A., Greischar, L., Rawlings, N., Ricard, M. & Davidson, R. (2004). Long-term meditators self-induce high-amplitude gamma synchrony during mental practice. *PNAS, 101* (46), 16369–16373. doi: 10.1073/pnas.0407401101

Lyubomirsky, S. (2007). *The How of Happiness: A Scientific Approach to Getting the Life You Want.* New York, NY: Penguin Press.

Lyubomirsky, S. (2013). *The Myths of Happiness.* New York, NY: Penguin Press.

Lyubomirsky, S., Sheldon, K. & Schkade, D. (2005). Pursuing happiness: The architecture of sustainable change. *Review of General Psychology, 9* (2), 111–131. doi: 10.1037/1089-2680.9.2.111

Lyubomirsky, S. & Layous, K. (2103). How do simple positive activities increase well-being? *Associations for Psychological Studies, 22* (1), 57–62. doi: 10.1177/0963721412469809. Retrieved from http://sonjalyubomirsky.com/files/2012/09/Lyubomirsky-Layous-20132.pdf

McCullough, M., Emmons, R. & Tsang, J. (2002). The grateful disposition: A conceptual and empirical tool. *Journal of Personality and Social Psychology, 82* (1), 112–127. doi: 10.1.1.579.2458&rep=rep1&type=pdf

Miller, A. (2014). When thankfulness can hurt us. *USNews.* Retrieved from https://health.usnews.com/health-news/health-wellness/articles/2014/11/24/when-thankfulness-can-hurt-us

National Coalition against Domestic Violence. (n.d.). Statistics. Retrieved from https://ncadv.org/statistics

National Geographic Live. (n.d.). The science of happiness, part 1. Retrieved from https://video.nationalgeographic.com/video/ng-live/160321-davidson-healthy-mind-part1-lecture-nglive

Park, S., Kahnt, T., Dogan, A., Strang, S., Fehr, E. & Toble, P. (2017). A neural link between generosity and happiness. *Nature Communications, 8* (15964). doi: 10.1038/ncomms15964

Perich, T., Manicavasagar, V., Michell, P., Ball, J. & Hadzi-Pavlovic, D. (2012). A randomized controlled trial of mindfulness-based cognitive therapy for bipolar disorder. *Acta Psychiatricia Scandinavica, 127* (5), 333–343. doi: 10.1111/acps.12033

Richard, M. (2003). *Happiness.* New York, NY: Little, Brown and Company.

Riess, H. & Neporent, L. (2018). *The Empathy Effect: Seven Neuroscience-Based Keys for Transforming the Way We Live, Love, Work, and Connect Across Differences.* Boulder, CO: Sounds True.

Rosenberg, M. (2003). *Nonviolent Communication: A Language of Life.* Encinitas, CA: PuddleDancer Press.

Sarafia, T. (2014). Forgiveness, gratitude, and happiness among college students. *International Journal of Public Health Science, 3* (4), 241–245. Retrieved from www.researchgate.net/profile/Safaria_Triantoro/publication/275025845_Forgiveness_Gratitude_and_Happiness_among_College_Students/links/552f3cf00cf2acd38cbbf270.pdf

Segrin, C. & Taylor, M. (2007). Positive interpersonal relationships mediate the association between social skills and psychological well-being. *Personality and Individual Differences, 43* (4), 637–646. doi: 10.1016/j.paid.2007.01.017

Seligman, M. (2011). *Flourish.* New York, NY: Free Press.

Smith, J., Suttie, J., Jazaieri, H. & Newman, K. (2017). The state of mindfulness science. *Greater Good Magazine*. Retrieve from https://greatergood.berkeley.edu/article/item/the_state_of_mindfulness_science

The St. Augustine Record. (2014). Story behind the song "count your blessings." *Staugustine.com*. Retrieved from www.staugustine.com/article/20141120/LIFESTYLE/311209948

Stierwalt, S. (2018). Mindfulness: The science behind the practice. *Quick and Dirty Tips*. Retrieved from www.quickanddirtytips.com/education/science/mindfulness-the-science-behind-the-practice?utm_source=sciam&utm_campaign=sciam

Thoits, P. (2012). Role-identity salience, purpose and meaning in life, and well-being among volunteers. *Social Psychology Quarterly*, *75* (4), 360–384. doi: 10.1177/0190272512459662

Thoits, P. & Hewitt, L. (2001). Volunteer work and well-being. *Journal of Health and Social Behavior*, *42* (2), 115–131. Retrieved from www.jstor.org/stable/3090173

Toepfer, S., Cichy, K. & Peters, P. (2012). Letters of gratitude. *Journal of Happiness Studies*, *13* (1), 187–201. doi: 10.1007/s10902-011-9257-7

Treleaven, S. (2018). The science behind healthy relationships. *Time*. Retrieved from https://time.com/5321262/science-behind-happy-healthy-relationships

Tsvetkova, M. & Macy, M. (2014). The social contagion of generosity. *PLoS One*, *9* (2), e87275. https://doi.org/10.1371/journal.pone.0087275

Watkins, P., Grimm, D. L. & Kolts, R. (2004). Counting your blessings: Positive memories among grateful persons. *Current Psychology*, *23* (1), 52–67. doi: 10.1007/s12144-004-1008-z

Watkins, P., McLaughlin, T. & Parker, J. (2019). Gratitude and subjective well-being: Cultivating gratitude for a harvest of happiness. In N. Silton (Ed.) *Scientific Concepts Behind Happiness, Kindness, and Empathy in Contemporary Society* (pp. 20–42). Hershey, PA: IGI Global.

Wei, M. (2018). New research suggests mindfulness improves job satisfaction. *Psychology Today*. Retrieved from www.psychologytoday.com/us/blog/urban-survival/201810/new-research-suggests-mindfulness-improves-job-satisfaction

Wood, A., Joseph, S. & Maltby, J. (2009). Gratitude predicts psychological well-being above the big five facets. *Personality and Individual Differences*, *46* (4), 443–447. doi: 10.1016/j.paid.2008.11.012

5

NEEDS

Needs learning objectives

The objectives of this chapter are for students to be able to:

- Learn what needs are.
- Identify needs.
- Understand the connections between needs, happiness, well-being and sustainability.
- Learn about Maslow's hierarchy of needs.
- Learn about Max-Neef theory of needs.
- Learn about Wilber's modes of development.

Preliminary questions

- What are your needs?
- Are needs different for different people?
- Are humans' needs different from other animals' needs? If so, how? If not, why?
- What happens when a person is unable to meet a need?
- What does it mean to be fully self-actualized?
- Is it possible for a person to meet all their needs entirely on their own? If so, how?

Needs identified

All living beings have needs. We need shelter from the elements, healthy food to eat, clean water to drink, clean air to breathe and a sense of safety. We can go for about three weeks without food, about 11 days without sleep, three days without water, three hours without warmth and three minutes without air. Without meeting basic needs, humans do not live long.

One of the first scholars to classify human needs into categories was Abraham Maslow (Maslow, 1943). Abraham Maslow was a psychologist and one of the first to see that the field of psychology was too focused on what was wrong with people. He thought that psychologists should be trying to figure out what made people happy. Maslow thought that the key to happiness and the way out of mental illness was meeting our basic and higher needs (Maslow, 1998). His theories were among the first in the field now known as positive psychology.

Abraham Maslow created a hierarchy of needs (Fig. 5.1). The basic needs are at the bottom of a pyramid, with the higher needs on top. The basic

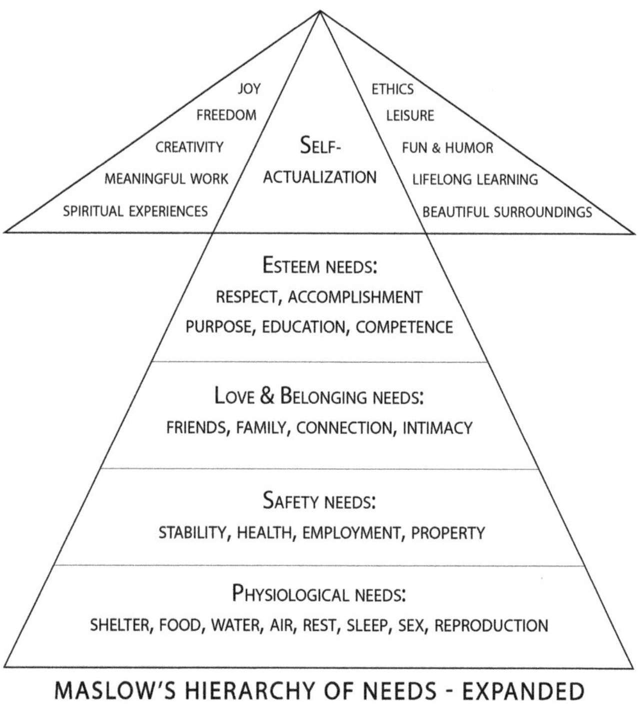

FIGURE 5.1 Maslow's Hierarchy of Needs

Source: Revised by the authors

needs he identified are physiological needs. Physiological refers to the functions of a living organism. Physiological needs are shelter, food, water and air. The next level of needs in Maslow's hierarchy are safety and security. Above that are the needs for belonging and love. The top two levels in his hierarchy are called higher needs. The second from top is the need for respect and esteem. The highest level of need is that of self-actualization.

Maslow believed that if a person's lower-level needs were deeply unmet, they would strongly assert their demands, and the person's decisions and actions would be driven by these needs. He believed that basic needs have to be met at least to a modest degree before higher needs could satisfactorily be met (Maslow, 1943). For example, if someone is hungry and homeless most of the time, they will have a hard time staying in school to get an education so they can get a good job. Esteem needs are met when there is healthy self-esteem and self-respect. Esteem needs are met through other people when they respect and admire you. Self-actualization needs are met when you are realizing your full potential. There are many aspects of self-actualization (de Graaf, 2018). One way to think about self-actualization is being the person you were born to be. Doing this is no easy task. It means seeing beyond the expectations of your family, friends, school and society and knowing what is right for you, as a unique being. Joseph Campbell, a famous mythologist, called this the *hero's journey* (Campbell, 1973).

Another important scholar contributing to the understanding of human needs is Manfred Max-Neef, an economist. He expanded Maslow's needs theory because he saw the need for economists to think about meeting more needs than money can buy. He was motivated by his exposure to extreme poverty. He saw that very poor people were meeting some needs wealthy people did not have but also that they had no hope of meeting other needs (Wake Up World Education, 2015). Max-Neef formed a taxonomy called *Fundamental Human Needs and Human-Scale Development* (Max-Neef, 1991). A taxonomy is a system of classification or organization. Max-Neef's taxonomy has nine different needs. Five of the needs Max-Neef identifies are similar to Maslow's basic needs. These are subsistence, protection, affection, participation and understanding. The other four needs Max-Neef identifies are similar to Maslow's higher needs. They are leisure, identity, freedom and creation.

Max-Neef identified ways to meet the higher needs of leisure, identity, freedom and creation (Max-Neef, 1991). The need for leisure is met by relaxing, having fun, daydreaming, remembering, playing games and enjoying the company of other people. When your imagination is sparked, you feel tranquil and are able to be spontaneous; then your leisure needs are met. The need for identity is met by getting to know oneself, growing and learning. You know you have met identity needs when you have high self-esteem, feel like you belong and are consistent in what you say and do. The need for creation is met by inventing, designing, writing, building and working. You know you have met creation needs when you are imaginative, curious, inventive and courageous in your ideas. The need for freedom is met through equal rights guaranteed to everyone in your society, having choices, being able to disagree with dominant people and ideas, developing an understanding of life's circumstances and taking risks. You know freedom needs are met when you have autonomy and can be open-minded and are passionate about your values.

Ken Wilber is a philosopher who expanded on both Maslow's and Max-Neef's theories (Wilber, 2000). He uses the term *modes of development*. According to his theory, a person progresses in each mode of development throughout their entire lives until the day they die. The modes of development he identified are kinesthetic, strategic, emotional, interpersonal, intrapersonal, social and cultural, intellectual, artistic, moral and spiritual.

Each of Wilber's modes of development have dimensions, meaning each one is about different aspects of personality. Kinesthetic development is about physical acumen, your senses (touch, taste, smell, sight, hearing) as well as how your body is feeling and what your body is communicating to you. An example is paying attention to a "gut feeling." Strategic development is about the ability to see what needs to get done, make plans and implement them. Emotional development is about being able to identify your own and other people's feelings, as well as manage your own feelings. Interpersonal development is about your ability to interact and communicate with others. Intrapersonal development is about your ability to understand how you impact others around you. Social and cultural development is about your ability to navigate the values, expectations, beliefs and customs of your culture. Intellectual development is about your ability to learn and organize ideas and thoughts. Artistic development is about your ability to express yourself artistically. Moral development is about your ability to understand the difference between right and wrong and follow morally and ethically upright principals, such as not harming others, not stealing and not lying or gossiping. Spiritual development is about your ability to feel connected to something larger than yourself.

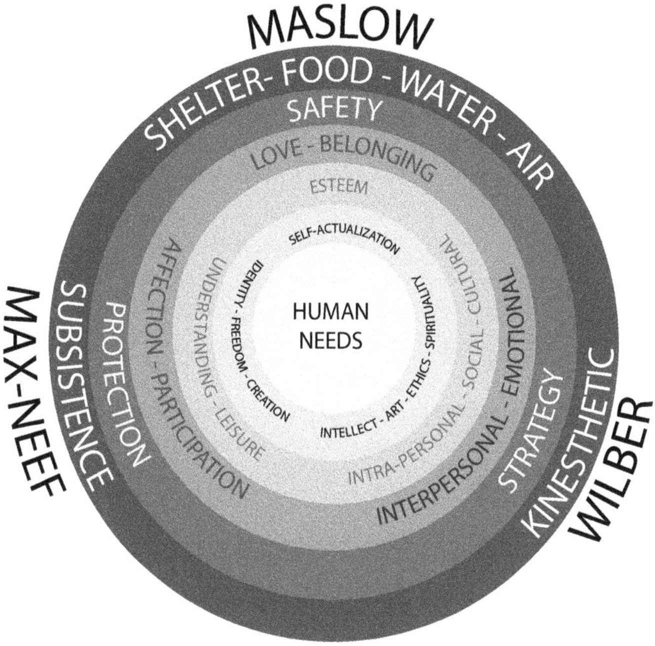

FIGURE 5.2 Needs taxonomy comparisons

Maslow, Max-Neef and Wilber have three different and important perspectives on human needs and development. Their concepts overlap in many ways. Figure 5.2 is one way to show the overlaps.

Not meeting needs: the rich-poor gap

People will do things they did not imagine they were capable of doing to get food when starving, water when thirsty enough or shelter when it's cold enough. People have braved bullets to get water for themselves and their family when the other choice is dying of thirst. People have risked imprisonment or loss of a limb to get food when the other choice is starvation. Even just being hungry without facing starvation can cause a person to do risky things they would not ordinarily do (Symmonds et al., 2010).

Income inequality is a factor contributing to the situation where some people are unable to meet their needs. The rich–poor gap in many countries is growing (World Watch Institute, 2003). Globally, 1% of the population owns about 99% of all the wealth in the world (BBC News, 2016). One of every nine people in the world does not have enough food to be healthy. This means that over 790 million people are malnourished (World Hunger Education Service, 2016). About 10% of the world's population lives in extreme poverty, equivalent to living on less than $2 a day (The World Bank, n.d.). About 400 million people in the world do not have access to basic health care. This means that if they get sick, break a leg or get cancer, they can't see a doctor (World Health Organization, 2015).

In the UK, about 7.7% of the population experiences homelessness at some point in their lives (Ortiz-Ospina & Roser, 2017). In the US, about 6.2% of the population experiences homelessness at some point in their life. Today, in almost every large city in the richest nations, a short stroll in the center of the city will include an encounter with or sighting of a person who is spending their day or night on the street.

HIGHLIGHT: SUSTAINABLE DEVELOPMENT

In 1987, the Brundtland Commission released the report *Our Common Future*. It defines sustainable development as "meeting the needs of the current generation without compromising the ability of future generations to meet their needs" (p. 41). Six challenges to meeting needs were included: (1) overpopulation and human resources, (2) sustainable food security, (3) sustainable use of species and other natural resources, (4) development of clean energy, (5) efficiency in industry, and (6) urban growth. Seven core strategies were set to achieve sustainable development. They were:

- reviving growth;
- changing the quality of growth;
- meeting essential needs for jobs, food, energy, water and sanitation;
- ensuring a sustainable level of population;
- conserving and enhancing the resource base;
- reorienting technology and managing risk; and
- merging environment and economics in decision making.

(Brundtland, 1987, p. 41)

Five years later, in response to the report and in an effort to bring about sustainable development, the United Nations convened the first Earth

Summit, officially called the United Nations Conference on Environment and Development, in Rio de Janeiro. Emerging from the Earth Summit were a number of plans and projects, including Agenda 21, a global plan for sustainable development; eventually, a number of projects, including the Intergovernmental Panel on Climate Change (IPCC); and much later, in 2015, the Sustainable Development Goals (SDGs, which are listed in Chapter 3 about measuring happiness).

For this book, sustainability is defined as the sustainability of nature now and in the future. We propose that a healthy natural environment is necessary and provides the resources to meet our needs but also that nature is intrinsically valuable. What do you think?

HIGHLIGHT: CAN NEEDS BE SUSTAINABLY MET?

An ecological footprint is a measure of the amount of Earth's resources needed to sustain a lifestyle indefinitely. There are a number of ecological footprint tools online. With them you can measure your use of energy and other resources and your waste production. The answer provided will tell you how many planets are needed to ensure everyone has the same lifestyle as you now and in the future. For most people, more than one planet is needed. This puts us in a dilemma.

Environmental and sustainability researchers Daniel O'Neill et al., (2018) wrote a report called *A Good Life for All Within Planetary Boundaries* in which they found that basic needs such as sustenance, housing, energy and elimination of poverty could be met, but there are not enough natural resources in the world to bring everyone to a point whereby they had high satisfaction with life via the strategy of economic growth. They also found that it was not biologically possible to meet the 17 SDGs.

Some alternatives that have been suggested are no economic growth, de-growth (meaning a decrease in GDP) and redefining growth. Considering the domains included in the Happiness Index as areas of need, how could you imagine redefining growth in each domain and overall so everybody could equitably and fairly experience high satisfaction with life? Listed alphabetically, the domains are:

- Community needs (include sense of belonging, sense of safety, volunteerism and donating to charities)

- Culture needs (include culture, recreation, diversity and inclusion)
- Economic needs (include housing, food and financial security)
- Learning and education needs (include access to education as well as lifelong learning)
- Government needs (include trust in and participation in government)
- Natural environment needs (include healthy environment, access to nature and biodiversity)
- Social support needs (include relationship and safety needs)
- Physical health needs (include health care, sense of being healthy and exercise)
- Psychological health needs (include a sense of purpose, meaning, optimism and autonomy)

How would you change the Brundtland Commission strategies to ensure sustainable development with your own redefinition of development?

Inequality, misery and happiness

These are somber facts, and reading them is probably depressing to you. This is because most humans have an innate empathy. When they hear of others suffering, it hurts. Scientists call this the empathy effect (Batson, 1990; Iacoboni, 2007; Bernhardt & Singer, 2012).

When there is so much income inequality that people cannot meet their basic needs, everybody is less happy (Wilkinson & Pickett, 2010). It seems to make sense that the people who have more than they need could share with the people who do not have enough to meet their basic needs because it would make everybody happier. But this appeal does not inspire action in those who are ignorant of others' suffering, lack empathy, believe that it is the fault of the poor that they are not wealthy or do not understand the connection between themselves and others.

When it is up to people who do have empathy to try to help those in need, the people helping others often end up sacrificing their own well-being for the sake of others. Often the helping people are underpaid or not paid at all because they are volunteers. They may feel underappreciated by society.

Government can and should step in to ensure all beings have the opportunity to meet their basic needs. There is a subtle distinction between providing the opportunity to meet needs and ensuring all beings' needs are met. When people have the opportunity to meet their needs, they have a choice. They can choose to have an education, housing, a job, health care or healthy food. They can also choose to develop the skills for loving relationships and a strong sense of belonging to community. If a person is required to use a service, then they lose a sense of freedom and agency, both of which are important to happiness. Studies show that when people do not have the opportunity to choose the education, housing or jobs they would like, they are less happy than when they do have these options (Nikolaev, 2014; Ott, 2016).

HIGHLIGHT: HALT

HALT is a commonly used acronym for the states of being hungry, angry, lonely or tired. The acronym tells you to stop and not make any decisions or take any action when you are hungry, angry, tired or lonely. Another way of thinking of HALT is that it is a way to signal that you should stop what you are doing and take care of yourself. The idea is that you are not thinking well or at your best in terms of decision making when in these states. Instead, HALT, and if you are hungry, eat; angry, cool down; lonely, spend time with someone you can talk to; or tired, get rested. Then come back to the matter and see if you have a different perspective and would take a different action.

What do you think? In your experience, have you ever done something you regretted when you made a decision because you were hungry, angry, lonely, tired or any combination of these? Surely you have noticed other people making bad decisions or acting badly when they are hungry, angry, lonely, tired or a combination of these states.

Could you take this acronym to a population level? What happens when a crowd or even a nation is hungry or angry? We can look back on history and see that wars have erupted out of starvation or anger. In terms of lonely, if we consider isolation and exclusivity or cultures where people resist diversity or people who are not like them in race, nationality, religion, political affiliation or other ways of identification, then we can see also that wars are fought over being lonely. If we think of tired as being downtrodden, discriminated against or misused, again we can see how this state can erupt into war.

What do you think? What do you think happens at a population level that brings people to war? How would you change the HALT acronym or states of hungry, angry, lonely and tired to describe what happens to a population that leads them to war?

We want to give a caveat to the idea of HALT for you and for populations; we do not suggest that no good can come from being angry. Anger is an important emotion that everybody experiences at some point in their lives. Anger tells you that something is wrong. Anger can give you important clues about what is not working in your life for you or about what is wrong with the world. Anger can also fuel you to make something right. When you pay attention to your anger but do not act out of it, you can also get clarity on how to right a wrong. Once you are calm, you will be better able to right the wrong in a way that puts things right for you and does not lead to more anger, hurt or harm.

Needs and sustainability

At the base of Maslow's pyramid of needs are the needs for food, air and water. We draw from natural resources that come from our planet to meet many of our most basic needs. It seems obvious that to meet our basic needs, we must care for our planet's natural systems, but this is not how things usually play out.

One reason for this is that faced with the choice of meeting needs or caring for the environment, more often than not, a person will choose meeting short-term needs over long-term needs. This is a reason it is key to prioritize meeting people's basic needs when addressing sustainability. This challenge can be met through ecologically sustainable ways to meet basic human needs.

Another reason that people are willing to overuse or pollute the environment is that for many people, it is hard to differentiate what they need from what they want. Advertising and other marketing encourage people to consume more than they need. The use of wealth and appearance as a measure of success adds to the confusion between what a person needs and what they want (Cole, 2010). Consumption needs and wants are met by the use of the earth's natural resources. Chapter 6 on sustainability explores the connections between humans and the environment.

Meeting our sustenance needs is directly tied to the natural environment. Our sustenance needs are met by food, shelter, clothing, water and air.

Meeting these needs requires the use of natural resources, which are services provided by our ecosystems.

People safeguard their ability to meet their needs through ensuring the sustainability of the natural environment. However, no one can meet their needs from food, air, water or other ecosystems services alone. Some needs are essentially non-material. Higher needs are primarily met through how you spend your time and your relationships with others. None of the needs – esteem, self-actualization, leisure, freedom, creativity or identity – can be entirely met in isolation. Meeting each need requires that people work together. Meeting your needs is tied to society and government and their organizations.

Our needs include safety and protection, love and affection, connection and understanding. You may survive without meeting these needs, but you cannot flourish without meeting them. For most people, there is a lot of overlap between the different kinds of needs. For example, a gardener can meet sustenance needs while also meeting self-esteem, freedom and identity needs and developing creatively and artistically.

One thing Maslow, Max-Neef and Wilber's theories have in common is that to meet needs, we need each other. Relationships, including our relationship to the self, are the core element for meeting needs. Happier people have healthier relationships and are better able to meet their basic and higher needs. Happier people are generally more successful. Yet humans are not born with the skills needed to be happy and must learn them. This is a reason why developing your own skills for achieving happiness is a worthy effort.

However, many of the circumstances necessary to meet our needs are outside our control. For example, if your calling in life is to be a programmer, therapist, manager, engineer, physician assistant, scientist or researcher, you need access to the appropriate education or training and the right to choose the job you want. Or if you become deeply depressed or anxious, you need access to the right kind of help and support to get healthy. To fully meet our higher needs, the external conditions must be favorable.

Our society, government, economy, natural environment and personal lives are strongly affected by the policies created by organizations. Changing policies changes lives and culture, which has a cascading effect changing our society, government, economy, natural environment and personal lives. This is way that policy is connected to needs.

HIGHLIGHT: A BACKPACKER'S THEORY OF LIFE

John de Graaf, one of the authors of this book, co-authored the books *Affluenza, What's the Economy For, Anyway?* and *Take Back Your Time*. He is also an award-winning documentary producer and speaker and an innovator and change agent who has influenced people's lives and changed government policies through his work on ecological preservation, time balance, happiness and well-being measurements, and beauty. A backpacker since early childhood, he developed his backpacker's theory of life shortly after the death of his father, who taught him to backpack (de Graaf, 2017). The theory is synopsized here.

Overconsumption in rich countries, and occasionally even in poor ones, threatens the natural environment and human life. Since World War II, humans have consumed more resources than in all previous history, while reducing forests, fisheries, soil, fossil fuels and wildlife by about one half (de Graaf, Wann & Naylor, 2001). The Global Footprint Network found that by August 1, 2018, the earth's population had consumed a full year's share of renewable resources and possible sinks for waste for that year (Global Footprint Network, 2003–2020). This phenomenon is called *overshoot*. An ecological footprint, the amount of consumption the earth can sustain over the long run, is limited. We humans are currently overshooting that sustainable footprint every year. Overconsumption is sometimes thought of as a disease, which John refers to as *affluenza*. Affluenza includes such fanciful symptoms as *shopping fever, resource exhaustion* and *industrial diarrhea* (de Graaf, Wann & Naylor, 2001).

The backpacker's theory of life posits that rich countries operate like backpackers who continually add new items to an already-overloaded pack, regardless of their value for well-being. Successful backpackers seek to achieve a balanced load that is as light as possible while still meeting real necessities. They ask: "How much food do we really need? How much water must we carry? How much protection do we need against the elements?" If they are short of these necessities, they suffer and may even perish. But if they carry more than they need, the added weight causes increasing discomfort as the trip progresses. It behooves them to be careful in their planning. Nations can be seen, metaphorically, as backpackers on earth. Instead of adding undifferentiated consumer goods, to successfully carry their people into the future, they must assess which aspects of economic growth will actually contribute to greater happiness and well-being and which may actually produce *negative externalities* that detract from both well-being and sustainability.

Our needs theory

People whose needs are fulfilled are happier (Tay & Diener, 2011). We propose that being happy can help fulfill your needs. We also propose that mindfulness, gratitude and generosity practices help with meeting needs because, over time, you train yourself to see things as they really are, be friendly towards yourself and others and live in greater balance. Mindfulness helps to find the life that is right for you instead of trying to fit into an idea of what success is or trying to fulfill somebody else's wishes for you. Happiness skill, practiced regularly, helps you to overcome low self-esteem and build up a healthy sense of self-esteem and self-respect. Communication skills are also very helpful in meeting needs because these are met, in no small part, through interacting with other people. When you have good listening and speaking skills, you are more capable of finding ways to meet needs that are beneficial to you and the people around you. In terms of Wilber's different modes, as you develop in each, you are more able to meet needs. As you become more grateful and generous, you develop emotional bandwidth, and interpersonal and intrapersonal skills get stronger. These in turn further ability to develop in the other modes. Then development occurs in many modes instead of developing in one mode at the expense of another.

For example, let's say you really need a vacation. Someone who has not developed their communication skills might blurt out how tired they are and how much they need a vacation. This could be off-putting or ignored by other people. With good communication skills, you can communicate your feelings and needs and work with your boss, friends or family members to find a solution that fulfills the needs for everybody. In this scenario, imagine that instead of complaining, you tell your best friend that you are feeling tired and stressed, and rest and calm is needed. The friend might then express that she or he has the same feelings and needs. Your friend can't give you a vacation, but together you might decide together to take half of your lunch break each day and rest quietly. The two of you might make an arrangement with the school librarian or a sympathetic teacher to use a room for a quiet lunch and place to spend some quiet time.

Let's imagine a different scenario in which money is needed. You may devise creative strategies that are against the rules or require that someone else lose money. You might be fabulously successful at making money, but your moral, interpersonal, intrapersonal and spiritual development would probably be stymied. On the other hand, if you were to find ways to make money that helped other people and gave you joy, then you would be developing along many different modes and not to the detriment of any aspect of yourself.

But to fully meet your needs, favorable external circumstances are needed that provide opportunities to pursue happiness. External circumstances include access to affordable education and to work you love and resources needed to do the things you love. They ensure a sense of safety in your home and neighborhood. Other circumstances that support happiness are income equality (closing unfair rich–poor gaps), a healthy natural environment, access to nature, tolerance and inclusion of different cultures and peoples, equal rights for women and children, and equal pay for men and women. Other circumstances in life include civil rights, vacation laws and social safety nets. Examples of social safety nets are affordable health care for the sick and access to jobs for the unemployed seeking work. External circumstances are created by organizations through policies.

Needs exercises

- Create your own version of a list of human needs based on your understanding. Jot down your ideas about the differences between needs and wants.
- A human can go for about three weeks without food, about 11 days without sleep, three days without water, three hours without warmth and three minutes without air. Hold your breath for as long as you comfortably can, while you imagine what it would be like if our world ran out of breathable air. Write down your thoughts. Next, try to go for two hours longer than you usually take between lunch and dinner (do not do this if you have diabetes, feel like you are getting sick or otherwise have a health challenge). When you feel hungry, imagine what it is like for people who do not have access to food. Jot down your thoughts throughout the day. When you finally do eat, note what it feels like to eat again. Share this experience with one or two others and write down what you learned from sharing your experiences.
- Watch this video, *A New Hierarchy of Needs* by Kennard Kim, TEDx-WhitneyHigh, at www.youtube.com/watch?v=PmRLm5qmk0k, and then answer these questions:
    - What do you agree with? What do you not agree with?
    - Does the speaker describe your own experience or observation of how to meet needs? How are your experiences and observations different?

- Jot down your ideas about hunger and poverty. Learn from the Hunger Project about the facts on hunger and poverty in the world by visiting www.thp.org/knowledge-center/know-your-world-facts-about-hunger-poverty. Was there anything that surprised you about the facts? Using systems thinking, how would you solve this problem?
- Read the article "How Women Can Save the Planet" in *Scientific American*: www.scientificamerican.com/article/how-women-can-save-the-planet. Did anything about the article surprise you? How did reading the article make you feel? What are some other solutions you can imagine that will solve problems of hunger and poverty? For inspiration, check out the solutions from the project Drawdown at www.drawdown.org/solutions.
- Do you own a cell phone, laptop or other device? If someone told you that as of right now, all your devices no longer work and you will never have access to new ones, how would you feel? Once feelings are identified, write them down. For each feeling, identify the needs associated and how that need is met by your device. How many of these needs are listed by Maslow, Max-Neef or Wilber? Are there any needs that your device meets that are not listed? Now cast your mind back to a time when you did not have a device, or imagine that you lived 50 years ago, before cell phones, laptops and other devices existed. How would you meet these same needs? What are some of the good things about having devices? What are some of the good things about not having devices? After completing this exercise, discuss your findings with one or two others.
- Imagine that for your birthday, you are given a companion robot that could have a conversation with you, learn from conversations it had with you and then help you develop your interpersonal, emotional, moral and intrapersonal modes. Would this robot be a good substitute for a human friend? Why or why not? List at least three reasons why it would be good for you and three reasons for why it would not.

Needs discussion questions

- What do you really need to live? How is what you need different from what you have and from what you want? What do you think about the difference between what you need, what you have and what you want?
- Do you think that there are basic needs that all animals share? If so, do you agree that they are shelter, food, water, air and safety? Are there other needs all animals share? How about love?

- Do you think it is the role of government to secure the rights of all people to life and liberty? If so, why? If not, why not?
- Do you think it is the role of government to protect the environment? If so, why? If not, why not?
- Do you think it is true that income inequality results in everybody having less well-being? Why do you think so, if so, and why not, if not?
- Why do you think people live in a world where some people die of starvation or struggle to have adequate clean water? What do you think should be done about it?
- Do you agree with the needs that Maslow and Max-Neef have identified? Would you take any away, add any or change the description in any way?
- Do you think the development tracks that Wilber identifies overlap with Maslow and Max-Neef's needs?
- Do you think all people have the same needs, or do some people have different needs or not have certain needs? If so, why? If not, why?
- Under what circumstances might somebody's esteem or self-actualization needs change?
- Why do you think a person would choose not to meet a need when they had the resources and capacity to do so? Give an example of a need and explain why.
- Do you think it would be possible to meet needs without a shared currency (i.e. money)?
- If you had unlimited money, how would you meet your needs? How does this differ from the way you meet your needs today? What is the most money you think you need to meet your needs?
- How do you think the world would be different or the same if all people had equitable access to meeting all their needs? Is it possible to live in a world where all people have equitable opportunities to meet their needs?

Needs resources

Videos

- *Maslow's Hierarchy of Needs* by Spouts. www.youtube.com/watch?v=O-4ithG_07Q
- *WUWE Presents: Manfred Max-Neef – Barefoot Economics* by Wake Up World Education. www.youtube.com/watch?v=H8wfXczQ8Ew
- *The Economics of Enough* by Dan O'Neill, TEDxOxbridge. www.youtube.com/watch?v=WIG33QtLRyA

- *The Hero's Journey* by Joseph Campbell. www.youtube.com/watch?v=RchePX5gElc
- *The Definition of Genius* by Michael Meade. www.youtube.com/watch?v=O-Pnkp6r6mo
- *Social Sustainability: Satisfying Human Needs* by Sustainability Illustrated. www.youtube.com/watch?v=FyT9TMlzC6s

Movies

- *Enough is Enough* by Tom Bliss. www.youtube.com/watch?v=xQ-LYElvtEU
    - Book form: *Enough is Enough: Building a Sustainable Economy in a World of Finite Resources* by Rob Dietz and Dan O'Neill
- *Escape from Affluenza* by John de Graaf
- *Affluenza: The All Consuming Epidemic* by John de Graaf, David Wann and Thomas H. Naylor.

References

Batson, C. (1990). How social an animal? The human capacity for caring. *American Psychologist, 45* (3), 336–346. doi: 10.1037/0003-066X.45.3.336

BBC News. (2016). Oxfam says wealth of richest 1% equal to the other 99%. Retrieved from www.bbc.com/news/business-35339475

Bernhardt, B. & Singer, T. (2012). The neural basis of empathy. *Annual Review of Neuroscience, 35*, 1–23. doi: 10.1146/annurev-neuro-062111-150536

Brundtland, G. (1987). Report of the world commission on environment and development: Our common future. *United Nations General Assembly Document A/42/427*. Retrieved from www.un-documents.net/our-common-future.pdf

Campbell, J. (1973). *The Hero with a Thousand Faces*. Princeton, NJ: Princeton University Press Print.

Cole, C. (2010). Overconsumption is costing us the earth and human happiness. *The Guardian*. Retrieved from https://integralwithoutborders.net/sites/default/files/resources/Overview%20of%20Developmental%20Levels.pdf

de Graaf, J. (2017). A backpacker's theory of life. *Sierra*. Retrieved from www.sierraclub.org/sierra/green-life/backpacker-s-theory-life

de Graaf, J. (2018). Families and children in the new system. *The Next System Project*. Retrieved from https://thenextsystem.org/learn/stories/families-and-children-next-system

de Graaf, J., Wann, D. & Naylor, T. (2001). *Affluenza: The All-Consuming Epidemic*. San Francisco, CA: Berrett-Koehler.

Global Footprint Network. (2003–2020). Earth overshoot day. Retrieved from www.footprintnetwork.org/our-work/earth-overshoot-day/

Iacoboni, M. (2007). Face to face: The neural basis of social mirroring and empathy. *Psychiatric Annals, 37* (4), 236–241. Retrieved from https://m2.healio.com/~/media/journals/psycann/2007/04_april/3704iacoboni.pdf

Maslow, A. (1943). A theory of human motivation. *Psychological Review, 50* (4), 370–396. doi: 10.1037/h0054346

Maslow, A. (1998). *Toward a Psychology of Being.* New York, NY: Wiley & Sons.

Max-Neef, M. (1991). *Human Scale Development.* London, UK: The Apex Press. Retrieved from www.wtf.tw/ref/max-neef.pdf

Nikolaev, B. (2014). Economic freedom and quality of life: Evidence from the OECD's your better life index. *The Journal of Private Enterprise, 29* (3), x–xx. Retrieved from http://borisnikolaev.com/wp-content/uploads/2014/08/Economic-Freedom-and-Quality-of-Life.pdf

O'Neill, D., Fanning, A., Lamb, W. & Steinberger, J. (2018). A good life for all within planetary boundaries. *Nature Sustainability, 1,* 88–95. doi: 10.1038/s41893-018-0021-4. Retrieved from https://tinyurl.com/y3jg44wn

Ortiz-Ospina, E. & Roser, M. (2017). Homelessness. *OurWorldInData.org.* Retrieved from https://ourworldindata.org/homelessness

Ott, J. (2016). Measuring economic freedom: Better without size of government. *Social Indicator Research, 135* (2), 479–498. doi: 10.1007/s11205-016-1508-x

Symmonds, M., Emmanuel, J., Drew, M., Batterham, R. & Dolan, R. (2010). Metabolic state alters economic decision making under risk in humans. *PLoS One, 5* (6). doi: 10.1371/journal.pone.0011090

Tay, L. & Diener, E. (2011). Needs and subjective well-being around the world. *Journal of Personality and Social Psychology, 101* (2), 354–365. doi: 10.1037/a0023779

Wake Up World Education. (2015). WUWE presents: Manfred Max-Neef-Barefoot economics | An alternative to GDP? Retrieved from www.youtube.com/watch?v=H8wfXczQ8Ew

Wilber, K. (2000). *Integral Psychology: Consciousness, Spirit, Psychology, Therapy.* Boulder, CO: Shambhala Publications.

Wilkinson, R. & Pickett, K. (2010). *The Spirit Level: Why Greater Equality Makes Societies Stronger.* New York, NY: Bloomsbury Press.

The World Bank. (n.d.). Poverty. Retrieved from. https://data.worldbank.org/topic/poverty (click the link for data).

World Health Organization. (2015). New report shows that 400 million do not have access to essential health services. Retrieved from www.who.int/mediacentre/news/releases/2015/uhc-report/en/

World Hunger Education Service. (2016). 2016 world hunger and poverty facts and statistics. Retrieved from www.worldhunger.org/2015-world-hunger-and-poverty-facts-and-statistics/

World Watch Institute. (2003). Rich poor gap is widening. Retrieved from www.worldwatch.com

6
SUSTAINABILITY

Sustainability learning objectives

The objectives of this chapter are for students to be able to:

- Understand the concepts of sustainability and planetary boundaries.
- Understand four growth trends impacting the carrying capacity of the planet.
- Understand ways to increase personal happiness through sustainable practices.

Preliminary questions

- What does the statement "we are playing a global endgame" mean to you?
- What might be some of the consequences of the rapid increase in global population?
- Do you feel your lifestyle is compatible with saving the environment?
- How is our changing climate also likely to change your life?
- Can you think of some actions we might take to reduce the damage to the natural environment that is now occurring?

Defining sustainability

We have been using the word *sustainability* in this book to mean ecological sustainability in terms of maintaining nature in a healthy state now and in the future. Chapter 1 stated a belief that individual happiness, community well-being and the natural environment, or nature, are inextricably connected. We also believe that while we need natural resources to live, from clean air to the trees, minerals and healthy soils, nature also has an intrinsic value separate from any direct benefit we derive from it. Chapter 5 on needs examined how sustainable development is defined in the Brundtland Commission report *Our Common Future* as "meeting the needs of the current generation without compromising the ability of future generations to meet their needs" (Brundtland Commission, 1987, p. 41). In this book, the definition of *sustainable development* encompasses the happiness and well-being of humans (both individually and collectively) and the health of ecosystems. What do you think?

Humans have changed the Earth and its atmosphere dramatically in the past two centuries. Since the advent of the industrial age in 1790, humans have changed the environment more than any other animal that has lived on the planet. Some scientists are even calling it a new era: the Anthropocene era (Crutzen, 2006). *Anthropo* means human, and *cene* means epoch or age. Our tremendous ability to reshape our environment, drive other species to extinction and destroy each other has been and can be balanced by our tremendous ability to restore our environment, care for other species and treat each other well. Thinking and acting within the framework of sustainability requires a skill set that can be taught and cultivated. Learning how to think and act for a sustainable future helps us navigate our way through environmental, governmental and social crises and is fundamental for our happiness and well-being.

We have the capacity to invent solutions to seemingly insurmountable challenges when working together with others. By orienting ourselves and society to engage in the crucially important mission of sustainability, individually and collectively, it is possible to surmount the challenges to humanity. Along the way, it's good to work with friends and neighbors towards sustainability in ways that bring joy. When working towards a large and meaningful goal with others, you may find an increased personal sense of worth, happiness and the well-being of those around you as well.

Researchers have shown that people experience satisfaction and happiness when they engage in sustainable practices, such as reducing carbon footprints, reducing the rich–poor gap, assisting those who are less fortunate, inventing a new water purification system or cleaning up trails in the wilderness (Helm, 2019; Corral-Verdugo et al., 2011; Venhoeven, Bolderdijk & Steg, 2016). Denmark, Sweden and Norway are very supportive of policies that are sustainable and increase people's well-being. Policies such as encouraging biking, using renewable energy and minimizing production of trash add to people's happiness and are good for the environment. It is no coincidence that these Scandinavian countries consistently have the highest happiness scores in the world (Zamora, 2017).

HIGHLIGHT: SUSTAINABLE AND HAPPY COMMUNITIES

One of the authors of this book, Rhonda Phillips, is a community planning and development specialist. She has worked with many communities and regions throughout her career and has seen first-hand what can happen when people decide to make positive change. Growing up in the poorest state in the US, she decided as a teenager to work in the area of development. It did not seem fair that most people in that area had to leave for work to places far from family and friends, especially when surrounded by some of the richest and most productive land in the entire country.

Her background led to exploring ways of development that are more sustainable and could meet needs of people while protecting the environment. Local food systems have become a passion because they can provide ways to encourage livelihoods as well as improve well-being of people and land. Explore her book on this topic, *Growing Livelihoods: Local Food Systems and Community Development* at www.taylorfrancis.com/books/e/9781315688596.

Community development is all about making places better, and part of this focuses on both process and outcomes. Being inclusive and listening to the voices of those impacted by decisions are important. Doing so includes developing capacities and protecting resources while taking action for community improvements. If you're interested in learning more about community development, see the book *Introduction to Community Development* at www.routledge.com/An-Introduction-to-Community-Development-2nd-Edition/Phillips-Pittman/p/book/9780415703550.

There are many resources available about community development and well-being and sustainable development approaches. One of Phillips' favorite experiences was being able to live in Vermont several years ago and seeing what has been accomplished there. Along with colleagues, she wrote a book about what Burlington and other places in the state did to foster sustainable approaches to development. See the book *Sustainable Development: Creating a Durable Local Economy* at www.routledge.com/Sustainable-Communities-Creating-a-Durable-Local-Economy/Phillips-Seifer-Antczak/p/book/9780415820172.

All three of these books offer at least one chapter to download freely or check with your school's library to obtain a copy. Better yet, visit with the community or economic development department where you live and talk with them about approaches they use. Perhaps there will be a project or program that you would like to participate in or learn more about.

Her vision for communities is that community well-being is at the forefront for both residents and policy makers to enable more sustainability now and in the future. How would your vision work to change communities you are familiar with for those who live there?

HIGHLIGHT: BEAUTY, HAPPINESS, WELL-BEING AND SUSTAINABILITY

Research is proving what common sense tells many: that natural beauty is important to our happiness and well-being (Sifferlin, 2016). It is healing and is a source for happiness and health. The natural beauty of a place and the beauty in the design of spaces also makes a big difference in people's attachment to where they live and life satisfaction (Knight Foundation, 2010; Delistraty, 2014). Elaine Scarry (2013), a professor of literature and writer, suggests that natural beauty encourages altruism, gratitude, tolerance and support for social justice.

People of all cultures are drawn to natural and human-designed beauty, whether the wilderness, a city park or a historic site or well-designed building or neighborhood. Hermann Knoflacher (2007), a transportation engineer, found that urban dwellers are more likely to walk longer distances on forested paths separated from traffic-filled streets than shorter distances on streets with traffic and ride public transportation more where stations are decorated with art. Walking in green areas as opposed to sidewalks devoid of nature can also reduce stress and enhance health (South et al., 2014).

Do you think that ecological sustainability is beautiful? If so, is there a positive feedback loop for beauty, sustainability, happiness and well-being? In Chapter 1, you were asked to design a city or town for happiness, well-being and sustainability. Did beauty feature in your design? If not, how would you integrate it now? If so, how did it feature, and why did you include consideration of it?

Global problems and solutions

The past 100 years of life have been radically different from any other time in human existence. We humans have been agents of massive damage to the natural environment of the planet as a result of human activities. This section briefly goes over some major challenges facing humanity and many other species. You probably already know the facts in this section. They are presented as stepping stones to think about the challenges in terms of the systems that created them and how could the system be redesigned to avoid ending up with the same or similar problems. At the end of each section, there are a few prompts for redesign and solutions. The intent is to encourage and empower for changing systems for realizing happiness, well-being and sustainability now and in the future.

Climate change

Pollution of our planet's air, waters and soils has increased exponentially, following ever-increasing production and consumption of goods and services. Greenhouse gas emissions (GHGs) are a form of air pollution. There are six kinds of greenhouse gases. Carbon dioxide (CO_2) accounts for about 75% of greenhouse gases and is primarily emitted from using gas, oil and coal in transportation and for electricity, including cooling and heating buildings (Environmental Protection Agency, n.d.a., n.d.b.). Methane accounts for about 16% of GHGs. Methane comes from decaying garbage in landfills and from farms with compost and emissions from animals. Other types of GHGs, nitrous oxide and three other types, come from manufacturing of cars, electronics and other things. Greenhouse gases absorb the radiation of the sun that would otherwise bounce off the Earth back up through the atmosphere and into space. This absorption heats up the atmosphere. It changes air temperatures, precipitation patterns and wind patterns. It leads to increases in ocean acidity and temperature. This is why we use the terms *global warming* and *climate change*. Major consequences of climate change include ocean acidification, severe storms, loss of species through habitat changes, drought and decreased food supplies (Intergovernmental Panel on Climate Change, 2018).

Many governments have taken steps to reduce the rate of damage caused by greenhouse gas emissions by reducing the use of fossil fuels and increasing production and use of renewable fuels through various incentives such as taxes on gasoline and tax breaks for the use of renewable energy. Other steps include global agreements to limit these emissions through economic incentives and penalties, such as the Kyoto Protocol and Paris Agreement.

These agreements to increase the use of renewable energy have resulted in less expensive wind and solar energy in over 25 countries (Harrington, 2017).

Some countries provide incentives for decreasing deforestation rates. Bhutan, Denmark and Iceland are examples of countries that have long-range effective policies and encourage people to get involved in conservation and sustainable practices (World Wildlife Fund, 2019; Nordic Timber, n.d.; Soil Conservation Service of Iceland, n.d.). In some cities, vehicles and roads are being renovated for efficiency and resilience to rising sea levels and to support the use of renewable and clean energy (Frangoul, 2015: Milman et al., 2017; Sammy, 2017). Leadership in Energy and Environmental Design (LEED) certification for green buildings and the Living Building Challenge are two of a proliferation of green building certification schemes that have been helpful in the redesign of buildings around the world, as well as some campuses and cities adopting green building rules and protocols (Vierra, 2019, Vyas, 2018). Desalination plants are the main source of water in the United Arab Emirates (Mathews, 2019). Other solutions could be the capture and storage of carbon dioxide, injection of sulphur into the atmosphere and nuclear energy (Metz et al., 2005; Berandell, 2018; Rotman, 2013; World Nuclear Association, n.d.).

One thing you may have noticed that these solutions have in common is that they change an element of a system that meets needs but not the overall system itself. The degrowth or beyond-growth movement got its start in the 1970s (Degrowth, n.d.). It is one way to change a system. Some ways transitions towards degrowth are conducted is by meeting needs by spending time in nature, in community and on cultural, recreational and artistic activities, and through shorter work weeks and restructuring of tax and financial systems instead of through consumption of goods and services (Mastini, 2017). A few solutions to climate change that can be implemented in daily lives are to live within walking or biking distance of work, drive energy-efficient cars, consume less, eat less meat, plant trees, unplug devices when not in use and have one-child families (Biello, 2007). Some of these solutions are more controversial than others. Why do you think that is? What role do values and assumptions play in the acceptability of these and other solutions?

Only a few facts and ideas were presented in this section with the hope that they will inspire a new perspective for reflecting and acting on the many facts, falsehoods and activities you will encounter in your life with regard to climate change. Shifting perspective can be a powerful means to understanding the interactions, feedback loops and leverage points of a global system when a problem seems overpowering, as climate change can. Your perspective also influences personal resilience to the challenges facing your own life from climate change and for being a change agent for positive change in your community and globally. With that, let's proceed to the next problem.

Human population and our ecological footprint

The growth in human population is an example of a feedback loop. It increased more than four-fold in the past 100 years, from 1.6 to 7 billion people (Annenberg Learner, 2017). In 1804, the human population was 1 billion people. One hundred and twenty years later, in 1927, the population was 2 billion. Fifty years later, in 1974, it was 4 billion. By 2023, it is forecasted to be 8 billion. By 2100, the population is expected to reach 10 billion.

Humans have impacted over 80% of the land on earth (Mayell, 2002). Today, humans use about 75% of the land on earth for agriculture, transportation, industry and human habitats (Mason, 2016). The damage to our planet's natural environment from our activities includes:

- Absolute water scarcity (meaning that there is actually no water available), infrastructure water scarcity (meaning that the means to supply available water is inadequate or nonexistent), or economic water scarcity (meaning that people can't afford water). Absolute water scarcity is expected to affect 1.8 billion people by 2025. Today about one quarter of the world's population experiences some kind of water scarcity (UN Water, n.d.).
- The destruction of biodiversity worldwide (biodiversity is measured by the number of different species of animals and plants in an ecosystem). The number of species of mammals, birds, amphibians and corals that are threatened with extinction grew from 10,000 species in 2010 to 25,000 species in 2017 (IUCN Red List, n.d.).
- Forest cover loss as forests are cut down for food production and expansion of towns and cities (Food and Agricultural Organization of the United Nations, 2016).
- Climate change, bringing on drought, extreme weather, coastal flooding, ocean heating and acidification, rising temperatures and challenges to human health from extreme weather, flooding, agricultural disruption and migration of insects and animals (IPCC, 2018).

Donella Meadows and her colleagues did research to find that the various damaging effects are largely the consequence of growth in five variables which impacts the ability of the planet to be a hospitable home to humans as well as many other species (Meadows, Randers & Meadows, 2004). They are called variables because they can and do change. The five variables are:

- Human population
- Nonrenewable natural resource consumption
- Food production
- Commercial production of goods and services
- Pollution of the atmosphere, water and soil

With regard to the variable of human population, given the damage already occurring, it is unlikely that our Earth will support 10 billion people with our current standard of living and, with its current population of 7.5 billion people, the standard of living experienced in wealthy nations almost certainly cannot be sustained for all nations (UNEP Global Environmental Alert Service (GEAS), 2012; O'Neill et al., 2018). The question of how to change lifestyles today so future generations will be able to live on this planet is yet to be answered. This question has at its heart the concept of the earth's carrying capacity.

GUEST COURSEBOOK CONTRIBUTION FROM BETH ALLGOOD: WILDLIFE PROTECTION

Beth Allgood was educated in management sciences and works for non-profits, governments and companies. Her focus is helping policy makers understand the value of vulnerable wildlife populations and how to make policy that protects wildlife. She bridges national-level work as a policy advisor and program director with grassroots activism as a member of nonprofits and a generator of cutting-edge conservation projects. She wrote this essay to encourage the readers of this coursebook.

This is an exciting time in human history to be alive even though many species are facing an extinction crisis because of, in part, a relentless drive to consume ever more in the pursuit of growth. Never before have our choices mattered so much or has our leadership been so important.

In my 20 years of working in conservation and development policy and programs in Washington, DC, I have worked to preserve our public lands from commercial exploitation and to protect elephants from illegal or unsustainable trade. These issues are critical, as urgent threats like these need to be addressed as they happen. For example, stopping the flow of illegal ivory into the US and China was critical to stop the scourge of elephant poaching in Africa and Asia. But these issues are just symptoms of a bigger problem – our global system measures and promotes things that do not matter the most to people, animals and the planet.

Most people don't even realize that we can do things differently. Once you do realize this, there is no way to go back to business as usual. I know that animals make people happier and contribute to human and planetary well-being. There are scientific studies that prove it, yet there are examples in communities around the world that demonstrate it and we can feel it in our hearts. I knew I needed to devote myself to promoting policies and practices for human happiness and well-being that reflect our connection with animals.

We are all connected. When you do the work that calls you, the impacts will ripple around the world. It has to – because you too are connected to everything. That is the gift of the most challenging and the most exciting time in human history.

The earth's carrying capacity means how many people and other species can have a decent life on our earth. Another way of understanding the earth's carrying capacity is the concept of an ecological footprint (Weinzettel et al., 2004). Your ecological footprint is the amount of natural resources, measured in land, it takes to sustain your lifestyle and that same lifestyle for all people on the planet.

Our earth's carrying capacity depends on many things, and one of the foremost is the lifestyle we have today. Lifestyle is determined by the amount of stuff consumed, everything from clothes to technology, to the food eaten, how cities are built, types of transportation systems and energy consumption. The five areas described – population, food production, natural resource consumption, commercial production and pollution – are another way of understanding the impact lifestyle has on our earth's carrying capacity. Lifestyles vary hugely around the world, but it is important to realize that many of their effects on the planet do not recognize political boundaries. The richer countries, with their emphasis on GDP as the leading measure of progress, use more natural resources and produce more pollution than other countries. This affects everyone, no matter what country they live in around the globe.

Taking the five domains that Donella Meadows and her colleagues identified, how would the system be changed if there were no growth or de-growth in any one of them? The zero waste movement is one way to change the system via de-growth (Planet Aid, n.d.). Germany's packaging take back law, called *Verpackungsverordnung* (*verpackungs* is the word for packaging, and *verordnung* is the word for regulation), requires companies to take back packaging. Cities around the world, including Hout Bay, South Africa; Ljubljana, Slovenia; Pune, India; Taiwan; and Vancouver, Canada, have set zero waste goals (National Geographic, 2018). The local food system movement is another way to change the system through production and delivery of food within a community or city (Community-wealth.org, n.d.). Some cities, such as Portland, Oregon, and Edinburgh, UK, are adopting ordinances to allow for urban agriculture, protecting agricultural lands outside of cities, promoting local farmers' markets and other distribution of local food and providing local food for school lunches in schools (Breitenbach, 2016; Mellino, 2014).

Let's imagine once again that you are the ruler but this time of the world. Your goal is to ensure sustainability of all systems so people can meet their needs today and in the future and so nature is healthy. What would you do? Would you take one of the variables Donella Meadows and her colleagues identified and work towards de-growth, or would you take another path?

HIGHLIGHT: WILL TECHNOLOGY SAVE US?

There is a theory that technological advances will allow for infinite increases in production and cures for problems of climate change (Rau, Toker & Howard, 2010; Jackson, 2019). Technological innovations do allow for extraction of greater value from natural resources, so that it is possible to make more stuff from fewer natural resources. It is true that some technological advances have vastly improved our impact on the environment. You are familiar with these technological innovations in your own life. Plastic bottles are reused for clothing, carpets and building materials. Electronic media has cut down on our use of trees and transportation to communicate and keep records. For the most part, energy production, delivery and use are much more efficient in buildings. However, increasing consumption and population rates means that overall use of natural resources is increasing. Use of natural resources is outstripping the ability of nature to replenish them. In the future, it is quite likely there will not be the access to natural resources that there is today. Access to the natural resources that people had 100 years ago is very different than today. What do you think? How do you think technological advances have changed the economic system with regard to nature and sustainability for natural resources? How would you imagine technological advances bringing about happiness, well-being and sustainability? This is a big question, and the solutions will likely evolve over time as you seek them, so don't expect to have the right answer just now! However, it is an important question to contemplate.

There is also a theory that technology will replace humans, rending the quest for sustainability moot. According to this theory, the majority of humans will become redundant and obsolete due to technology (Sample, 2016). Yuval Harari is a historian who wrote the book *Homo Deus: A Brief History of Tomorrow*. In it he predicts that people who have to work to make a living will lose their jobs to artificial intelligence (AI), the tax base will all but disappear, and with it, the social support systems that provide for the needs of people who do not have a way to make a living.

For the majority of people, life will become very difficult or meaningless. For a few wealthy people, AI will be used to improve their lives, starting with health care, extending to augmenting human intelligence and ending with AI-augmented immortality. Harari paints a bleak picture of the future for the majority of humans and leaves unanswered the question of what will happen to nature. He has essentially conducted a thought experiment with his book. In the resources section of this chapter, there are two recordings of his talks. If you watch one, or better yet, read his book, consider contemplating how you would design a future where AI is a part of life and there is happiness, well-being and sustainability for all beings.

HIGHLIGHT: UNIVERSAL BASIC INCOME

Imagine that today you just heard that you will have a guaranteed monthly payment of the amount of money it would take you to rent a nice apartment; pay your utilities, buy food, clothing and other necessities; and have a little left over each month. You will have this for the rest of your life. If you decide to work for money, you will get the amount over your guaranteed monthly payments, so you will not be penalized for working.

This concept is called universal basic income or guaranteed basic income. Some also call it citizens income, social dividend or negative income tax. Much of the discussion about it is fueled by the expectation that AI will take away jobs (Associated Press, 2019). A few cities and nations have experimented with it, but there is not yet much data about its benefits or problems. There are many questions about whether it would discourage people from getting an education or working or if it would encourage people towards addiction to drugs or alcohol, unhealthy and anti-social behaviors or despair and suicide. There are also questions about whether it would encourage more prosocial behaviors, such as helping neighbors, volunteering and spending time to restore or preserve the local environment, or encourage people to discover what they love to do and realize self-actualization (the top level in Maslow's hierarchy of needs).

What do you think? Would you keep pursuing an education if you never had to worry about meeting your basic needs? Not taking into consideration the question of where all this money would come from, how do you think a universal basic income would affect your community or city? How about your nation? If you take a systems approach and play out the long-term effects, identifying the elements, interactions and feedback loops, what happens?

Sustainable business

Sustainable business represents the possibility of a new way to do business. Some businesses have the goal of making profit, protecting the environment and caring for people. Sometimes this way of doing business is called *People, Planet, Profit* or the *Triple Bottom Line*. Social entrepreneurship, for-cause businesses and cooperatives are a few examples of ways businesses are formed for a purpose beyond profit.

Another term for sustainable business is *Green Economy* (UN Environment, n.d.; United Nations Development Programme, 2012). The United Nations Development Programme defines a green economy as an economy "that results in improved human well-being and social equity, while significantly reducing environmental risks and ecological scarcities" (United Nations Sustainable Development Knowledge Platform, n.d., p. 5) A green economy is low carbon, resource efficient and socially inclusive. Another new way of doing business is called the circular economy. In the circular economy, production of goods is a closed loop system so that there is no waste or pollution, and resources are used in a sustainable way (Het Groene Brein, n.d.).

In Chapter 3 about happiness measurements, the idea of what you measure is what you get was introduced. Perhaps nowhere does this resonate more than in business. In 2000, the Global Reporting Initiative (GRI) issued the first set of global guidelines for measuring sustainability performance of companies, also sometimes called corporate social responsibility (Global Reporting Initiative, n.d.). The GRI covers guidance and indicators for economic, environmental and social performance. A year earlier, in 1999, the first sustainability benchmark for investors was issued, called the Dow Jones Sustainability Index (S&P Global, 2019). By 2018, 78% of the 500 largest companies traded on the stock market were issuing reports for environmental or social performance and over 2,000 publicly traded companies had been evaluated with the Dow Jones Sustainability Index (Lukomnik, 2018; RebecoSAM, 2018). In the US, where for many years it was the law that a corporation's purpose must be to make a profit and managers of companies had to prioritize the goal of profit, laws are changing to allow the formation of for-benefit companies or social entrepreneurship that exist with the goals of helping people and caring for the environment as well as making a profit.

Some businesses that operate with the objective of minimizing their negative impact on the environment include Patagonia and Levis (Boynton, 2013). Some of the businesses that are working in the circular economic method are Dell, Caterpillar and Royal DSM (DSM, n.d.; Hower, 2015). However, the question remains of how much harm or benefit is realized in the environment and society by measuring and managing environmental and social performance in businesses. To date, while there are some countries where companies are required to report their environmental and social performance (Denmark, France, India, Indonesia, Malaysia, Norway, South Africa, the UK and Norway), there are no laws requiring companies to be socially or environmentally responsible, beyond environmental protection laws (Kaya, 2016).

Perhaps you have been told that you can make a difference towards sustainability by your purchasing decisions. The amount spent on ecofriendly products rose from $107 billion to $128 billion between 2014 and 2018 in the US (Gelski, 2019). In 2018, the US GDP was $20.89 trillion, and about one quarter of that is what is called non-durable goods, meaning food, clothing and other things you buy that are not expected to last (BEA, 2019; Amadeo, 2019). This means eco-friendly products account for 2.45% of the market. This is kind of depressing news, but at the same time, there is good reason to believe purchasing decisions do make a difference at a local and global level. Buying green and sustainable products encourages companies to produce more of the same rather than unsustainable products and also sends a signal to companies about their behavior – because they know the kind of consumer who buys green is more likely to be watching and to raise awareness among other consumers when companies behave badly (O'Rourke, 2012).

Let's again imagine that you are a ruler. This time you are the governor of an island, and you can make any laws desired. Your goal is to have an ecologically sustainable, socially responsible, just and equitable island. The people and the businesses that operate on your island are 100% behind you, but not all the goods people buy are from the businesses located on the island. What would you do to reach your goal?

HIGHLIGHT: THE CIRCULAR ECONOMY

A circular economy has no waste and resources are infinitely used. Other terms for a circular economy are *biomimicry, circularity, closed loop, cradle-to-cradle, ecological, regenerative* and *zero waste* (Hobson, 2015; Dijk, Tenpierik & Dobbelsteen, 2014). This is similar to nature, where the waste or end of life of one element such as manure, a leaf falling from a tree, or even the death of an animal provides an input for other elements. A basic tenet of the circular economy is that all outputs are inputs for another process or product, or refurbished, remanufactured, repaired or reused rather than wasted. In addition to ecological benefits, efforts towards circular economies yield economic benefits of job creation and entrepreneurship, which in turn advances an area towards achievement of sustainable development goals.

The European Union adopted a Circular Economy Action Plan in 2015, with member nations then following suit (United Nations, 2019). Some examples of cities with circular economy programs can be found on the Ellen MacArthur Foundation Circular Economies In Cities Case Studies page at www.ellenmacarthurfoundation.org/our-work/

activities/circular-economy-in-cities/case-studies. Amsterdam's plan for a circular economy can be downloaded via the cooperative business Circle Economy website at www.circle-economy.com/case/developing-a-roadmap-for-the-first-circular-city-amsterdam/#.XhAm2ZNKgk9.

What are some of the impacts a circle economy would have on your life? How would your life be better? What things would be more difficult? Would you like to live in a city or nation where the economy is circular?

HIGHLIGHT: EXTERNALITIES

We are producing and consuming goods at an ever-increasing rate. Goods include everything from a toothbrush to a car or airplane. Goods are different from services in that services are not tangible. Services are the ways we help each other. Baristas, engineers, doctors, lawyers, artists and teachers are some examples of service jobs. Service providers use some goods to do their jobs. A barista needs an espresso machine. A doctor needs medicine. An artist needs supplies. Thus, a service-based economy still relies upon production of goods. Our world's production of goods and services in 1900 in current US dollars was about $1 trillion (Delong, 1998). In 1925, it was about $2 trillion. In 1950, it was about $4 trillion. In 1970, it was about $12 trillion. In 1995, it was about $34 trillion. In 2010, it was about $66 trillion. By 2020, it is forecasted to be $81 trillion (OECD Data, n.d.).

Almost every nation in the world is under pressure to increase production, trading off other policy objectives to focus on economic growth. People are pressured to increase consumption of goods and services with advertisements that they will be happier and life will be easier when they buy this or that. Many people buy more than they need and dispose of things before they are used up. Businesses are pressured to increase profits, often at the expense of the environment. This expense is called an *externality*, which is another impact of our economic systems on the environment and our happiness and well-being. Externalities are the impacts that are not included in the cost of things sold or traded.

For example, imagine a steel plant that makes metal rods for high rises. Some of its externalities may be ash pollution in the air from burning coal to forge the steel and the heating up of water to cool the steel. The people living by the steel plant may have a high chance of getting asthma or lung disease. Those people pay a price with their health, and the society pays the price of the health care costs. The fish pay the price with their lives (most fish need cool water to reproduce and live). The price of the good produced by the industrial plant is lower than it would be if the business invested in technology to reduce or eliminate air and water pollution. This is just one example of externalities. There are lots of other kinds of externalities. Pollution in the form of greenhouse gases, landslides from clear-cutting trees and the death of bees from the use of pesticides are three examples of environmental externalities. High stress rates from the outsourcing of jobs, traffic from urban sprawl and loss of access to nature from development that does not include parks are some examples of social externalities.

What would the economic system look like if the costs of externalities were included in the price of goods and services? Try starting first with changing prices for goods, assuming the cost of externalities at a certain price. What else would be necessary to both account for and change the outcome to society and nature if externalities and the impacts they reflect on society and nature were no longer unaccounted for? This is not an easy question; contemplating it may reveal pathways for systems change.

Connecting sustainability and happiness

There are many challenges facing humanity, from climate change to the economy, human rights to health care. When addressing one system, connections with other systems will be found. This is because all systems, in one way or another, are linked. For example, climate change is connected to the economic system via the emphasis on production of goods and services at a cost to the environment and connected to homelessness via health and safety risks from exposure to extreme weather. Any one system is complicated, and when considering the many ways systems are linked and the possible outcomes of a change, the possibilities are difficult to comprehend. This means that a small act of kindness or a project embarked on today could eventually ripple into a complete system change. It also means that when a system is being addressed, some assumptions are made about the boundaries of that system.

Changing our systems to live in a sustainable world where people are happy is an enormous task. It will take many people doing many different things to realize sustainability. Finding a way to contribute towards our earth's sustainability and the well-being of others that makes you happy is a very beneficial thing you can do.

In the words of philosopher and mythologist Michael Meade, "Each person born, regardless of race or ethnicity, gender identity or social status participates in the genius of life in some unique way. Everyone has something to give if they give from their essential nature" (Meade, n.d., p. 2). By being who you want to be, doing no harm to others and living on this planet in ways that help others and the earth, sustainability and happiness can be connected.

Sustainability exercises

- How do you define sustainability? How do you define sustainable development? Do you think individual happiness, community well-being and the natural environment are different sides of the same thing, and if so, why? If not, how are they different?
- Do you think that humans are part of the planet, like trees, bees or other animals, or that humans are separate and distinct from the planet and life forms on it? Why do you feel this way? Write down your thoughts in a paragraph or bullet points. Now consider the opposite perspective. What would be the reasons for this perspective? Write down the counter-argument to your thoughts. Once you have done this, look at both sides of the issue and see where you can find agreement between the two perspectives. Next, pair off and take turns explaining to each other, in a helpful and friendly way, the different perspectives: in the first debate, one takes the perspective that humans are a part of the planet, and the other the perspective that humans are masters of their environment; then switch. Rather than argue, try to understand each other's perspective and find things you have in common.
- Take your ecological footprint using the following tool: www.footprintcalculator.org. Notice that this tool is composed of the following elements: (1) food, (2) shelter, (3) mobility, (4) goods and (5) services. What do you think about your ecological footprint? How many planets would be needed for everyone to have the same standard of living as you? What does this mean to you? Is there anything you are inspired to change in your life? Is there anything you think should change but that is not in

your control? Note your ideas. Share your ecological footprint with one or two other people; also share your ideas for changes in your own life and changes in our systems. Note the ideas that your conversation yields. If the conversation seems to yield nothing or leaves a sense of hopelessness, spend a little time contemplating the hopelessness in silence without trying to change the feeling; then come back to the conversation in a day or two.

- Look at the pie charts for the types of greenhouse gases and the causes of greenhouse gases at https://wri.org/blog/2014/11/6-graphs-explain-world%E2%80%99s-top-10-emitters. Some actions that have been called for are (1) educating all generations, from preschoolers to those in senior facilities and in between, about pathways to sustainability, including conservation, recycling, sharing and minimalism; (2) developing and requiring sustainable approaches for agriculture, energy production and transportation; (3) designating at least half of the earth as a protected reserve (that amount is now about 15%) to preserve forests and reduce loss of species; and (4) planning new urban environments around sustainability. Do any of these resonate with you? What changes would you like to see happen in the world to decrease greenhouse gas emissions? What changes would you like to see happen to prepare for climate change? If you are inspired, make your own charts for greenhouse gases and for how to decrease greenhouse gases.
- Graph the growth of the human population: 1804, 1 billion people; 1927, 2 billion; 1974, 4 billion; 2023, 8 billion; and 2100, 10 billion. Note your reflections on human population growth. Next gather data for the population of a large non-human mammal and graph it. Note your reflections about that animal's population trend.
- Graph the world's production of goods and services from the data provided in US dollars or convert to another currency: 1900, $1 trillion; 1925, $2 trillion; 1950, $4 trillion; 1970, $12 trillion; 1995, $34 trillion; 2010, $62.2 trillion; and 2020, $81 trillion. Note your reflections about the trend line.
- A relatively new impact on the environment arises from online shopping. Some may say that online shopping is more eco-friendly because the delivery to the door is much more efficient than each person going out in their car to the store. Others say it encourages overconsumption. Taking a systems approach, what would happen to your household purchasing patterns if you could no longer shop online? What would you do differently, and how might this change the happiness level for you and those you know? You probably would not be at all happy if your ability to buy online were taken away, but what if you never had it in the first

place? How would your life be different, and how would your community and the companies you do business with operate differently?

- Watch the video *6 Ways Mushrooms Can Save the World* by Paul Stamets at https://embed.ted.com/talks/paul_stamets_on_6_ways_mushrooms_can_save_the_world. What do you think about the idea of how mycelial mats, humanity and technology are similar systems? Does it make sense to you? If not, what is missing? What elements of the system Stamets describes are missing in his description?

Sustainability discussion questions

- Do you agree with the Brundtland Commission's definition of sustainability: "meeting the needs of the current generation without compromising the ability of future generations to meet their needs"? Do you agree that the sustainability movement prioritizes the environment over people? Do you think that meeting people's needs can be done while also protecting our environment? If so, why? If not, why not?
- Can you think of an example of a good or service you use that is from the green economy? Is there something you use that is not from the green economy but could be? How would you change how it is made so it would be from the green economy?
- How would you explain what externalities are to your friend or your parent? What are some externalities of business activities you can think of? What are some ways to address or fix these problems?
- Facebook, Apple, Amazon, Microsoft, Google and other large social media companies have the ability to affect your mental state and what you do. How might they also affect your desire and ability to bring about sustainability? Discuss how they can hinder your desire to bring about sustainability. Discuss how they can help.
- Do you believe humans have an obligation to act as stewards of the environment?
- Minimalism means living a life with the minimum amount of stuff. What kinds of things and activities would you no longer have in your life if you were to live minimally?

Sustainability resources

Videos

- *Homo Deus: A Brief History of Tomorrow* by Yuval Noah Harari for Making Ethics Matter, 2017. www.youtube.com/watch?v=ldTV4qowNms

- *Will the Future Be Human?* by Yuval Noah Harari for World Economics Forum, 2018. www.youtube.com/watch?v=hL9uk4hKyg4
- *Shoulders* by Shane Koyczan and *The Short Story Long* (contains explicit language). www.youtube.com/watch?time_continue=421&v=An4a-_NjilY
- *World Population* by Population Education. www.youtube.com/watch?v=khFjdmp9sZk
- *Sustainable Happiness* by Randy Taran, TEDxMission. www.youtube.com/watch?v=C_AoilMFFzI
- *Truly Sustainable Economic Development* by Ernesto Sirolli TEDxEQChCh (contains explicit language). www.youtube.com/watch?v=SpIxZiBpGU0
- *Why Leading a Sustainable Lifestyle Can Make You Happier* by Colin Beavin. www.un.org/sustainabledevelopment/blog/2016/02/colin-beavan/

Websites

- Drawdown Solutions by Paul Hawkins at www.drawdown.org/solutions
- About Limits to Growth at http://donellameadows.org/archives/a-synopsis-limits-to-growth-the-30-year-update/
- United Nations Strategic Plan for Forests 2017–2030 by the United Nations at www.un.org/esa/forests/documents/un-strategic-plan-for-forests-2030/index.html

Reading materials

- *Encyclical Letter Laudato Si' of the Holy Father Francis on the Care for Our Common Home* by Pope Francis. http://w2.vatican.va/content/francesco/en/encyclicals/documents/papa-francesco_20150524_enciclica-laudato-si.html

References

Amadeo, K. (2019). Consumer spending trends and current statistics. *The Balance*. Retrieved from www.thebalance.com/consumer-spending-trends-and-current-statistics-3305916

Annenberg Learner. (2017). Unit 5: Human population dynamics // section 4: World population growth through history. Retrieved from www.learner.org/courses/envsci/unit/text.php?unit=5&secNum=4

Associated Press. (2019). Over 30 million U.S. workers will lose their jobs because of AI. *Market Watch*. Retrieve from www.marketwatch.com/story/ai-is-set-to-replace-36-million-us-workers-2019-01-24

BEA. (2019). Gross domestic product, fourth quarter and annual 2018 (initial estimate). Retrieved from www.bea.gov/news/2019/initial-gross-domestic-product-4th-quarter-and-annual-2018

Berandell, J. (2018). Controversial spaying method aims to curb global warming. *CBS News*. Retrieved from www.cbsnews.com/news/geoengineering-treatment-stratospheric-aerosol-injection-climate-change-study-today-2018-11-23/

Biello, D. (2007). 10 solutions for climate change. *Scientific American*. Retrieved from www.scientificamerican.com/article/10-solutions-for-climate-change/

Boynton, J. (2013). How Patagonia, Levi Strauss, connect with customers through sustainability. *The Triple Pundit*. Retrieved from www.triplepundit.com/2013/01/patagonia-levi-strauss-customer-engagemen-sustainability-initiatives/

Breitenbach, S. (2016). Beyond farmer's markets: Cities, states champion locally grown food. Retrieved from www.pewtrusts.org/en/research-and-analysis/blogs/stateline/2016/11/07/beyond-farmers-markets-cities-states-champion-locally-grown-food

Brundtland, G. (1987). Report of the world commission on environment and development: Our common future. *United Nations General Assembly Document A/42/427*. Retrieved from www.un-documents.net/our-common-future.pdf

Community-wealth.org. (n.d.). Overview local food systems. Retrieved from https://community-wealth.org/strategies/panel/urban-ag/index.html

Corral-Verdugo, V., Mireles-Acosta, J., Tapia-Fonllem, C. & Fraijo-Sing, B. (2011). Happiness as correlate of sustainable behavior: A study of pro-ecological, frugal, equitable and altruistic actions that promote subjective wellbeing. *Human Ecology Review, 18* (2), 95–104. Retrieved from www.jstor.org/stable/24707465

Crutzen, P. (2006). The anthropocene. In E. Ehlers & T. Krafft (Eds.) *Earth System Science in the Anthropocene*. New York, NY: Springer.

Degrowth. (n.d.). History of degrowth. Retrieved from www.degrowth.info/en/a-history-of-degrowth/

Delistraty, C. (2014, August 15). The beauty-happiness connection. *The Atlantic*. Retrieved January 2020, from www.theatlantic.com/health/archive/2014/08/the-beautyhappiness-connection/375678/

DeLong, J. (1998). Estimating world GDP, one million B.C-present. *Holtz for Congress, Holtz for Congress*. Retrieved from http://holtz.org/Library/Social%20Science/Economics/Estimating%20World%20GDP%20by%20DeLong/Estimating%20World%20GDP.htm

Dijk, S., Tenpierik, M. & Dobbelsteen, A. (2014). Continuing the building's cycles: A literature review and analysis of current systems theories in comparison with the theory of Cradle to Cradle: Resources. *Conservation and Recycling, 82*, 21–34. doi: 10.1016/j.resconrec.2013.10.007

DSM. (n.d.). DSM bio-based products & services. Retrieved from www.dsm.com/corporate/about/business-entities/dsm-biobased-productsandservices.html

Environmental Protection Agency (EPA). (n.d.a.). Overview of greenhouse gases. Retrieved from www.epa.gov/ghgemissions/overview-greenhouse-gases

Environmental Protection Agency (EPA). (n.d.b.). Sources of greenhouse gas emissions. Retrieved from www.epa.gov/ghgemissions/sources-greenhouse-gas-emissions

Food and Agriculture Organization of the United Nations. (2016). State of the world's forests. Retrieved from www.fao.org/3/a-C0176e.pdf

Frangoul, A. (2015). World's most sustainable transport systems. *CNBC.com*. Retrieved from www.cnbc.com/2015/07/15/worlds-most-sustainable-transport-systems.html

Gelski, J. (2019). Sustainable product market could hit $150 billion in U.S. by 2021. *Food Business News*. Retrieved from www.foodbusinessnews.net/articles/13133-sustainable-product-market-could-hit-150-billion-in-us-by-2021

Global Reporting Initiative. (n.d.). GRI history. Retrieved from https://tinyurl.com/y5hyxad7

Harrington, D. (2017). Spectacular drop in renewable energy costs leads to record global boost. *The Guardian*. Retrieved from www.theguardian.com/environment/2017/jun/06/spectacular-drop-in-renewable-energy-costs-leads-to-record-global-boost

Helm, S., Serido, J., Ahn, S., Ligon, V. & Shim, S. (2019). Materialist values, financial and pro-environmental behaviors, and well-being. *Young Consumers*, *20* (4), 264–284. doi: 10.1108/YC-10-2018-0867

Het Groene Brein. (n.d.). What is the definition of a circular economy. Retrieved from https://kenniskaarten.hetgroenebrein.nl/en/knowledge-map-circular-economy/what-is-the-definition-a-circular-economy/

Hobson, K. (2015). Closing the loop or squaring the circle? Locating generative spaces for the circular economy. *Progress in Human Geography*, *40* (1), 88–104. doi: 10.1177/0309132514566342

Hower, M. (2015). Dell cuts e-waste with recycled carbon fiber. *Green Biz*. Retrieved from www.greenbiz.com/article/dell-cuts-e-waste-recycled-carbon-fiber

Intergovernmental Panel on Climate Change (IPCC). (2018). Global warming of I.5 C summary for policy makers. Retrieved from www.ipcc.ch/site/assets/uploads/2018/11/SR1.5_SPM_Low_Res.pdf

IUCN Red List. (n.d.). Summary statistics. Retrieved from www.iucnredlist.org/about/summary-statistics

Jackson, F. (2019). Top ten technologies to save the world. *Forbes*. Retrieved from www.forbes.com/sites/feliciajackson/2019/01/17/top-ten-technologies-to-save-the-world/#1ba854b68742

Kaya, I. (2016). The mandatory social and environmental reporting: Evidence from France. *Procedia-Social and Behavioral Sciences*, *229*, 206–213. doi: 10.1016/j.sbspro.2016.07.130

Knight Foundation. (2010). Knight soul of the community 2010. Retrieved from www.issuelab.org/resources/10006/10006.pdf

Knoflacher, H. (2007). Success and failures in urban transport planning in Europe-understanding the transport system. *Sadhana*, *32*, 293–307. doi: 10.1007/s12046-007-0026-6

Lukomnik, J. (2018). State of integrated and sustainability reporting 2018. *Harvard Law Forum on Corporate Governance and Financial Regulation*. Retrieved from https://corpgov.law.harvard.edu/2018/12/03/state-of-integrated-and-sustainability-reporting-2018/

Mason, B. (2016). Maps show humans' growing impact on the planet. *National Geographic News*. Retrieved from https://news.nationalgeographic.com/2016/08/human-footprint-map-ecological-impact/

Mastini, R. (2017). Degrowth: The case for a new economic paradigm. *Open Democracy*. Retrieved from www.opendemocracy.net/en/degrowth-case-for-constructing-new-economic-paradigm/

Mathews, R. (2019). Impact of Middle East's water desalination in the spotlight. *The National UAE*. Retrieved from www.thenational.ae/uae/science/impact-of-middle-east-s-water-desalination-in-the-spotlight-1.823091

Mayell, H. (2002). Human 'footprint' seen on 83 percent of earth's land. *National Geographic News*. Retrieved from https://news.nationalgeographic.com/news/2002/10/1025_021025_HumanFootprint.html

Meade. M. (n.d.). The myth of genius, the genius of myth. Retrieved from https://retreat.pacifica.edu/the-myth-of-genius-the-genius-of-myth/

Meadows, D., Randers, J. & Meadows, D. (2004). *The Limits to Growth: The 30-Year Update*. White River Junction, VT: Chelsea Green Publishing Company.

Mellino, C. (2014). 10 cities revolutionizing local food. *EcoWatch*. Retrieved from www.ecowatch.com/10-cities-revolutionizing-local-food-1881972342.html

Metz, B., Davidson, O., Coninck, H., Loos, M. & Meyer, L. (2005.). *IPCC Special Report on Carbon Dioxide Capture and Storage*. Cambridge, UK: Cambridge University Press. Retrieved from www.ipcc.ch/site/assets/uploads/2018/03/srccs_wholereport-1.pdf

Milman, O., Eskenazi, J., Luscombe, R. & Dart, T. (2017). The fight against climate change: Four cities leading the way in the Trump era. *The Guardian*. Retrieved from www.theguardian.com/cities/2017/jun/12/climate-change-trump-new-york-city-san-francisco-houston-miami

National Geographic. (2018). 25 cities that are committed to going zero-waste soon. Retrieved from www.nationalgeographic.com/travel/lists/zero-waste-eliminate-sustainable-travel-destination-plastic/#/green-cities-taiwan.jpg

Nordic Timber. (n.d.). Danish forests and Danish stance on sustainability. Retrieved from www.nordictimber.org/danish-forests-and-denmarks-stance-on-sustainability

OECD Data. (n.d.). GDP long-term forecast. Retrieved from https://data.oecd.org/gdp/gdp-long-term-forecast.htm#indicator-chart

O'Neill, D., Fanning, A., Lamb, W. & Steinberger, J. (2018). A good life for all within planetary boundaries. *Nature Sustainability*, *1*, 88–95. doi: 10.1038/s41893-018-0021-4. Retrieved from https://tinyurl.com/y3jg44wn

O'Rourke, D. (2012). The power of environmentally conscious shopping. *New York Times*. Retrieved from www.nytimes.com/roomfordebate/2012/07/30/responsible-shoppers-but-bad-citizens/the-power-of-environmentally-conscious-shopping

Planet Aid. (n.d.). What is the zero-waste movement? Retrieved from www.planetaid.org/blog/what-is-the-zero-waste-movement

Rau, A., Toker, R. & Howard, J. (2010). Can technology really save us from climate change? *Harvard Business Review*. Retrieved from https://hbr.org/2010/01/can-technology-really-save-us-from-climate-change

RebecoSAM. (2018). DJSI 2018 review results. Retrieved from www.robecosam.com/media/0/2/1/02188034046af5db919d7ce87dd72b98_djsi-review-presentation-results_tcm1016-14658.pdf

Rotman, D. (2013). A cheap and easy way to stop global warming. *MIT Technology Review.* Retrieved from www.technologyreview.com/s/511016/a-cheap-and-easy-plan-to-stop-global-warming/

Sammy, J. (2017). How Taiwan is pushing for sustainable urban mobility. *Motion Digest.* Retrieved from https://motiondigest.com/2017/06/08/how-taiwan-is-pushing-for-sustainable-urban-mobility/

Sample, I. (2016). AI will create 'useless class' of human, predicts bestselling historian. *The Guardian.* Retrieved from www.theguardian.com/technology/2016/may/20/silicon-assassins-condemn-humans-life-useless-artificial-intelligence

Scarry, E. (2013). *On Beauty and Being Just.* Princeton, NJ: Princeton University Press.

Sifferlin, A. (2016). The healing power of nature. *Time.* Retrieved from https://time.com/4405827/the-healing-power-of-nature/

Soil Conservation Service of Iceland. (n.d.). The soil conservation service of Iceland (SCSI, Landgræðsla ríkisins) was founded in 1907. Retrieved from www.land.is/english/

South, E., Kondo, M., Cheney, R. & Branas, C. (2015). Neighborhood blight, stress, and health: A walking trial of urban greening and ambulatory heart rate. *American Journal of Public Health, 105*, 909–913. doi: 10.2105/AJPH.2014.302526

S&P Global. (2019). The benchmark that changed the world: Celebrating 20 years of the Dow Jones Sustainability Indices. Retrieved from www.spglobal.com/en/research-insights/articles/accounting-for-climate-the-next-frontier-in-esg-shell

UN Environment. (n.d.). Green economy. Retrieved from www.unenvironment.org/explore-topics/green-economy

UNEP Global Environmental Alert Service (GEAS). (2012). One planet, how many people? A review of Earth's carrying capacity A discussion paper for the year of RIO+20. Retrieved from https://na.unep.net/geas/archive/pdfs/geas_jun_12_carrying_capacity.pdf

United Nations. (2016). The world's cities in 2016. Retrieved from www.un.org/en/development/desa/population/publications/pdf/urbanization/the_worlds_cities_in_2016_data_booklet.pdf

United Nations. (2019). 'Waste not, want not': European Union goes circular. Retrieved from www.un.org/development/desa/en/news/sustainable/good-practice-circular-economy.html

United Nations Development Programme. (2012). Green economy in action. Retrieved from www.undp.org/content/dam/aplaws/publication/en/publications/environment-energy/www-ee-library/mainstreaming/Green%20Economy%20in%20Action/Green%20Economy%20Compilation%20Report.pdf

United Nations Sustainable Development Knowledge Platform. (n.d.6). *Green Economy.* Retrieved from https://sustainabledevelopment.un.org/index.php?menu=1446#:~:text=For%20example%2C%20UNEP%20has%20defined,%22%20(UNEP%2C%202011)

UN Water. (n.d.). Water scarcity. Retrieved from www.unwater.org/water-facts/scarcity/

Venhoeven, L., Bolderdijk, J. & Steg, L. (2016). Why acting environmentally-friendly feels good: Exploring the role of self-image. *Frontiers in Psychology*, 7, 1846. doi: 10.3389/fpsyg.2016.01846

Vierra, S. (2019). Green building standards and certification systems. *Whole Building Design Guide*. Retrieved from www.wbdg.org/resources/green-building-standards-and-certification-systems

Vyas, K. (2018). Top 17 greenest university campuses around the world. *Interesting Engineering*. Retrieved from https://interestingengineering.com/top-17-greenest-university-campuses-around-the-world

Weinzettel, J., Steen-Olseb, K., Hertwich, E., Borucke, M. & Gallid, A. (2004). Ecological footprint of nations: Comparison of process analysis, and standard and hybrid multiregional input-output analysis. *Ecological Economics*, *101*, 115–126. doi: 10.1016/j.ecolecon.2014.02.020

World Nuclear Association. (n.d.). Nuclear energy and climate change. Retrieved from www.world-nuclear.org/focus/climate-change-and-nuclear-energy/nuclear-energy-and-climate-change.aspx

World Wildlife Fund. (2019). Bhutan: Committed to conservation. Retrieved from www.worldwildlife.org/projects/bhutan-committed-to-conservation

Zamora, R. (2017). Norway is the happiest country in the world: What's the secret? *Time*. Retrieved from http://time.com/4706590/scandinavia-world-happiness-report-nordics/

7

POLICY

Policy learning objectives

The objectives of this chapter are for students to be able to:

- Understand what policy is.
- Understand the role of policy in society and in one's life.
- Learn about governments creating happiness, well-being and sustainability policy.
- Learn how to engage in policy making.

Preliminary questions

- What is policy?
- What are some policies that impact your life?
- What is happiness, well-being or sustainability policy? How is it different from other policies?
- What are some ways to get engaged in government?

Defining policy

Humans are one of the few species that are able to live together mostly peacefully. We can do this in part because of our ability to form and follow policies. We are the only large species that has organized at such density and intensity that we cover much of the land on earth. Today, there are 90 cities with more than 3 million people living together in them (United Nations, 2016). There are super cities, too (giant metropolises covering large geographic areas stretching far beyond the original city limits); for example, over 20 million people live in each of these places: Shanghai, Beijing, Seoul, Mexico City and New York, and 38 million live in Tokyo. Contemplating the Earth's history, one could say that no other species of animal has so successfully lived together or formed so many different kinds of organizations. While humans do suffer wars, plagues and epidemics, for the most part, the majority of people in the world enjoy a daily life without wars near their home (Marc, n.d.). If you contemplate the simple daily experience of life without war, what is your assessment of the capacity for humans to be peaceful and harmonious?

Policy is an action, law or principle undertaken by a government, organization or other entity. Policies affect every aspect of life: education, economic opportunities, ownership, marriage and so on. At school, there may be a policy that cell phone use or eating is not allowed in class. Different countries have different policies. In both China and Switzerland, one has to be at least 18 years old to drive. In Brazil, Australia and 16 other countries, people 18 years and older are required by law to vote. Policies, in general, have six components. They are:

1. A statement of the purpose and intent. This is the highest level of a policy. It may be composed of envisioned outcomes, the mission or vision.
2. An explanation of the reason for the policy. This may include the scientific findings, the historical circumstances and the principles or values.
3. Strategies. These includes the long-term goals, sometimes called objectives; mid- and short-term goals, sometimes called targets; and the tactics, or specific actions to achieve the goals.
4. Measurements to measure the outcome of the policy. Measurements should help to explain if the policy realizes its purpose and intent and be tied to the goals.
5. Resources. Resources include the appointment of a lead for the strategy, staffing and budget for the implementation of the policy
6. Means of accountability. These may include a review process for the policy and a description of roles and responsibilities to ensure accountability.

In most countries in the world, policy is guided by the assumption that happiness and well-being come from a strong economy. There is a belief that if people are wealthy, then they can be happy, and hence this is why

GDP is the primary guiding measurement for policy makers (Diener et al., 1993). When a government believes that the most important way to increase people's happiness and well-being is strong and rapid economic growth, it often makes policies that have unintended negative consequences on the environment, society and individuals.

Researchers have produced the evidence that other factors besides GDP, income and consumption have a larger impact on our happiness and well-being (Diener & Diener-McGavran, 2008; Diener et al., 2009; Easterlin, 1974, 1995, 2001; Helliwell, Layard & Sachs, 2018; Ovaska & Takashima, 2006). Their findings might seem like common sense. Happiness policies, like well-being and sustainability policies, vary from other types of policies due to the main purpose being to foster happiness for those who live in the jurisdiction where implemented. In their book *The Happiness Policy Handbook*, the authors of this coursebook explain:

> Happiness and well-being policy encompasses feelings of joy and satisfaction with life, ecological and human health, wealth and prosperity, and many other factors because it is founded on an understanding that personal happiness and well-being are intrinsically linked to the sustainability of our planet, health of economies, and well-being of society. . . . It is policy that is connected to all aspects of human existence, because individual and collective happiness and well-being are connected to (all these aspects).
>
> *(Musikanski, Phillips & Crowder, 2019, p. 21)*

Happiness, well-being and sustainability policies

Table 7.1 provides a starting place for policies organized in terms of five variables for the sustainability of human existence introduced in Chapter 6 on sustainability (Meadows, Randers & Meadows, 2004). The policy concepts provided are based on actual policies in place. However, the intent of this section is to inspire and embolden you to contribute to the creation of policies, whether it is for government or any other organization, for happiness, well-being and sustainability.

Organizational changes for happiness, well-being and sustainability policy

Change in the organization of government (as well as any businesses, educational institutions, nonprofits and so on) support consistency in the creation and implementation of happiness, well-being and sustainability policy. One

TABLE 7.1 Happiness, well-being and sustainability policy concepts

Variable	*Policy concept*
Human population	Equal representation of women in political decisions and processes
	Equal representation of women in management and board rooms of businesses
	Education of girls and women
	Family planning and health care, including mental health care
	Equal rights for women
	Affordable higher education
	Protection of human rights
Non-renewable natural resource consumption	Conservation, preservation and restoration of forests, prairies, grasslands, rivers, lakes and oceans
	Green and renewable energy production and consumption
	Desalination of water
	Sustainable forestry, mining and other extraction of natural resources
	Urban and rural sprawl ordinances
Food production	Local food production and local food self-reliance and resilient food network
	Organic agriculture and banning of some pesticides, herbicides and fertilizers
	Food waste reduction
	Indigenous food production
Commercial production of goods and services	Circular economy, green economy and so on
	Worker-owned corporations, worker representation in corporate governance
	Bans on advertising to children
	Work share and part-time work protection laws
	Vacation, sick and parental leave laws
	Campaign finance reform
	Personal and corporate income tax reform
Pollution of the atmosphere, water and soil	Climate change agreements and greenhouse gas reduction (e.g. Paris Accord, carbon taxes, cap and trade)
	Plastic bag and other plastic and packaging bans
	Public and green transportation systems
	Ocean waste cessation and clean-up

way to do this is by appointing an office, having a plan and providing evaluation tools to policy makers.

An office in government can be a separate department or within another office, such as that of the top level of government (prime minister, president, governor and so on) or as part of another department. It usually includes a high-level leader of the office, who has the title of administrator, commissioner, minister, secretary or another title. The leader has a staff and resources. In Bhutan, where gross national happiness (GNH) is written into the constitution, there is a GNH Commission composed of the leaders of each governmental department and a GNH Commission Secretary, who works with the leaders (Gross National Happiness Commission, n.d.; Innovations for Successful Societies, 2009). This is also an approach taken in the United Arab Emirates, where the Minister of the State of Happiness and Well-being works with all the departments in the government (McKenzie, 2016). Ecuador has also appointed a high-level office for Bien Vivir, which is also written into the constitution (Stiglitz, Fitoussi & Durand, 2019). In Indonesia, the national planning department is in charge of happiness and well-being and sustainability for the nation (Iriarte & Musikanski, 2019). Some cities and other nations around the world have also appointed happiness, well-being or sustainability officers (Aman & Uanikhehi, 2017).

The parts of a plan are the same or very similar to the parts of a policy. Planning for happiness, well-being and sustainability has been undertaken in various ways. In some governments, from city or town to national governments, sustainability is integrated into the planning, strategic or another department, and in others, there is an office of sustainability (ICMA, 2016). In Bhutan, the nation produces GNH five-year plans and uses their GNH data, which they began gathering in 2008, to monitor performance (Musikanski, 2017).

Some tools policy makers use include policy screening tools, policy manuals and measurements. In Bhutan, before a policy becomes law, it is first screened by the GNH Commission (Ura et al., 2012) using a screening tool. One example of a policy decision that the GNH Commission screened was joining the World Trade Organization (WTO). According to the screening tool, joining the WTO rated high in economic impact but low in cultural and environmental impact, so it was determined not to join (Musikanski, 2014). A Happiness Policy Manual is provided to all the governmental departments in the United Arab Emirates to educate government officials about setting goals, forming or adapting policies and measuring success (Ministry of Cabinet Affairs and the Future, 2017). The United Kingdom was one of the first nations to measure and report happiness data in an easy to access format (United Kingdom Office for National Statistics, 2015), with many nations following suit (Stiglitz, Fitoussi, & Durand, 2019). Chapter 3 on happiness measurements provides information about measurements.

HIGHLIGHT: THREE FACTORS FOR HAPPINESS AND WELL-BEING IN CITIES

Research on 26 American cities with more than 43,000 people found that three factors provide happiness and well-being for cities (Knight Foundation, 2010). The three factors are:

- Social offerings: Access to affordable and accessible cultural, social and artistic activities that bring people together and support people's sense of community have a large positive impact on satisfaction with their city and their lives. Social offerings include events such as art walks, concerts, farmers' markets and ethnic celebrations, as well as features such as parks, community centers and museums. Some policies that support social offerings include zoning laws and building codes that encourage community space, art and parks, ordinances that encourage urban agriculture and farmers' markets and permits that support local events.
- Openness: This includes degree of tolerance for diversity, acceptance of newcomers, including immigrants and refugees, friendliness and opportunities to engage with government. These all increase people's positive feelings about their cities and their happiness and well-being. Some policies that support openness include awareness campaigns and promotion of inclusion, compensation for government employees and resources for government departments based on satisfaction with services, and laws that penalize discrimination.
- Beauty: The aesthetics of urban design and public places make a big difference in how people feel about their city. Features of beauty in a city include access to nature, preservation of historic sites and buildings that are pleasing to look at and support plants as well as human living. Some policies that promote beauty include zoning laws to encourage green buildings, conservation easements, historical site preservation and awareness raising campaigns.

These three factors proved to be more important than basic services, economic growth, education, safety and other features for the cities in the study. One reason for this may be that the cities included in this study by and large had not experienced social unrest, wars, natural disasters or other catastrophes that would interrupt access to water, sewage or education; disrupt the economy; or result in unsafe and violent neighborhoods.

In the previous chapters, you made plans for a city or town for happiness, well-being and sustainability. This time imagine that disaster will strike your city or town in one year, but you are the only person who knows about it. It may be a tremendous earthquake, a heat wave that melts roads and destroys power plants, or a pandemic. You have the power to plan for the disaster but must do so through the three factors of social offerings, openness and beauty. Your first step is to form policies. What policies will you form, and how will your plans prepare your city or town for the impending disaster?

How to engage in policy making

Public policy and legislation shape the directions of our lives, for better or for worse. Policies include everything from which neighborhoods get playgrounds and potholes repaired to policies that shape access to such vital services as education and health. When you are ready to get engaged in policy making, the first step is to determine what kind of policy you want to engage in and the scope of your involvement. Anyone has the ability to shape public policy on small and large scales. Having a large-scale impact is not easy, but it is possible. It takes planning, energy, commitment and sustained pressure to make it happen. There are a variety of ways for you to engage with your governments and policy makers.

Some ways you can influence policy on a small scale are to sign petitions; write letters to the editor of newspapers; and monitor blogs, websites and social media sites on issues that are important to you. You can meet with or write to the political representative for your area (whether that is city council, state or national). You could join an existing group or organization that is focused on the issues that are important to you.

There are also many ways to get involved on a large scale. You can join a political party of your choice to attempt to influence the kinds of policies that political party thinks are important. Check out the websites of the parties to find which one most suits your values and then attend meetings and meet with local representatives of the party to decide if it is the political party that best matches your interests. You can even run for political office. Most political parties offer some kind of information and training for potential candidates, and there are sources listed later on how to put together an election campaign.

Initiating your own petitions is another way to have a larger impact. Petitions are good ways to spread your message, generate interest and gather contact information for people who support your initiative, particularly when you find no one else is tackling a particular problem that you are passionate about. In some countries, such as Canada, it is possible to present electronic petitions. You can also form a group of like-minded people and prepare to lobby your political representatives.

If you become a policy maker or policy influencer, you will find that change requires planning and persistence. Sometimes what you want happens quickly, and sometimes it takes a large amount of sustained effort with what feels like lots of failures. There needs to be a willingness to accept that things do not necessarily change overnight.

GUEST COURSEBOOK CONTRIBUTION FROM JEAN CROWDER: LOBBYING

Jean Crowder served as a Member of Parliament (MP) for the Canadian Government after a career as a policy maker and human resources and organizational consultant. She wrote the following tips based on her experience before she became an MP and worked with governments at the local, provincial and national levels, and afterward, when she worked with lobbyists, to encourage and empower readers of this coursebook.

Lobbying has a bad name for many because of associations with abuse of power, but the truth is anyone can lobby. Collins Dictionary (n.d.) defines lobbying as trying to "persuade them [a member of a government or council] that a particular law should be changed or that a particular thing should be done" (p. 1). If you want to lobby a politician for a change in policy, you will need to develop a detailed plan. The essential steps for preparing to lobby are the following:

- *Form a team or join an existing group to help with the work.*
- *Do your research and develop your key message.*
- *Define what you want as an outcome.*
- *Get your facts straight. Make sure everything you say and write is true.*

- *Prepare a report about the change you want that gives an explanation of the problem, the causes of the problem and the solutions to the problem. If possible, include similar policies adopted in other areas.*
- *Prepare a one- or two-page summary of the report explaining the change you want, with the key facts and a clear statement of your desired policy change.*
- *Develop a plan to lobby.*
- *Identify who the decision makers are (local, state or regional, or national).*
- *Find out how the decision makers have voted on similar issues.*
- *Find out who your supporters are and who is against you.*
- *Prepare to either persuade your detractors (those who are against you) to support you or to refute their arguments.*
- *Schedule your meeting with the decision maker. Give them your report.*
- *When you meet, ask for something doable and within their authority. Be specific in what you ask for. Ask them when they can follow up with you. (Will they have it done in two weeks? In two months?)*
- *Use print and social media to spread the word and gain support for your policy change.*
- *Follow up with the decision makers. This is critical and may be the most important tip. Meeting and getting a promise to follow up is not enough. You must call or visit again and again to follow up. Never give up!*

This section introduced the idea of happiness, well-being and sustainability policy; gave some examples of these policies; discussed a few ways governments are integrating happiness, well-being and sustainability into all aspects of government; and gave ideas on how to engage in policy making. These approaches are relatively new. The exercises provided next are aimed at identifying some ways that governments may have not thought of, in the hope that you, as a new leader, will continue this transformation in government and other organizations.

Policy exercises

- If you could redesign our economic and social systems, what changes would you make? If you would not make any changes, why?

- Happiness movement researchers Andrew Clark, Sarah Fleche, Richard Layard, Nattavudh Powdthavee and George Ward wrote that while governments are gathering subjective well-being data with the intent to explore their use for public policy, most governments will not use it until the evidence supports its use (http://voxeu.org/article/origins-happiness). Gus O'Donnell, former UK Cabinet Secretary, stated that 1,000 examples of evidence were necessary for governments to promulgate policy based on subjective well-being or happiness data. (Listen to the talk at www.youtube.com/watch?v=wKmwweYJOnQ&t=217s.) Do you think it makes sense for governments to wait for evidence before forming happiness, well-being and sustainability policy? If so, why? If not, why not?
- Choose a subject and draft a policy for it based on the six components in this chapter. Write a paragraph on how it will change the system. Be bold and don't worry if it's not perfect.
- Write a happiness, well-being and sustainability proclamation for your classroom or campus. If you do so for your campus, bring it to the highest-level administrator. Ask them to sign it. When they do, write to the press about it and release it to your school newspaper, the local radio and other news sources.
- Review the steps for lobbying in the contribution from Jean Crowder. What issue are you passionate enough about to consider taking these steps? Sketch a plan for lobbying for your issue.

Policy discussion questions

- Is policy important? If so, why? If not, why not?
- What are some policies in place that already contribute to your happiness? What are some policies that, if put in place, would contribute to your happiness? Now imagine that you are 80 years old and answer the same questions.
- How would you define happiness, well-being and sustainability policy? How is it different from some policy today? How is it the same or similar to some policy today?
- What factors make it easier or harder for a government to prioritize happiness, well-being and sustainability over or as much as economic growth?
- What is the job description of a government official responsible for integrating happiness, well-being and sustainability into government?
- What do you think would need to happen for your nation, state, city or town to adopt happiness, well-being and sustainability instead of

economic growth as the main goal and measurement for government and society?

Policy resources

Videos

- *Making Public Policy Fun* by Vasiliki (Vass) Bendar, TedX Toronto. www.youtube.com/watch?v=wXYSsA5yVSY
- *Gross National Happiness Explained* by Prime Minister of Bhutan by GNHcentreMedia. www.youtube.com/watch?v=SPujYdcWCFU
- *Gross National Happiness* by Maarten Desmet, TEDx Flanders. www.youtube.com/watch?v=i43X0pS094Q
- *Making Personal Happiness and Well-being a Goal of Public Policy* by the London School of Economics and Political Science. www.youtube.com/watch?v=dpA73a9bbuU&t=5s

Reading material

- *What is Policy?* http://partcfood.msvu.ca/section4/4.pdf
- *The Happiness Policy Handbook* by Laura Musikanski, Rhonda Phillips and Jean Crowder
- *Global Happiness and Well-being Policy Report* by Global Happiness and Well-being Council www.happinesscouncil.org/
- *Happiness and Public Policy* by Richard Layard. http://eprints.lse.ac.uk/47483/1/Happiness%20and%20public%20policy%28lsero%29.pdf
- *Community: The Structure of Belonging* by Peter Block
- *The Troublemaker's Teaparty: A Manual for Effective Citizen Action* by Charles Dobson
- *The World We Want: Virtue, Vice, and the Good Citizen* by Mark Kingwell.
- *Getting to Maybe: How the World is Changed* by Frances Westley, Brenda Zimmerman and Michael Patton

References

Aman, M. & Uanikhehi, I. (2017). Not everyone is happy about this new 'happiness minister' in Nigeria. *CNN*. Retrieved from www.cnn.com/2017/12/07/africa/nigerian-governor-appoints-happiness-minister/index.html

Collins Dictionary. (n.d.). Policy. Retrieved from www.collinsdictionary.com/us/dictionary/english/policy

Diener, E., Lucas, R., Schimmack, U. & Helliwell, J. (2009). *Well-Being for Public Policy*. Oxford, UK: Oxford University Press.

Diener, E., Sandvik, E., Seidlitz, L. & Diener, M. (1993). The relationship between income and subjective well-being: Relative or absolute? *Social Indicators Research, 28* (3), 195–223. doi: 10.1007/BF01079018

Diener, M. & Diener-McGavran, M. (2008). What makes people happy? In M. Eid & R. Larsen (Eds.) *The Science of Subjective Well-Being*. New York: The Guilford Press.

Easterlin, R. (1974). Does economic growth improve the human lot? In P. David & M. Reder (Eds.) *Nations and Households in Economic Growth: Essays in Honor of Moses* (pp. 89–125). New York: Academic Press, Inc. Retrieved from http://graphics8.nytimes.com/images/2008/04/16/business/Easterlin1974.pdf

Easterlin, R. (1995). Will raising the incomes of all increase the happiness of all? *Journal of Economic Behavior and Organization, 27* (1), 35–48. doi: 10.1016/0167-2681(95)00003-B

Easterlin, R. (2001). Income and happiness: Towards a unified theory. *The Economic Journal, 11* (473), 465–484. doi: 10.1111/1468-0297.00646

Gross National Happiness Commission. (n.d.). Mandate. Retrieved from www.gnhc.gov.bt/en/mandate/

Helliwell, J., Layard, R. & Sachs, J. (2018). *World Happiness Report 2018*. New York, NY: Sustainable Development Solutions Network. Retrieved from http://worldhappiness.report/

ICMA. (2016). Local government sustainability practices, 2015. Retrieved from https://icma.org/sites/default/files/308135_2015%20Sustainability%20Survey%20Report%20Final.pdf

Innovations for Successful Societies. (2009). *Karma Tshiteem*. Princeton, NJ: Princeton University Press. Retrieved from https://successfulsocieties.princeton.edu/interviews/karma-tshiteem

Iriarte, L. & Musikanski, L. (2019). Bridging the gap between the sustainable development goals and happiness metrics. *International Journal of Community Well-Being, 1*, 115–135. doi: 10.1007/s42413-018-0012-2

Knight Foundation. (2010). Knight soul of the community 2010. Retrieved from www.issuelab.org/resources/10006/10006.pdf

Marc, A. (n.d.). Conflict and violence in the 21st century: Current trends as observed in empirical research and statistics. Retrieved from www.un.org/pga/70/wp-content/uploads/sites/10/2016/01/Conflict-and-violence-in-the-21st-century-Current-trends-as-observed-in-empirical-research-and-statistics-Mr.-Alexandre-Marc-Chief-Specialist-Fragility-Conflict-and-Violence-World-Bank-Group.pdf

McKenzie, S. (2016). Happy says? United Arab Emirates appoints first minister of happiness. *CNN*. Retrieved from https://edition.cnn.com/2016/02/15/middleeast/united-arab-emirates-minister-of-happiness/index.html

Meadows, D., Randers, J. & Meadows, D. (2004). *The Limits to Growth: The 30-Year Update*. White River Junction, VT: Chelsea Green Publishing Company.

Ministry of Cabinet Affairs and the Future. (2017). HE Ohood Al Roumi: UAE has developed world's first 'happiness policy manual.' Retrieved from www.mocaf.

gov.ae/en/media/news/he-ohood-al-roumi-uae-has-developed-world-s-first-happiness-policy-manual

Musikanski, L. (2014). Happiness in public policy. *Journal of Social Change, 6* (1), 55–85. Retrieved from http://scholarworks.waldenu.edu/jsc/vol6/iss1/5/

Musikanski, L. (2017). Bhutan's recipe for happiness. *Happiness Alliance Blog*. Retrieved http://happycounts.blogspot.com/2017/02/bhutans-recipe-for-happiness.html

Musikanski, L., Phillips, R. & Crowder, J. (2019). *The Happiness Policy Handbook, How to Make Happiness and Well-Being the Purpose of Your Government.* Gabriola Island, BC: New Society Press.

Ovaska, T. & Takashima, R. (2006). Economic policy and the level of self-perceived well-being: An international comparison. *The Journal of Socio-Economics, 35* (2), 308–325. doi: 10.1016/j.socec.2005.11.054

Stiglitz, J., Fitoussi, J. & Durand, M. (2019). *Measuring What Counts.* New York, NY: The New Press.

United Kingdom Office for National Statistics. (2015). Measuring personal well-being in the U.K. Retrieved from www.ons.gov.uk/ons/rel/wellbeing/measuring-national-well-being/personal-well-being-in-the-uk-2014-15/stb-personal-well-being-in-the-uk-2014-15.html#tab-3-Measuring-personal-well-being-in-the-UK

United Nations. (2016). The world's cities in 2016. Retrieved from www.un.org/en/development/desa/population/publications/pdf/urbanization/the_worlds_cities_in_2016_data_booklet.pdf

Ura, K., Alkire, S., Zangmo, S. & Wangdi, K. (2012). An extensive analysis of GNH index. *Centre for Bhutan Studies.* Retrieved from www.grossnationalhappiness.com/wp-content/uploads/2012/10/An%20Extensive%20Analysis%20of%20GNH%20Index.pdf

CLOSING

Your future, our future

The intent of this coursebook is to inspire and empower you by providing knowledge, tools and resources. For this closing, instead of providing more resources, we submit that the most important resource is you. All humans on the planet have a role to play and will influence, in however small or large a scope, the future. It is our sincere hope that we have inspired you to learn more and apply some of the lessons from the coursebook for your happiness, the well-being of others and the sustainability of our beautiful Earth.

In conclusion, we leave you with four tips.

Play: Take time to play every day. Have fun. Never underestimate the power of play. It brings joy, opens your heart and mind and can provide space and place to discover your purpose (which changes and evolves over the course of one's life). Play can facilitate thinking about solutions to small and global problems, and by so doing, inspire you and provide happiness by implementing them. Make the promise to yourself to spend time with family or friends hanging out and having fun at least three times a week and keep this promise. Live a life in which most of your work and most of the time spent with family and friends feels good and is full of play. Choose work and a career that feel like play.

Nature: Spend time in nature. Take long walks as often as possible. On vacations, seek out places to spend time in natural settings. Go to parks, large and small, in your own community and wherever you visit. Have meetings where you go for a walk in the park or natural area instead of meeting at a coffee shop and staying there or in an office. Go out with friends and watch the moon rise or sun set or have fun in a park. When you can't go into nature, bring it to you. Have potted plants nearby in your work and home. Place a bouquet of cut flowers on your desk, within a few inches of the sightline of your computer. Nature has tremendous wisdom. By spending time in it, whether gazing at flowers or a plant placed nearby where you spend time or even a picture of nature on a desktop, benefits are achieved by immersing one's self in nature.

Be aware: Take the profound step of setting the intention to being aware of what is happening in the moment. With awareness, there are choices about how you feel, what you think and what you do. It is not a complicated thing. In fact, it is so simple that most people entirely miss it. Once an intention to be aware is set, it develops through mindfulness practice or any other way. What we think about and focus on make a difference, and decisions are made this way. Through awareness, one becomes alert to what they can and cannot change, so find leverage points in their own life and in the world around them. If there is something that can't be changed, then stop spending time and energy on it. Decisions and actions will be better and possibly easier as awareness increases.

Believe: Believe in yourself, in your values and dreams, and in others. When you believe in yourself, you realize your dreams. The list of things that you are not is endless. Instead of focusing on what you are not or what you do not want, focus on what is good about you and what you do want. Celebrate who you are. When you believe in and celebrate yourself, it is easier to see the good in others too.

INDEX

Note: Page numbers in **bold** refer to information in highlights and guest contributions; those in *italics* refer to figures, tables, or images.

For Product Safety Concerns and Information please contact our EU
representative GPSR@taylorandfrancis.com
Taylor & Francis Verlag GmbH, Kaufingerstraße 24, 80331 München, Germany

www.ingramcontent.com/pod-product-compliance
Ingram Content Group UK Ltd.
Pitfield, Milton Keynes, MK11 3LW, UK
UKHW021955180926
475701UK00003B/48

* 9 7 8 0 3 6 7 4 8 8 7 0 3 *